THE EUROPEAN P
THE NATIONAL PARLIAMENTS, AND
EUROPEAN INTEGRATION

The European Parliament, the National Parliaments, and European Integration

Edited by

RICHARD S. KATZ

and

BERNHARD WESSELS

OXFORD
UNIVERSITY PRESS

OXFORD
UNIVERSITY PRESS

Great Clarendon Street, Oxford OX2 6DP

Oxford University Press is a department of the University of Oxford.
It furthers the University's objective of excellence in research, scholarship,
and education by publishing worldwide in

Oxford New York

Athens Auckland Bangkok Bogotá Buenos Aires Calcutta
Cape Town Chennai Dar es Salaam Delhi Florence Hong Kong Istanbul
Karachi Kuala Lumpur Madrid Melbourne Mexico City Mumbai
Nairobi Paris São Paulo Shanghai Singapore Taipei Tokyo Toronto Warsaw
with associated companies in Berlin Ibadan

Oxford is a registered trade mark of Oxford University Press
in the UK and in certain other countries

Published in the United States
by Oxford University Press Inc., New York

British Library Cataloguing in Publication Data
Data available

Library of Congress Cataloging in Publication Data
The European Parliament, the national parliaments, and European
integration / edited by Richard S. Katz and Bernhard Wessels.
p. cm.
Includes bibliographical references and index.
1. European Parliament. 2. Legislative bodies—European Union
countries. I. Katz, Richard S. II. Wessels, Bernhard, 1955- .
JN36.E9545 1999
328.4—dc21 99-28123
ISBN 0-19-829660-6

3 5 7 9 10 8 6 4 2

Printed in Great Britain
on acid-free paper by
Biddles Ltd.
Guildford and King's Lynn

Preface

THIS book is the result of a collective effort that started in 1993. It is the companion to the volume *Political Representation and Legitimacy in the European Union*, edited by Hermann Schmitt and Jacques Thomassen, also published with Oxford University Press. In 1993, Hermann Schmitt and Jacques Thomassen proposed a fascinating idea in conjunction with plans for the 1994 European Election Study. This idea was to study "Political Representation in Europe", and this became the project name. It was not long before a whole group of people were engaged to realize a research design in which European elections could be studied comprehensively, but also in connection to the attitudes, backgrounds, roles and reported actions of parliamentarians over what was then the European Community.

In a sort of division of labor, but with close co-operation and co-ordination, four larger empirical studies soon were on their way; the *European Elections Study* of 1994, a comparative EC-wide survey among mass publics; the *European Candidate Survey*, a mail survey conducted before the elections in eleven of the then twelve member states; the *Members of the European Parliament Study*, a face-to-face survey conducted in spring 1996; and the *European Study of Members of Parliament*, a mail survey carried out in 1996 and 1997 in eleven member states.

Those who worked in conjunction with the overall project on *Political Representation in Europe* or its sub-projects, have enjoyed something that is relatively rare but none the less needed—at least the editors of the two companion volumes feel so: a kind of gluing together to get the big tanker launched. It was a real comparative undertaking and given the topics of our books one might say, a real European project. At least it furthered the integration of Europe between many social scientists.

Acknowledgements

THE book and the whole study would not have been possible without support from many people and institutions. First of all we would like to thank those members of the European Parliament and the national parliaments of Belgium, France, Germany, Greece, Ireland, Italy, Luxembourg, the Netherlands, Portugal, Spain, and Sweden, and the candidates who run in the 1994 European Elections, who had the willingness and found the time to take part in the survey.

Thanks also are due to our collaborators in the member states, who carried out the mail surveys for the candidates to the European Parliament and the members of national parliaments. These are, in alphabetic order of the countries they represent: *Patrick Dumont* and *Lieven de Winter* (Belgium and Luxembourg); *Colette Ysmal* (France); *Achim Kielhorn* (Germany); *Manina Kakepati* (Greece); *Michael Marsh* and *Mary Clare O'Sullivan* (Ireland); *Louisa Gardella* (Italy); *Henk van der Kolk* and *Jacques Thomassen* (The Netherlands); *Christina Leston Bandeira* (Portugal); *Irene Delgado* and *Lourdes López Nieto* (Spain); and *Martin Brothen, Peter Esaiasson,* and *Soren Holmberg* (Sweden); *Peter Lynch* and *Pippa Norris* (Britain); *Tom Bryder* (Denmark); *Cecile Chavel* (France); *Giorgio Sola* (Italy); *Peter Geurts* (the Netherlands); and *Maria José Stock* (Portugal) carried out the candidate surveys in their countries, either together with the above mentioned colleagues or alone.

The universities of Mannheim and Twente, and the *Wissenschafts-zentrum Berlin (WZB)*, Research Unit "Institutions and Social Change" provided resources for translating and printing the questionnaires, data punching and cleaning and co-ordinating the whole effort. A generous research grant of the German Science Foundation (*Deutsche For-schungsgemeinschaft*) made possible the survey among the members of the European Parliament. These institutions deserves our thanks.

Finally, special thanks to *Katarina Pollner*, Wissenschaftszentrum Berlin, who managed to handle all the manuscripts, tables and figures, worked in revisions, corrected errors, and brought the whole book into a printable form. Without her extraordinary engagement, everything would have taken much longer.

Contents

List of Figures

List of Tables

Abbreviations

ARE	Group of the European Radical Alliance
AU	Austria
BE	Belgium
COPA	Committee of Professional Agricultural Organizations in the European Community
COREPER	Committee of Permanent Representatives
DE	Denmark
EC	European Communities
ECSC	European Coal and Steel Community
EDN	Europe of Nations Group
EEB	European Environmental Bureau
EEC	European Economic Community
EFG	European Federation of Green Parties
ELDR	Group of the European Liberal Democrats and Reformist Party
EP	The European Parliament
ETUC	European Trade Union Confederation
EU	European Union
EUROCOOP	European Community of Consumers' Co-operatives
FI	Finland
FIPMEC	International Federation of Small and Medium Sized Commercial Enterprises
FR	France
GB	Great Britain
GCECEE	Savings Banks Group of the EC
GE	Germany
GR	Greece
GUE	Confederal Group of the European United Left
IR	Ireland
IT	Italy

LC/IRU	Liaison Committee of Professional Road Transport of the European Communities
LU	Luxembourg
MEP	Member of the European Parliament
MNP	Member of national parliaments
MP	Member of Parliament
NE	The Netherlands
NP	National Parliament
PO	Portugal
PPE	Group of the European People's Party
PSE	Group of the Party of European Socialists
SEPLIS	European Secretariat of the Liberal, Intellectual and Social Professions
SP	Spain
SW	Sweden
UK	United Kingdom
UNICE	Union of Industrial and Employers' Confederations
UPE	Group Union for Europe
V	The Green Group in the European Parliament

List of Contributors

PETER ESAIASSON, Associate Professor, Department of Political Science, Göteborg University, Göteborg, Sweden.

MARK N. FRANKLIN, Reitemeyer Professor of Political Science, Trinity College, Hartford, Connecticut, USA.

RICHARD S. KATZ, Professor, Department of Political Science, The Johns Hopkins University, Baltimore, Maryland, USA.

ACHIM KIELHORN, Research Scholar at the Faculty of Public Administration and Public Policy, University of Twente, Netherlands.

MICHAEL MARSH, Senior Lecturer, and Head of Department of Political Science, Trinity College, Dublin, Ireland.

PIPPA NORRIS, Associate Director of the Joan Shorenstein Center on the Press, Politics and Public Policy and Lecturer at the Kennedy School of Government, Harvard University, Cambridge, Massachusetts, USA.

SUSAN SCARROW, Associate Professor, Department of Political Science, University of Houston, Houston, Texas, USA.

HERMANN SCHMITT, Senior Research Fellow, Mannheimer Zentrum für Europäische Sozialforschung, Mannheim, Germany.

JACQUES THOMASSEN, Professor of Political Science, Faculty of Public Administration and Public Policy, University of Twente, the Netherlands.

BERNHARD WESSELS, Senior Fellow at the Wissenschaftszentrum Berlin für Sozialforschung (WZB), Research Unit "Institutions and Social Change", Berlin, Germany.

The European Parliament,
the National Parliaments,
and European Integration

1

Introduction:
European Parliament, National Parliaments, and European Integration

BERNHARD WESSELS AND RICHARD S. KATZ

EUROPEAN integration is progressing at an ever more rapid rate. Accompanying this progress is increasing debate about the institutional shape and legitimacy of this new political order. Positions of the protagonists range from euphoric support for the "European Project" to strong and deep-seated scepticism. While this debate is driven in part by conflicting values, in part it is driven by uncertainty. There is no historical precedent for the emerging European system, and the institutional imaginations of observers are both limited and imprecise (Schmitter 1996a: 131), leaving room for all kinds of speculation.

If the emerging European political order is to qualify as democratic in any meaningful sense, parliaments as representative institutions will have to play a central role. Although major steps to increase the role of the European Parliament have already been taken however, increasing the importance of parliament to political decision-making in the European Union does not mean increasing the importance only of the European Parliament. While this might solve some of the problems of the so-called democratic deficit of the EU, it addresses only one side of the question of European democracy. As Scharpf (1996a) has pointed out, focusing on the European level alone is insufficient, since the increase of powers at the European level has also called into question democratic legitimacy at the level of the nation-state. Thus the role that national parliaments should, can, and want to play in European policy-making is also of central importance to the future of the European order.

What roles should be played by which level of parliament depends very much on one's political vision. The views of those who support a confederal model differ from the views of those who support a federal model (W. Wessels 1996), views of neoliberals differ from those of advocates of a social democratic model of regulated capitalism (Hooghe and Marks 1999). There is consensus that democracy requires parliaments to play a major role, but dissensus about the proper place for parliamentary control at the national or at the European level.

This book addresses the question of parliamentary involvement in the emerging European political system by looking at both national and European levels of parliamentary representation. In doing this, it gives greater attention to the role of national parliaments than is usual in discussions about democracy in the European Union. We address the problems and prospects of European integration from the perspectives of the members of the European Parliament and of their counterparts at the national level. The views, evaluations, and wishes concerning the current and future development of Europe expressed by MPs at the European level thus are complemented and contrasted with the views, evaluations, and wishes of members of the national parliaments of eleven of the fifteen members states. In this way, this book tries to address important questions about European integration as perceived by key actors—the peoples' elected representatives at the European and national levels. The book provides analyses of the *views from within* concerning European integration and the role of parliaments in this process.

THE DEMOCRATIC QUESTION

Sensitivity to a variety of shortcomings of the integration process has increased tremendously in recent years. The 1991 signing of the Maastricht Treaty, in particular, triggered an intense public debate concerning the legitimacy of European political institutions. In a sense it is surprising that the trigger for this debate was the signing of the Maastricht Treaty rather than the 1986 ratification of the Single European Act, since the SEA had much greater and more immediate impact on the daily lives of the citizens, affecting everything "from boar meat to banking" as the *Financial Times* put it (Schmitter 1996a: 121). Perhaps it was the Maastricht Treaty's greater focus on the reform of institutions rather than movement of goods, capital, persons, etc. that increased sensibility for the democratic deficit. It might also be that the consequences of integration became more obvious because the Maastricht Treaty sought not only political integration through institutional means, but monetary union as well. This added a symbolic dimension that, to a certain extent, threatened national identity (Risse 1998). In Germany, for example, the public debate about the risks of a common currency was inspired largely by such concerns, but this was not only a German phenomenon. There was a general downward trend in public support for European integration, and in particular for monetary union, after Maastricht. The reasons may lie, in part, in purely economic, cost-benefit, calculations, but certainly also lie to some extent in an increasing fear about loss of national identity (Niedermayer 1995a: 71-2). With the Maastricht Treaty, the EC negotiated simultaneously rather than sequentially across a broad and interdependent spectrum of issues for the first time (Schmitter 1996b).

Whatever the trigger, the democratic question is on the agenda, and with it a big and complex debate about possible institutional solutions to the problem of EU legitimacy. This problem has emerged because the European Community eroded the basic ordering principle of the modern European state, which is autonomy within and independence without—in a word, sovereignty. Without force or violence, the European Union has crossed the border from horizontal interstate cooperation to vertical (i.e., hierarchical) policy-making. The European Union possesses enormous redistributive powers, and in exercising these powers has supremacy over national laws. This naturally raises the democratic question of how the system of institutions exercising this power is to be controlled and held accountable. The system is still under construction, but that construction has to take account of problems of legitimacy and democracy.

Democratic legitimation rests both on the effectiveness of policy achievements and on popular representation and participation. Democracy as an ideal combines these two criteria of governance and representation that are often seen as being in tension (Shepsle 1988; Katz 1997). There is an inevitable trade-off between output legitimacy and input legitimacy, between an emphasis on government *for* the people and an emphasis on government *by* the people, to draw on Abraham Lincoln's famous triad. Every liberal democracy has its particular combination of these two basic aspects of legitimation. Some political structures emphasize effective government more strongly, others emphasize representation, but all legitimate democracies must achieve at least minimal levels on both dimensions.

The European Union, and especially its predecessors, put most emphasis on effective governance, that is, on government *for* the people. But while in this respect the European institutional system appears to be largely crystallized, the institutions for participation and representation are still very much under construction. The European Parliament has continuously increased its powers, and, by default, it is the key institution at the European level with regard to popular participation and representation. It is, however, not much of a parliament by the traditional standards of democracy at the level of the European nation-state. The national parliaments are generally regarded as legislative bodies; operating in a very different institutional setting, the European Parliament is not yet a legislature in the strict sense, although it is moving in that direction. It also does not elect a government, since there is no European government in the traditional, national, sense. Moreover, one major task of the European Parliament is the construction of its institutional setting; it is "interested in system change" (i.e., fundamentally modifying the nature of the relationships between it and the other Union institutions), whereas national parliaments in established democracies such as those of western Europe can at most marginally alter their places in fundamentally fixed institutional settings (Corbett, Jacobs, and Shackleton 1995: 8).

The third aspect of Lincoln's triad, i.e., government *of* the people, also may present serious problems for the creation of a democratic order at the European level. Can we assume that there is a single European people in the same way that the concept of nation-state implies the coincidence of a single state with a single people? Is it necessary to have a single European people in order to have a European-level democracy? Can one conceive of government *by* the people that is not also a government *of* the people? While questions such as these cause few conceptual or "real world political" problems within the boundaries of most countries (although consider the cases of Belgium, Italy, and the United Kingdom), they may prove absolutely crucial at the European level.

EUROPEAN INTEGRATION, NATION-STATES,
AND DEMOCRACY

The "European project" from the beginning aimed at both economic *and* political integration. However, as the history of the European Union makes clear, the project started with economic integration. Whatever the ultimate intentions with regard to political integration, economic integration was, and still is, seen to be much more feasible. The market within the boundaries of the Union has been liberalized in the sense that European regulations apply equally within all member states, i.e., the economy has been liberated from particular national regulations. On one hand, economic integration was an early answer to processes nowadays identified as "globalization," while on the other hand it reinforced those processes. Economic integration in the European Union can be understood as a strategy of regionally enlarging political authority in order to (de)regulate the economy by keeping up with what was happening in the economy anyway. But by adding a political impulse to the extension of markets, the "state" fell even farther behind (Scharpf 1996a). This is the major reason why progress in political integration has become so urgent. Although globalization has become one of those "buzz words of our time" (Tsoukalis 1998), the process it identifies touches the most central concerns of European integration. Some liberal economists welcome globalization since it frees the market from hypertrophic state regulations. Other observers fear that the loss of states' steering capacity against a globalized economy will spell the end of democracy (Guéhenno 1995). Still others hope that the loss of authority at the national level can be compensated by extending the state, i.e., by establishing supranational authority (Delors 1992) and cosmopolitan democracy (Held 1996: ch. 10). This perspective, however, returns the question of democracy to the table. To adapt the scope of European state authority to the scope of markets requires that the complex relationships among European integration, the institution of the nation-state, and democracy be considered.

   Democracy can be understood as a form of collective self-determination. "Democracy means a form of governance in which, in contradistinction to monarchies and aristocracies, the people rule" (Held 1996: 1). With respect to inputs, democracy requires that political choices be derived from the preferences of the people. With respect to outputs, it implies "effective fate control" (Scharpf 1996a: 2). The right balance between input and output legitimacy is crucial for democracy; neither input nor output legitimacy is adequate by itself.

Until recently, the European Union, and its predecessor the EC, could rely almost exclusively on output legitimacy because its actions were perceived to be serving everybody's interests. This was the principal basis of the so-called "permissive consensus." Since the launching of the Single European Act in 1986 and its completion in 1992, however, the situation has changed on both the institutional and the mass levels.

Institutionally, national governments are losing effective control over redistributive policies due to the pressures of economic competition in the integrated European market. They are, thus, losing output legitimacy. This aspect of the democratic deficit is widely overlooked. As Scharpf (1996a: 1) observes, the "debate is deficient in so far as its focus is on the democratic deficit of *the European Union*, rather than the democratic deficit *in Europe*." It appears that the only way to regain political control is to extend the scope of the state, i.e., to shift responsibility to the European level, and this, indeed, is what appears to be happening (Schmitter 1996a: 124-7).

This, however, brings with it the demand for more input legitimacy at the European level, exacerbated by two further developments. First, most EU decisions no longer are made by unanimous agreement among national governments, each of which possesses an absolute veto power. Second, EU policy competence has expanded into areas (e.g., welfare and social policy) in which the obvious differences between member states with respect to wealth, social policy regimes, or dependence on agricultural subsidies make it unlikely that consensus will be obtained; the resulting tensions can only increase with the accession of new members (Tsoukalis 1998).

This problem of input legitimacy then is aggravated by the absence of a true European political community. Even if decisions, for example to require Portugal to implement social policy standards similar to those in Germany or to require Sweden to bring its level of social provision down to the European average, were to result from a parliamentary majority vote or an electorally legitimated European government, this would not solve the problem. Weiler (1996: 523) has highlighted the situation with an example: "imagine an *Anschluss* between Germany and Denmark. Try and tell the Danes that they should not worry since they have full representation in the Bundestag." Democracy is so closely connected to the coincidence of a people and their state that majority rule seems only to legitimate within a singular *demos*.

The nation-state has lost authority and the supranational level has gained authority, but without the capacity to make effective use of it. EU decisions still depend very much on negotiation. In terms of the legitimacy of outcomes, this may not be a bad solution, since it is unlikely that major interests will be ignored. This is even more the case now that the role of the European Parliament has been significantly strengthened. But it also means that the number of veto players has increased, again reducing the capacity for political action (Tsebelis 1995). Thus, the legitimacy of the outcomes of decisions might be increased but the possibility of reaching agreement is decreased (Scharpf 1996a). As Scharpf (1988, 1996b) put it, "the 'joint decision trap' is still in good repair."

The situation of representation in Europe and the European Union is characterized by a puzzle: (economic) integration policies have increased competition between economies with the consequence that the nation-state has lost autonomous capacity to handle the (social) consequences. Output legitimacy, i.e., government *for* the people, has decreased at the national level. The shift of authority to the European level that is taking place could, in principle, compensate for this, but it is still missing input legitimacy, i.e., government *by* the people. This severely limits the capacity of the European level to exercise the authority that it has in principle, because "citizens of countries whose governments are outvoted have no reason to consider such decisions as having democratic legitimation" (Scharpf 1996b: 26). Thus, input legitimacy of European governance still must rest primarily on the agreement of democratically accountable national governments, i.e., on the European negotiation system that has become more complicated as a result of the strengthening of the European Parliament to a point at which it can be regarded as a veto player. Decisions reached by this route may have extremely high legitimacy, but such decisions are unlikely to be reached at all in areas where conflicts are "pre-programmed," i.e., social and welfare policies as well as agricultural policies at least as far as eastward enlargement of the European Union is concerned.

Which kind of order will emerge and which route to European integration is likely to solve these problems is still an open debate. But procedures have to be developed to guarantee input as well as output legitimacy at the national as well as at the European level. A crucial question in this regard is the one concerning the role of the European Parliament and the national parliaments.

In the European tradition, parliaments are the central institutions for political legitimacy. As institutions they live through the behaviour of their individual members. As bodies they are collective actors that constrain or facilitate executive action. For European integration, the process is a multi-actor, multi-level game. European institutions are faced with an increasing demand for the European Parliament to play a stronger role in political decision-making. At the same time, many national parliaments, reacting to an increasing erosion of national sovereignty and a decline of parliamentary decision-making capacity, have sought to institutionalize parliamentary control over their governments' action at the European level (W. Wessels 1996). The part parliaments want and will play in the ongoing integration process is crucial for policy development as well as for the development of democracy at the European level. The interplay between the national and the European level, as well as between nations, has shaped and will shape the course of development.

In this context, Scharpfs' idea that the democratic deficit is not only a deficit at the European level, but at the national level as well, is of crucial importance. The development of the EU is shifting the locus of legitimacy in a special, maybe paradoxical, way. The most general goals emphasized by the pioneers of European integration—peace, democracy, and political stability—so far have been realized at the national level. The ongoing process of integration, however, has challenged the sovereignty and thus the legitimizing mechanisms of the nation-state without at the same time replacing them or compensating with comparable democratic mechanisms at the European level.

ACTORS: THE ROLE OF PARLIAMENTS AND
PARLIAMENTARIANS

The institutional setting of the European Union is marked by an aston-
ishing autonomy of its institutions from direct democratic control. As
opposed to traditional international organizations and confederal systems, European institutions "which take part in the policy cycle are *de
jure* and to a large degree *de facto* independent of national governments ... this implies that 'sovereign' states have to deal with political
actors which are outside their immediate control" (W. Wessels 1996:
21). It can hardly be expected that this situation can hold up forever.
Parliament in conjunction with free and competitive elections is in the
European political tradition central for achieving democratic legitimation. The trend towards a parliamentarization of European politics is
obvious, given the continuous increase in competencies of the European Parliament.

Clearly, institutional factors matter for the ability of parliaments to
play their role (Döring 1995b). But at the same time, institutions can
only perform to the extent that their members are able to breathe life
into formal settings. The trend towards parliamentarization of politics
at the European level requires not only favourable institutional
reforms, but equally that MEPs play individual roles adequate for the
functions of the body as a whole. The performance of a system is to a
large degree dependent on the personnel acting within it (cf. Almond,
Powell, and Mundt 1993: 77-81; Lipset 1967). The efficiency of political institutions is likely to depend on the type of persons who join these
institutions (Blondel 1991: 187). Political leadership requires knowledge and skills (Almond, Powell, and Mundt 1993: 77), in particular
technical expertise, the ability to persuade and organize, as well as
loyalty and political reliability (Putnam 1976: 52).

The success of political integration in the EU will require guarantees
of democratic political representation. This raises a complex pattern of
questions not yet finally answered. These revolve around the grand
question of which model of politics for Europe one hopes to achieve.
But this question can be broken down into smaller parts, and the
answers relevant political actors choose for themselves will determine
the working of the institutions regardless of their formal structure. If
the European Parliament can be described as an institution that is con-

cerned with system change (Corbett, Jacobs, and Shackleton 1995: 8), the question is, what system changes do its members want. If MEPs were to aim to represent their national constituencies, the European Parliament would be quite different in its approach to representation than it would be if its members intended to represent "the European people," whatever that might be.

The European Parliament does not represent citizens in isolation, but in an environment that also includes the national parliaments. The role that the parliament plays in policy-making varies considerably across nations. In addition to the question of MEPs' orientations, there is the question of the congruity or incongruity of their orientations with those of members of the national parliaments. These MNPs may have rather different objectives for the emerging European system, and these too will have implications for the future development of European integration. The interplay among institutions and individuals acting in them will determine the performance of parliaments, and in particular of the European Parliament, in the integration process. This interplay can be described in terms of at least four elements: the goals and preferences of political actors in the institutions; the norms and rules (the culture) of the organization; the institutional capacity and constraints for autonomous action; and the ability and capacity of individual actors to breathe life into formal organization and rules.

Knowing how members of parliament view the role of their institutions and their individual role as representatives, how the institution is able to socialize its members, and what political and professional capacities individuals bring into parliament, all facilitate some judgement about the prospects of European integration and the role of parliaments and their members in this process. Part I of the book addresses these questions.

PROCESSES: LINKAGES

Talking about parliament as a locus of democratic decision-making addresses only one aspect of the problem of establishing a democratic political order. Another question concerns the way in which parliament is linked to society and people. Alternatives for EU democracy are not defined only by whether the national or European level is regarded as the proper locus of parliamentarization of European politics. The way in which one wants to see European level politics linked with nation-states' people leads to two principal alternatives.

The most common perspective regarding linkages between representatives and represented is the *responsible party model*. Political parties are regarded as the principal agents of democracy. It is sometimes even claimed that "modern democracy is unthinkable, save in terms of parties" (Schattschneider 1942: 1). Parties are "organizations which uniquely link particular social interests represented by their members or activists to ordinary voters, to parliamentarians (the elected candidates whom they have backed) and to members of the government who are usually the party leaders" (Budge, Newton, et al. 1997: 193). This perspective, having its roots in European democracy at the national level, has also been applied to the European level (Hix and Lord 1997). Article 138a of the Maastricht treaty emphasizes the relevance of parties not only as factors for integration but also as agents that express the political will of the citizens.

If one were to implement the responsible party model in European level politics, the result most likely would be some kind of federation (Schmitt and Thomassen 1999a), more or less based on majority rule and territorial representation. However, one of the great trade-offs of democracy is between size and scope. The European Union faces the *number problem of representation* which is discussed later in this volume (chapter 6) in particularly aggravated form. As a result, intermediary institutions are even more important at the European level than at the national level. This is why *functional* representation is so often stressed in the discussion about democracy at the European level (Schmitter 1996a; Andersen and Eliassen 1996b; Greenwood, Grote, and Ronit 1992).

The implications of this distinction are far reaching. Neo-functionalist integration theory first claimed that interest groups, i.e., functional representation, could and should play a significant role in compensating for the lack of direct contact between European level institutions and the citizens in the member states (Haas 1964). In present discussions, models of *post-parliamentary democracy* (Andersen and Burns 1996) or *associative democracy* (Schmalz-Bruns 1997) are presented as alternatives to parliamentary democracy. These approaches emphasize associative or corporatistic forms of bargaining democracy (*Verhandlungsdemokratie*) (Benz 1998: 347): "The 'democracy of organizations' tends to replace the democracy of citizens and their territorial representatives" (Andersen and Burns 1996: 230).

Arguments for this kind of democracy as an alternative to the responsible party model are based either on the diagnosis that such structures already exist *de facto* or that majority rule cannot work at the European level since there is not one united *demos*. Thus democracy must be based on negotiations including all major interests (Scharpf 1998). The appropriate decision rule to avoid the trap of majority decisions that nonetheless are not accepted is either *arguing* or *bargaining*. At the European level, such an arrangement would be characterized by *specialized representation*, distributed and only to a limited extent territorial, and *specialized sovereignty and authority*, again to an important degree non-territorial. The "overall development consists of the displacement of rule- and policy-making from parliamentary bodies to informal groups and networks..." (Andersen and Burns 1996: 237-9).

The two models of democracy arising from these different conceptions of linkages and representation clearly contradict one another in theory. The obvious tensions between parliamentary party representation and associative or functional representation that exist at the national level are multiplied at the European level. However, their *de facto* combination at the national level seems to confirm that they can complement each other. The *second circuit* (Offe 1981) or *two-tier-system* (Rokkan 1966) may become even more important for democracy at the European level than it is at the national level. Benz (1998) argues that the future order of the European Union must be one of functional differentiation among the arenas of governmental, parliamentary, and associative representation. One might also argue that functional representation should be embedded in party and parliamentary representation. However, this would need strong parties and strong parliaments that could resist particularistic demands and would be able to integrate the variety of interests into the public good.

It is doubtful that parties and parliaments are strong enough for that even at the national level. The most likely future appears to be a decline of parliamentary democracy (Andersen and Burns 1996), although everything is still possible in the course of European integration. It is not yet clear whether a real European party system can or will emerge. It is not clear what kind of interaction there will be among possible changes in the electoral law, the competencies of European and national parliaments, and the behaviour of the voters. It is not clear whether the result of such interactions will strengthen or weaken European level or national level democracy. It is not even clear what the actual situation is. Part II of the book takes up this question by investigating the role of interest groups in functional representation and party representation in the European Parliament.

STRUCTURES: PROBLEMS AND INSTITUTIONAL CHANGE

There is a great debate about whether national democracy should be used as a blueprint for the future political order of the European Union. Schmitter, provocatively, makes this clear by demanding that the reader imagine a polity that would *not* have a single locus of authority, a distinctive sphere of competency within which it can make binding decisions, a fixed territory, an overarching identity and political community of its members, effective monopoly over the legitimate means of coercion, or the capacity for direct implementation of its decisions, but *would* have the capability to take decisions, regulate markets, hold elections, incorporate new members, allocate expenditures, conclude international agreements, and even declare and wage war (Schmitter 1996a: 131). If these would indeed be the central characteristics of the future political order, it obviously would not be a democracy at all. And it can be doubted whether such a political order could work without clear and distinctive features to keep it accountable to the people over whom it rules.

Such an order would need institutional rules of decision-making. Current constitutional considerations range from democratic models of confederation to federation. The most general choice for the future of Europe is between a parliamentary structure and a regulatory system (Majone 1994). In the regulatory model, the Union is viewed as a special purpose organization with the primary task of addressing policy questions that can be handled more effectively at the European level than at the national level. The principal rationale of this model is expertise and legitimacy by outcomes. Purely intergovernmental solutions are regarded as inadequate since national representatives may lack sufficient expertise. Therefore, strong emphasis is put on delegation to more or less autonomous supranational institutions (Gatsios and Seabright 1989). Although the Amsterdam Treaty is strongly influenced by a parliamentary model, the extension of Union competencies in the fields of social regulations and, in particular, human health and consumer protection might bring the European Union closer to the regulatory model (Dehousse 1998). However, the provisions on transparency in the treaty point to the problem of democratic legitimacy. Only if the Commission consults widely before making legislative proposals, i.e., only if the negotiation system works and consensus is achieved, will decisions of autonomous regulatory bodies be accepted. This, on the other hand, reduces the possible range and areas of decision. In this sense, the regulatory model probably does not extend decision capacity beyond what is already known as intergovernmentalism.

In general terms, one might call the regulatory or intergovernmental model *confederal*. A confederal Europe is based on a "pooling of sovereignties, the member states, as the 'masters of the game' are always keeping the final say" (W. Wessels 1996: 23). Political legitimacy is based on national elections and transferred to national governments by national parliaments. In this case, the central decision-making body would be the European Council.

In contrast, a federal model of a "United States of Europe," is based on direct legitimation, with the Commission converted to be a government, with its head directly elected by the European Parliament which itself is directly elected. The European Parliament would become the first, and the Council the second chamber of a bicameral legislature (W. Wessels 1996: 25).

These two alternatives correspond to two different political ideologies, as has been pointed out by Hooghe and Marks (1999). They also imply different approaches to the role of the state. They represent two different political projects: the "neoliberal project" of deregulation of markets and intergovernmental decision-making, and the project of "regulated capitalism" in which a parliamentarized European liberal democracy is capable of regulating markets.

However, neither of these two alternatives will solve all the problems. The ongoing political and institutional developments suggest that the future order probably will be a mixture of three forms of representation: governmentalism; parliamentarism; and associationalism (Benz 1998). The trade-offs and tensions are, first, with respect to both parliamentary representation and (inter-)governmental representation, those between party competition and majority rule on the one hand and efficiency in decision-making on the other. The second tensions arise, with respect to governmental and associational representation, between territorial and sectoral cleavages. The third tensions, with respect to parliamentary and associational representation, arise between transparency and public debate on the one hand and selective bargaining on the other. In each case, the problem is how to find a balance within the European Union. To a considerable extent, this will depend on the analysis and diagnosis of the actors working in and on institution building in the EU. It will depend on their perceptions of problems, their evaluations of achievements, and their proposals regarding solutions. Part III of the book concentrates on these questions and tries to identify which kind of political order is wanted and which kind, in the views of parliamentarians in Europe, is likely to emerge.

PLAN OF THE BOOK AND STUDY DESIGN

The book is structured along the lines of the discussion in the pages above. Obviously, not all the questions raised can be answered, since prophecy is not one of the qualifications of political scientists. The book stresses the significance of the role of parliaments and their members at the European and national level for European integration and democratic development in Europe. It pursues an actor-centred approach. In a general sense, the book concentrates on three dimensions: the actors themselves; their embeddedness in processes; and their perspectives on institutional structures. Correspondingly, the book is divided into three parts, dealing with the *role of parliaments and their members* (part I) in European political representation, the *linkages* between the European and the national level (part II), and *problems and institutional change* of the existing institutions (part III).

The actor-centred approach to these questions is made possible by the specific research design on which the study is based. The empirical basis of the analyses is a series of surveys among members of parliament at the European and national levels as well as among candidates to the European Parliament. Before the 1994 European elections, a

mail survey was conducted among candidates to the European Parliament in ten member states (principal investigators: Jacques
Thomassen, University of Twente; Richard Katz, Johns Hopkins University; Pippa Norris, Harvard University; Bernhard Wessels, Wissenschaftszentrum Berlin). In 1996, personal interviews were conducted
with the members of the European Parliament (principal investigators:
Bernhard Wessels and Jacques Thomassen) and in the same year mail
surveys were conducted among members of national parliaments in
eleven member states of the Union (principal investigators: Jacques
Thomassen and Bernhard Wessels). Surveys among candidates and
members are comparable to a large degree, surveys among members of
the European and the national parliaments are almost identical. These
data allow a comparative cross-national, cross-level evaluation of attitudes, positions, and reported action. A detailed study description can
be found in the appendix.

PART I

Role of Parliaments and Parliamentarians

2

Representation, the Locus of Democratic Legitimation and the Role of the National Parliaments in the European Union

RICHARD S. KATZ

AS suggested later in this volume, the question of democratic legitimacy in the European Union generally is approached through the lens of the "responsible parties" (Ranney 1962) or "democratic party government" (Rose 1974; Castles and Wildenmann 1986; Katz 1986b, 1987) model of democracy. Within the context of sovereign unitary states, such as most west European states traditionally have been assumed to be, the meaning and requirements of this mode of government, and its connection to a "populist" (Riker 1982) or "popular sovereignty" (Katz 1997) conception of democracy are relatively unproblematic. The problem is only a bit more complex for states in which subnational governments exercise substantial independent power, even when the national and subnational party systems are not entirely congruent. Nonetheless, even in countries that are federal in formal constitutional terms, the democratic legitimacy of the central government (top tier) clearly rests on its own conformity to the generally accepted norms and requirements of democratic party government.

Democratic legitimation of the national governments thus involves the conformity of governmental institutions and practices to two generally accepted principles. The first principle is that national governments need to be legitimated through national institutions and with reference to a national *demos,* rather than through the transfer or delegation of legitimacy from subnational peoples and subnational institutions. The second principle is that democracy requires that both governors and government policy derive transparently from direct elections among coherent political parties competing precisely on the basis of who should form the government and what policies the government formed should pursue.

It is the manifest failure of the European Union to satisfy these principles, even as the competence of the EU and its direct impact on the daily lives of Europeans have increased, that has given rise to the idea of a "democratic deficit." Certainly, were European elections to be contested by coherent pan-European political parties and to result in the choice of a European Parliament that exercised powers comparable to those of the current national parliaments—including especially the power to choose and dismiss the European executive—the current democratic deficit would be eliminated. It might be replaced, however, by a different variety of democratic deficiency resulting from the scale of the EU and the inevitable distance of its institutions from the people (see Dahl and Tufte 1973). Moreover, the existence of pan-European parties presupposes the prior existence of a European polity and a European people; to the extent that these assumptions are not satisfied, an additional possibility of democratic deficiency might arise. Indeed, not only is the possibility of European democratic legitimation through the institution of a European party government questionable, so too is its desirability, with both the idea of direct rather than delegated legitimacy and the primacy of a popular sovereignty rather than a liberal conception of democracy, in fact, debatable.

Although direct legitimation through top-tier institutions of party government is the norm for discussions of European polities, it is not the only conceivable strategy for legitimation, nor is it the strategy originally envisioned for the European Economic Community (or its predecessor, the ECSC). Instead, these were understood to be legitimate because the governments that came together to form them were legitimate. The primary task of this chapter is to explore this alternative strategy of democratic legitimation for the EU—in particular reconciling the institutions of the EU with contemporary democratic norms by focusing on the national parliaments. In doing so, it will also give greater attention to the functions of parliaments in liberal models of democracy than is usually the case in discussions of European democracies, while recognizing that, as I have argued elsewhere (Katz 1997), the liberal and popular sovereignty conceptions of democracy are best understood as ideal types between which a compromise rather than a choice must be made.

NATIONAL OR EUROPEAN LEVEL LEGITIMATION?

The question of whether the EU should be legitimated through national or European level institutions is closely tied to the question of whether the EU itself should be understood principally as an international, inter-governmental organization or as a developing (almost certainly federal) state (See Newman 1996, ch. 7.). Whatever the aspirations of its founders, the EU in its earlier incarnations as the EEC or EC was in fact an inter-governmental organization, operating on the basis of a "permissive consensus", under which no one worried about the institution's lack of democratic legitimacy so long as it produced results to which the vast majority of citizens did not strenuously object.[1] At least at the elite level, economic success or necessity trumped democratic legitimacy, and the elites were the only ones consulted. To the limited extent that democratic legitimacy was a concern, it was presumed to derive from the legitimacy of the contracting national governments. So long as all important decisions in the Council were taken unanimously, one could at least rationalize a kind of indirect legitimation by assuming that every Council decision was tacitly endorsed by every national parliament, since the ministers were responsible to the parliaments, and the assent of all ministers was required to make any important decision. With the increased use of qualified majority voting, it is no longer possible to assume national parliamentary consent to every decision since any particular country's minister may have been outvoted, and moreover this possibility allows even a minister apparently on the winning side of a vote to argue that his or her assent was required to prevent something worse from being adopted by an alternative majority. Nonetheless, especially to the extent that one prefers an inter-governmental, or even a confederal, model of European cooperation (integration is perhaps too strong a word in this context), it is reasonable to suggest that the appropriate cure for this problem is to increase the accountability of the Council and of the rest of the EU institutions to the national parliaments as the true representatives of the sovereign European peoples.

The proper nature of democratic legitimation at the European level also is debatable. In the popular sovereignty model, the purpose of elections and representative institutions is to articulate the "national" (majority) will and further its translation into public policy. There is assumed to be a fusion of government, parliament, party, and popular majority. The primary function of a member of parliament is to facilitate the popular direction of government by supporting (or opposing) the executive based on partisanship, and the executive's fidelity to the policies that it (and he or she as a candidate of one of the parties) proposed in the last election. The liberal model, on the other hand, assumes a separation between government and parliament, with the primary function of the latter being to oversee and limit, rather than direct, the former. In place of a single majority (albeit one whose exact composition may shift over time with the formation and breakup of government coalitions) whose will is to be implemented, the liberal model assumes there to be a plurality of demands that must be articulated and interests that must be protected. From the perspective of members of parliament, party cohesion is less important and representation of particular constituencies, whether defined by geography or interest, is more important.

A liberal model of democracy in the EU could be implemented through the European Parliament, especially if the European executive were either directly elected or chosen on the basis of a European equivalent to the Swiss "magic formula" for allocation of seats in the Federal Council. So long as the individual national interests of the member states remain paramount among the interests that need to be protected, however, this conception of democracy also suggests the possibility of a significant role for the national parliaments. And to the extent that the powers of the European Union are perceived to be growing at the expense of the national governments, one might also expect the national parliaments to assert an active role not only in the name of the national interests that they claim to represent, but in their own institutional interest as well.

A third reason for interest in the role of the national parliaments in legitimating the European Union is that they are necessarily involved in EU decision-making and implementation under the current institutional arrangements (Laursen and Pappas 1995). Many EU policies are articulated in Brussels, but implemented through specific ministerial decrees, administrative decisions, and statutory changes that are made at the national level. The emphasis on subsidiarity under the Maastricht Treaty only furthers this long-standing principle. While the national parliament is only directly involved in amendments to or passage of legislation, in parliamentary democracies, actions of ministers and bureaucrats derive their legitimacy from the parliament. The same parliamentary oversight and control that reconcile administrative actions with the norms of democratic government for purely domestic issues might be expected to perform the same function with decisions concerning the implementation of EU policies. On the other hand, the effectiveness of these mechanisms as means of democratic legitimation is severely compromised to the extent that ministers and bureaucrats claim that parliamentary oversight is inappropriate in cases in which they are implementing policies of Brussels rather than policies of parliament.

As the preceding suggests, the national parliaments are, and always have been involved in European governance. Aside from such intermittent activities as the ratification of the treaties upon which the EU is based, this involvement takes, or has taken, several forms. Some of these involve actions by the parliaments as institutions, while others involve activities of individual members of parliament, albeit in their official roles.

At the institutional level, the national parliaments may be called upon to enact or modify legislation required by European directives. The degree to which this is required varies among policy areas and among the member states, depending on whether the relevant policies traditionally are controlled by statute or by administrative or ministerial decree/order, and depending on the constitutional arrangements of the country involved. In some cases there has been movement to increase the involvement of the parliament in the national implementation/ratification of European directives. For example, the Irish European Communities Act 1972 allowed ministers to repeal or amend existing Irish laws in order to conform to European regulations; in 1993, however, the Irish High Court ruled this provision contrary to the Irish constitution, ruling that only the Oireachtas (the Irish parliament in the full technical sense—the Dáil, the Seanad, and the President) could repeal Irish statutes (*John Meagher v The Minister for Agriculture and Food, Ireland and the Attorney General*).

Even if the assent of the national parliament is required for the implementation of European decisions, however, this may be more significant in form than in substance. On the one hand, the parliament may simply be presented with an annual omnibus bill, as was instituted in 1989 in Italy by the La Pergola Law, rather than being asked to debate and approve individual decisions as they arise. On the other hand, given the obligations imposed by the treaties and in particular the supremacy of EU law over national law, even when parliamentary assent is required, it is not clear that the parliament has the realistic option of withholding its assent. It is in this spirit, for example, that the British and Spanish parliaments have in effect permanently delegated to their governments the power to transpose Union directives into national law (Laprat 1995: 14).

Somewhat less directly, the national parliaments are involved in European decision-making as a result of their general capacity to influence and oversee the actions of the governments that are, at least nominally, responsible to them. In 1995, all the national parliaments except the Irish and Luxembourgeois had established special committees to deal with European Union affairs. The Danish Folketing has carried this to the greatest lengths, with a select committee on European Affairs that debates in advance of meetings of the Council the positions that should be taken by Danish ministers, although as must be the case when decisions will be made by negotiation and vote, the committee's decisions cannot be binding on the ministers. At other times, parliamentary influence may be exercised through the less formal means of speeches, resolutions, interpellations, or intervention with ministers or ministries on behalf of constituents.

A third route for MNPs to participate in European decision-making is through contacts with MEPs. In the early days of the EP, MNPs were the MEPs. While direct election of the EP may have contributed to the European democratic legitimacy of Europe, one potentially negative consequence was to weaken the link between the national parliaments and the EP. Nonetheless, formal meetings between a country's MEP delegation and members of the national parliament(ary committee), and even more the establishing, as in Belgium and Germany, of joint parliamentary committees including both MNPs and MEPs continue to provide MNPs with information about, and access to, decision-making at the European level. This then can be supplemented by informal contact between MEPs and MNPs of the same party or representing the same geographic area.

ATTITUDES CONCERNING LEGITIMATION

At the empirical level, the first question one might ask concerning the national parliaments and the problem of European legitimacy is what the MPs themselves, at both national and European levels, think about it. Confronted with the statement "Some people regard the European Parliament as the democratic heart of the Union, because democratic legitimacy of the Union can only be based on a supranational parliament. Others say that this is a wrong ambition because the legitimacy of the Union is already based on the national parliaments", respondents were asked to locate their personal opinions on a seven-point scale ranging between democratic legitimation based on the European Parliament (1) and the national parliaments (7).

As has been suggested above, there are plausible reasons for either answer. Nonetheless, given both the general debate about legitimacy in the EU, and the expectations that would be raised by the prevalence of the party government model in European political thinking, one would expect a strong inclination toward the EP end of the scale. At the same time, one would expect some tendency for respondents to privilege the institution in which they serve, and so for the MNPs to be more inclined than the MEPs to base the legitimacy of the EU on that of the national parliaments rather than the EP.

Table 2.1 shows the distribution of responses in the two surveys. In each case, the data have been weighted to make each national (sub)sample representative of the partisan population from which it is drawn and proportional to the relative size of that nation's delegation in the EP. As the table shows, both hypotheses are confirmed by the data. Nearly half of the MEPs (47.9% of the weighted sample) believe that the democratic legitimacy of the EU must be based primarily on the European Parliament (scores of 1 or 2), a view shared by less than a third (32.0%) of the MNPs. These figures are not strictly comparable, however, because the MEP sample includes respondents from all 15 member states, while the MNP sample includes data only from the 10 national parliaments for which we have data. Restricting attention to those MEPs from countries for which there also are MNP data available (still weighting so that the national contributions to each sample are proportional to the national seat allocation in the EP) shows an

TABLE 2.1. Preferred Locus of Legitimation by Level of Parliament
(Percentages)

The democratic legitimation of the Union should be based on	Members of the European Parliament		Members of the National Parliaments
	Full sample	Countries for which MNP data are available	
1 the European Parliament	30.1	35.7	14.0
2	17.8	20.4	18.0
3	16.5	16.3	15.0
4	14.2	16.8	27.1
5	5.5	2.6	9.3
6	6.5	3.6	9.6
7 the national parliaments	9.4	4.6	7.1
N (weighted)	308 (309)	217 (196)	1237 (794)

even greater difference, with 56.1% of the MEPs scored 1 or 2 on the 7-point scale.

While the majority of MEPs opt for democratic legitimacy through the EP, the majority of MNPs appear to favour a mixed solution, in which both the EP and the national parliaments contribute to the overall legitimacy of the EU. For respondents from both institutions, the mean score is on the EP side of the midpoint, but the mean, as expected, is closer to the EP end of the scale for the MEPs than it is for the MNPs. For the MEP sample, the mean is 3.04 on the 7-point scale with a median score of 3 (a mean of 2.59 and a median of 2 in the restricted sample); for the MNPs, the mean score is 3.57 with the median exactly on the midpoint of the scale (4).

The overall distributions reported in Table 2.1 conceal very large differences among the national samples, especially for the MEPs. The magnitude of the national differences is revealed in Table 2.2, which gives the mean response for each group. The finding that MEPs are likely to give greater prominence to the EP as the basis for the democratic legitimacy of the EU, while MNPs will give relatively greater prominence to the national parliaments, is reproduced for nine of the ten countries for which we have data from the MNPs.

The expectation that MEPs, and even MNPs, would, on balance, lean toward assuming that the democratic legitimacy of the EU must derive at least in large measure from the EP was not uniformly

TABLE 2.2. Mean Preferred Locus of Legitimation
by Level of Parliament and Nationality

	MEPs	MNPs	eta
Austria	3.73		
Belgium	2.65	3.17	.112
Denmark	5.84		
Finland	4.52		
France	4.40		
Germany	1.84	3.16	.320
Greece	2.28	4.27	.530
Ireland	3.77	4.85	.285
Italy	2.32	3.26	.248
Luxembourg	3.20	5.04	.485
Netherlands	2.62	3.60	.206
Portugal	3.86	4.56	.151
Spain	2.49	3.13	.164
Sweden	5.97	5.50	.135
United Kingdom	2.96		
Overall [full (restricted) samples]	3.04 (2.59)	3.57	.129 (.219)
Cross national eta [full (restricted) samples]	.551 (.566)	.390	

confirmed in the national samples. For five of the ten samples of MNPs, the mean response was higher than 4, indicating primary weight was given to the national parliaments as the source of EU legitimacy; moreover, this was true for four of the 15 national sub-samples of MEPs as well. Indeed, at least half of the respondents in the Swedish and Danish samples of MEPs chose the "national parliaments" end point of the 7-point scale, while only one respondent in either sample chose a point on the EP side of the midpoint. At the other extreme, not a single German, Luxembourgeois, or Spanish MEP chose a response on the "national parliaments" side of the midpoint.

In addition to identifying the proper locus for the democratic legitimation of the EU, each respondent was asked to identify on an 11-point scale "how much influence the following institutions and organs ought to have concerning decision-making in the European Union?" The first and last cues on this list were the European Parliament and the National Parliaments. Comparison of these responses provides an alternative approach to the question of the proper role of the national parliaments in the EU political system.

The overall pattern is very much like that observed with regard to strategy for legitimation. As shown in Table 2.3, respondents from each institution tend to believe that both institutions should have significant influence in EU decision-making; the lowest mean and median values (MEP views of the proper influence of the national parliaments) are each at or above the midpoint of the 11-point scale. Respondents from each institution tend to believe that the EP should have more influence that the national parliaments in European decision-making; on average, MEPs placed the European Parliament 2.20 points higher that the national parliaments on the 11-point scale (3.05 points in the restricted sample), while MNPs placed the European Parliament 1.18 points higher. Respondents from each institution tend to believe their own institution should have more influence than respondents from the other institution believe it should have. For the European Parliament the difference in means (but not in medians) actually is marginally the reverse of that expected when the full sample of MEPs is compared to the MNPs; this exception, however, is the result of the different national compositions of the sample, in particular the inclusion of the "anti-EP" Danes in the MEP but not in the MNP sample. When like is compared to like looking at the restricted MEP sample, the difference is both larger and in the expected direction. For the national parliaments the inter-institutional difference in preferred level of influence is quite substantial, with MNPs placing their institution nearly 1.5 points (mean; 2 points looking at the median) higher on the 11-point scale than it was place by the MEPs of the same countries.

TABLE 2.3. Mean and Median Preference Level of Influence in European Union Decision-making by Institution.

	Members of the European Parliament		Members of the National Parliaments
	full sample	restricted sample	
Preferred Influence of European Parliament	mean = 8.75 median = 10.00	mean = 9.26 median = 10.00	mean = 8.86 median = 9.00
Preferred Influence of National Parliaments	mean = 6.55 median = 7.00	mean = 6.21 median = 6.00	mean = 7.68 median = 8.00

Again, these aggregate figures conceal great national variations. Taking the difference between the preferred influence of the EP and the preferred influence of national parliaments (computed so that a negative score indicates a preference for the national parliaments to be the more influential), Table 2.4 shows again that the relative preference for EP influence generally is greater within each of the national pairs than it is overall, again with the Swedes standing out as a marked exception. Even among the MEPs from the other countries, however, the belief that greater influence should be exercised by the European Parliament is far from universal. As with the preferred strategy for legitimation, the Swedish and Danish MEPs are predominantly oriented toward the national rather than the European levels, with only one Dane of seven, and five Swedes of 14, suggesting that the greater influence should be exercised by the European Parliament. Although the differences are less dramatic, the Finnish MEPs and the Irish, Luxembourgeois, Portuguese, and Swedish MNPs also on average report that the influence of the national parliaments should be greater than that of the European Parliament, *in making European Union policy.*

INSTITUTIONAL EXPLANATIONS OF
INTERNATIONAL DIFFERENCES

The correlations between the mean scores for the ten MNP samples and the scores for the MEP samples of the same country are 0.82 for the strategy for legitimation scale and 0.73 for the relative preferred influence scale, underscoring the idea that there are systematic cross-national differences in preferred strategy of legitimation for the EU and in preferred relative influence of the two levels of parliaments. What, then, explains the differences among national mean scores?

One possible explanation is time in the EU. The ideas of parliamentary, or at least of national, sovereignty, and of democratic legitimacy rooted securely in the election of the national parliament have been established in European political thinking for a long time; presumably it takes time to adapt to the idea of a supranational alternative. If this is so, one would expect that the average scores for MEP and MNP samples from long-standing members would be closer to the EP end of the 7-point scale than those for samples from the newer members, and

TABLE 2.4. Mean Difference Between Preferred Influence for EP and NPs by
Level of Parliament and Nationality

	Members of the European Parliament	Members of the National Parliaments	eta
Austria	2.34		
Belgium	4.45	2.19	.222
Denmark	-4.63		
Finland	-.71		
France	.37		
Germany	3.63	1.83	.252
Greece	3.06	.81	.381
Ireland	1.47	-.50	.267
Italy	3.95	1.35	.330
Luxembourg	2.60	-1.71	.440
Netherlands	3.62	1.28	.264
Portugal	1.57	-.72	.328
Spain	2.85	1.70	.178
Sweden	-2.99	-1.47	.162
United Kingdom	2.04		
Overall	2.19 (3.05)	1.18	.132 (.230)
Cross-national eta	.494 (.472)	.290	

correspondingly that the average scores on the relative preferred influence scale would be greater (more weighted toward the EP) for respondents from long-standing members. The correlations between year of accession to the treaties and the national average score with regard to strategy for legitimation are .468 for the 15 MEP samples (.642 for the 10 MEP samples from the same countries as the MNP samples) and .497 for the ten MNP samples; the corresponding correlations between year of accession and national average relative preferred influence scores for the MEPs and MNPs are -.423 (-.751 for the 10 nation subsample) and -.412.

A second institutional explanation suggests that willingness to situate democratic legitimacy primarily in the EP depends on the weight that each country has within it. The larger the country's representation in the EP, the more willing respondents from that country might be to see the EP as the primary source of legitimacy at the European level, and the more willing they might be to see the primary locus of parliamentary influence on EU decision-making be the EP; conversely, this argument suggests that respondents from countries with little weight in

EU decision-making will insist that their national parliaments provide the primary basis for EU legitimacy and be the primary locus of parliamentary influence. This hypothesis can be tested by examining the correlations between the average strategy of legitimation and preferred relative influence of the parliaments scores, on the one hand, and the number of MEPs attributed to each country, on the other. For the 15 MEP delegations, the correlations are r = -.438 and r = .291 (-.539 and .377 for the 10 nation subsample), while for the 10 MNP samples, the correlations are r = -.720 and r = .640.

While both hypotheses are supported by the data from both levels of parliament, the strength of support differs in an entirely understandable way. The "national socialization" effect appears stronger for the MEPs, who are, after all, meeting regularly with their European colleagues and actually working in a transnational environment; whatever the process through which the national socialization effect operates, one would expect it to impact them most directly. Conversely, the "national defensiveness" effect appears to be substantially stronger for the MNPs, who do not have the experience of cross-national cooperation in the EP to mitigate fears of being submerged in a transnational pond in which their compatriots would be very small fish.

EXPLAINING INDIVIDUAL DIFFERENCES

While these institutional variables make an important contribution toward explaining the national differences in average scores, a large proportion of these differences still remains to be explained. With the individual MP as the unit of analysis, the impact of the institutional variables remains evident, but instead of accounting for as much as half of the variance in the dependent variables (adjusted R^2), they never account for more than 10% of the variance. (The multiple correlations between the two institutional variables and the strategy for legitimation and the relative preferred influence scales are shown in Table 2.5.) This suggests that one look to individual level influences to explain the within-delegation variance in these attitudes. One can then return to the national averages to see the extent to which the differences in national averages can be explained by national differences in the distributions of the individual level factors.

TABLE 2.5. Multiple Correlations of Length of EU Membership and Number of
MEPs with Preferred Strategy of Legitimation and Relative Parliamentary
Influence

Unit of analysis	Sample	Strategy of legitimation	Relative parliamentary influence
National averages	MEPs, all countries	.541	.443
	MEPs, 10 countries	.747	.773
	MNPs	.786	.687
Individuals	MEPs, all countries	.240	.170
	MEPs, 10 countries	.423	.343
	MNPs	.293	.214

The analysis and discussion so far suggest a number of hypotheses
concerning individual level explanations of individuals' preferred strategy for legitimation and relative influence of the European and national
parliaments in addition to the simple facts of their nationality and their
location in one institution or the other. First, while some of the effect of
institutional membership (in addition to a possible self-selection bias)
may come in an immediate recognition of institutional interest, much of
it is likely to come as the result of socialization and experience. If this
is so, one would expect the institutional effects already observed to be
strongest for those with the longest tenure in their institutions. Thus,
MEPs with longer service in the EP should be more inclined than other
MEPs to identify the EP as the necessary locus of EU legitimacy and to
prefer relatively greater EP influence in EU decision-making, while the
reverse should be true for MNPs with longer service in their national
parliament.

As suggested earlier, the choice between the EP and the national parliaments is associated with the choice between alternative conceptions
of the EU. Those who think of the EU in terms analogous to a national
state should favour greater prominence for the EP, while those who
think of the EU as a compact among states should favour greater
prominence for the national parliaments. While respondents were not
asked directly about their conceptions of the EU, one place in which
this distinction comes to the fore is with regard to decision-making in
the Council. Emphasis on national sovereignty is, in effect, only
compatible with a requirement of unanimity in the Council; all varieties
of voting, whether by qualified or simple majority, and whether with

votes counted on a one-country-one-vote basis or weighted by size or importance, imply a diminution or loss of sovereignty. MEPs were asked about their preferred Council decision rule, and the expectation is that those who opted for unanimity will have scores on both scales that assign greater importance to the national parliaments. (Unfortunately, the MNPs were not asked a comparable question.)

If democracy at the European level presupposes the existence of a European *demos*, one might expect that those individuals who feel themselves to be part of such a *demos* would be more likely than others to see the European Parliament as the necessary focus of democratic legitimation and to prefer relatively greater influence for the European Parliament. In order to test this hypothesis, a scale of European identity was constructed by combining the scores on three agree/disagree scales: "The differences between European countries are far less than the similarities"; "I feel proud to be a European"; "European unity threatens my country's cultural identity".[2] Those who score at the European end of this composite measure should also assign greater weight to the European Parliament.

One might also expect attitudes toward the basis of European legitimacy and the relative roles of European versus national institutions to be influenced by prudential concerns. In particular, the greater the respondent's confidence "that decisions made by the European Union will be in the interest of your country," the more inclined that person should be to identify the EP as the primary locus of democratic legitimacy for the Union and the greater the relative influence that person is likely to prefer for the EP. Analogously, those who are relatively more satisfied (in the vast majority of cases, relatively dissatisfied, but to a lesser degree) with "the way democracy works in the European Union" as compared to the way democracy works in their own country, and those who agree that "The European Union has strengthened democracy" should also be willing to give relatively greater prominence to the EP. At the same time, however, one must remember the possibility that dissatisfaction with the working of democracy at the European level may be caused by a feeling that the EP, as the "democratic" European institution, does not currently have adequate influence.

Table 2.6 reports the bivariate correlations testing each of these hypotheses. With two pairs of exceptions—the correlations with relative satisfaction with European-level democracy for the MNPs, and with tenure in parliament for the restricted sample of MEPs—the signs

TABLE 2.6. Correlations of Individual Level Predictors with Preferred Locus of Legitimation and Preferred Relative Influence

	MEPs, full sample		MEPs, 10 nation sample		MNPs	
	Locus of Legitimation	Relative Influence of the EP	Locus of Legitimation	Relative Influence of the EP	Locus of Legitimation	Relative Influence of the EP
Length of Tenure as an M(E)P	-.154	.091	.058	-.038	.105	-.065
Preference for Unanimity in the Council	-.681	.620	-.605	.485		
Sense of Europeanness	.623	-.544	.326	-.234	.275	-.170
EU Decisions Are in the Country's Interest	.684	-.602	.360	-.286	.271	-.184
Relative Satisfaction with European-level Democracy	.254	-.244	.017	-.036	-.026	.038
EU Has Strengthened Democracy	.487	-.487	.116	-.142	.054	-.074

of all the correlations are as hypothesized. Particularly for the full sample of MEPs, and particularly for the belief that EU decisions are in the interest of the respondent's country, his/her sense of Europeanness, and his/her attitude concerning unanimity as the decision rule for the Council (MEPs only), the correlations are quite impressive substantively as well.

The overall picture of strong relationships for the MEPs but much weaker relationships for the MNPs is continued in Table 2.7, in which the independent variables are taken together in a series of multiple regression analyses. Aside from this difference, several other observations may be made.

First, the degree to which attitudes about questions of EU structure are highly interrelated is demonstrated by the high betas attached to the preferred Council decision rule for the MEPs. Assuming that this variable may be taken as an indicator of the respondent's more general attitude about the EU as a compact among sovereign states as opposed to being a protostate itself, this attitude appears to be the most powerful explanation of attitudes about the proper basis of European legitimacy. Moreover, if the relationships between the preferred status of the EP and other preferred institutional arrangements presage reactions to changes in those other arrangements, one might anticipate that as such reforms as greater use of qualified majority voting in the Council proceed, pressure for the EP and European elections to play more prominent roles in European legitimation (or else that the negative consequences of their failure to play such a role) will increase.

Second, nationalism continues to exercise nearly as large an influence over attitudes about legitimation in the EU as attitudes about the nature of the EU. At the same time, however, the respondent's own sense of Europeanness also contributes to explaining the attitudes of members of parliaments about EU legitimation. Respondents from both the European and the national parliaments who believe that EU decisions are in the interest of their own country, and respondents who are more inclined to think of themselves as "European," are more likely than others to favour greater influence for the EP and a European basis for democratic legitimation.

Third, with these variables controlled, both parliamentary experience and evaluations of European-level democracy as it currently exists make no significant contribution to the explanation of attitudes regarding EU legitimation. (At the same time, however, it should be remem-

TABLE 2.7. Regression of Preferred Locus of Legitimation and Preferred Relative Influence with Individual Level Predictors (Table entries are standardized regression coefficients.)

	MEPs, full sample		MEPs, 10 nation sample		MNPs	
	Locus of Legitimation	Relative Influence of the EP	Locus of Legitimation	Relative Influence of the EP	Locus of Legitimation	Relative Influence of the EP
Length of Tenure as an M(E)P	-.074	.011	-.057	-.026	.129	-.091
Preference for Unanimity in the Council	-.376	.350	-.444	.302	.216	-.139
Sense of Europeanness	.162	-.091	.123	-.058	.186	-.096
EU Decisions Are in the Country's Interest	.325	-.254	.241	-.256	-.063	.069
Relative Satisfaction with European-level Democracy	.077	-.080	.023	-.155	-.026	-.034
EU Has Strengthened Democracy	.025	-.116	-.007	-.032		
Adjusted R^2	.617	.486	.458	.307	.118	.046
Adjusted R^2 with country dummies added	.653	.526	.504	.346	.162	.103
Adjusted R^2 with country dummies alone	.270	.202	.292	.180	.088	.073

bered that parliamentary experience may have an indirect impact on these attitudes by influencing their more proximate causes, and that negative evaluations of European-level democracy may reflect the belief either that the EP has too little influence at present, or that it—and indeed the whole European apparatus—has too much.)

By comparing the last three lines of Table 2.7, one can see the degree to which interpersonal differences with regard to the individual level explanatory variables account for national level differences among the respondents. The first of these lines shows the proportion of the individual level variance explained by the regression equations presented in the table. The second shows the variance explained by regression models in which the same independent variables are supplemented by national dummy variables. The smaller the difference between the two figures, the smaller the remaining "unexplained" national differences. Finally, the last line shows the variance explained by the national dummy variables alone.

Three reasons may be suggested for the relative incapacity of these individual level variables to account either for the individual variation in MNP attitudes about European legitimation or the aggregate differences among the members of the various national parliaments (and also, in part, the fact that the level of national distinctiveness reflected by those aggregate differences is so much smaller for the MNPs than the MEPs). The first is the omission from the MNP instrument of the question concerning the proper Council decision rule, or any other question addressing the respondent's conception of the EU as a compact among sovereign states or as a protostate itself. This is the most powerful single predictor of the attitudes of MEPs, and so its absence in the MNP models naturally reduces the proportion of the variance in the dependent variables that can be explained. On the other hand, even when it is omitted from the MEP regressions, these still explain substantially more variance than the corresponding regressions for the MNPs.

The second possibility is that the attitudes of MNPs regarding legitimation at the European level are to be explained differently from those of MEPs. While this cannot, of course, be disproven, especially given that nearly half of the MEPs were or had been members of their national parliaments there is no reason to suppose that the thinking of parliamentarians at these two different levels are sufficiently different as to account for the differences in levels of explained variance.

The third possibility is that the low level of explained variance for the MNPs reflects not that there is a different explanation but, in effect, that there is no explanation. In particular, it is possible that for MNPs, the "European question" is simply "more Europe" versus "less Europe," so that they have not thought about the subtler questions of how European institutions should be structured or what their proper relations to national institutions should be. In this case, the dependent variables in regressions for the MNPs might better be described as "nonattitudes," and inability to produce a powerful explanation of individual level variation in them is only to be expected.

NATIONAL PARLIAMENTARY OVERSIGHT

Whatever the views of MNPs and MEPs (and others) regarding the proper role of the national parliaments in the EU policy process, those parliaments currently do play a role, and one which under the scenario of subsidiarity might be expected to increase. In any event, the idea of democratic legitimation through the national parliaments is based on the presumption of effective national parliamentary oversight of the positions national ministers take in the Council—failing this, the members of the EU's most important decision-making body would be, in effect, responsible to no one.

Respondents from both levels of parliament were asked whether their national parliament "is exercising too much or too little supervision over the positions of the <COUNTRY> government in the Council of Ministers of the European Union?" using a scale ranging from 1 ("Too much") to 7 ("Too little"). The means of the distributions of responses are shown in Table 2.8.

What is most striking in the table is the degree of consensus among respondents from both levels of parliament that the national parliaments are not exercising enough supervision of the positions their countries take in the Council. Contrary to any expectation that MNPs would be anxious to exercise more control over their national ministers but that MEPs, taking a more "European" orientation (in which the Council would be seen as an institution of a European polity, rather than as a gathering of representatives of national polities) would want less national parliamentary oversight, roughly half of both MNPs and

TABLE 2.8. Mean Evaluation of Parliamentary Supervision over Ministers by
Level of Parliament and Nationality

	MEPs	MNPs	eta
Austria	3.94		
Belgium	5.48	5.67	.064
Denmark	5.18		
Finland	4.50		
France	5.46		
Germany	5.25	5.50	.079
Greece	6.38	5.90	.169
Ireland	4.44	5.09	.172
Italy	5.72	5.34	.127
Luxembourg	6.20	5.52	.236
Netherlands	5.52	5.58	.024
Portugal	5.02	4.93	.029
Spain	4.76	4.18	.146
Sweden	5.75	5.18	.189
United Kingdom	5.66		
Overall	5.35	5.22	.042
[full (restricted) samples]	(5.37)		(.044)
Cross national eta	.338	.374	
[full (restricted) samples]	(.328)		

MEPs chose one of the two points at the "Too little" end of the scale;
indeed, a larger proportion of MEPs than of MNPs chose the "Too
little" end-point. At the other end of the scale, fewer than 10% of either
sample chose any of the three scale points indicating a belief that their
national parliament was exercising too much oversight. While there are
only extremely minimal differences between the MEP and MNP samples from the same country, there are, however, more substantial cross-
national differences in evaluations of current levels of national parliamentary supervision.

One might suppose that the best explanation of satisfaction with parliamentary oversight would be the actual quality of that oversight. Unfortunately, we have no direct measure of this, but quality of oversight
ought to be reflected in MEPs' and MNPs' general evaluations of the
working of democracy in their country. Presumably, inadequate
parliamentary involvement is one reason for believing that democracy
is working less than optimally. Hence, one would hypothesize that
respondents who give less favourable evaluations of the working of

TABLE 2.9. Mean Evaluation of Parliamentary Supervision over Ministers by
Satisfaction with the Working of National Democracy and Level of Parliament

Satisfaction with the Way Democracy Works in <Country>	Members of the European Parliament		Members of the National Parliaments
	Full Sample	Restricted Sample	
Very satisfied	4.85	4.85	5.05
Fairly satisfied	5.23	5.35	5.06
Not very satisfied	5.76	5.58	5.73
Note at all satisfied	5.67	6.36	6.16
eta	.212	.207	.235

democracy in their country will be more likely to believe that parliamentary supervision over the positions of ministers within the Council
of Ministers of the EU should be increased. As Table 2.9 shows, this
expectation is supported by the data for both the MEPs and the MNPs;
those who are generally satisfied with the workings of democracy in
their own countries are less critical of the degree of supervision over
the positions taken by their national ministers in the Council exercised
by their national parliaments. Nonetheless, even among those who
report themselves to be "very satisfied" with the democracy in their
countries, the mean position for the MEPs is nearly a full point to the
"too little" side of the mid-point of the 7-point scale, while for the
MNPs, the mean is more than a full point to the "too little" side.

CONCLUSIONS

This analysis leads to two sets of conclusions. One set concerns the
differences between MEPs and MNPs, and the differences within each
group among respondents from the different member states of the EU
and among respondents as individuals. The other set concerns the
generalizations that can be drawn across institutional and national lines.

Looking first at the overall differences between MEPs and MNPs, it
is apparent that MEPs on average hold views more consistent with the
model of the EU as an emerging state than do their national level
counterparts. MEPs are more likely to believe that the democratic
legitimation of the EU should be based on European elections and

parliament, and they generally prefer a greater role for the European Parliament as compared to the national parliaments in the making of EU decisions. In part these differences might reflect self-interest; respondents are suggesting greater influence should be exercised by the institution of which they are members. In part, they might also reflect self selection; politicians are unlikely to seek election to positions that they believe should be unimportant. In part they reflect socialization into the norms of the institutions, regardless of the respondents' prior beliefs.

These differences between respondents from the two levels of parliament are apparent both across and within national samples. There also are significant differences between nations. Again, these differences are not surprising. Respondents from countries that have been in the EU for longer, and respondents from countries that have greater weight within the EU by virtue of their greater size, tend to take a more "European" view regarding the balance between national and supranational influence and legitimation. When individual differences in attitudes to questions such as preferred Council decision rule, personal sense of Europeanness, relative satisfaction with European-level democracy, and belief that EU decisions are in the interest of their own country are taken into account, the additional marginal explanatory power of nationality is reduced to practically nothing for the MEPs. For the MNPs, however, not only do these individual level variables explain a lot less, they also leave larger national differences so far only "explained" by the observation that "Portuguese are different from Dutch."

While these differences are significant, in the broader context of European democratic development excessive attention to the differences risks overlooking the more important and deeper similarities. When forced to make a choice or comparison, there is broad agreement, even among MNPs, that the EU's claim to democratic legitimacy should be based primarily on European rather than national institutions, and that the European Parliament should play a greater role than the national parliaments in EU decision-making. In this respect, both MNPs and MEPs are "Europeans." But as the data concerning national parliamentary supervision of ministerial positions in the Council indicate, both MNPs and MEPs also are parliamentarians. While both groups believe on average that the EP should exercise greater influence than it currently does in Brussels/Strasbourg/Luxembourg, both groups also think that the national parliaments should exercise greater supervision in their own national capitals. Thus if one conclusion is that the democratic deficit reflects the failure of European elections and the European Parliament to perform the functions expected of elections and parliaments in democratic systems at the national level, a second is that the democratic deficit reflects the nature of the European Union as an inter-ministerial cabal presiding over a technocracy, with national parliaments also unable to fulfil their representative and legitimizing functions.

NOTES

1   Note that failure to object is a very different thing from approval. For many citizens, it undoubtedly reflected indifference or obliviousness rather than approval. For others, it may have reflected the difficulty of organizing to manifest opposition in the absence of a clear focus and without the aid of "political entrepreneurs." On this last point, see Olson (1971).

2   The actual measure is the factors scores generated by a principal components analysis of these variables. The first component, derived in roughly equal measure from each of the three input variables, accounted for 52.3% of the variance in the three variables.

3

Making Europeans? The Socializing Power of the European Parliament

MARK N. FRANKLIN AND SUSAN E. SCARROW

IT often has been asserted or assumed that Members of the European Parliament, along with members of other institutions of the European Union, are more pro-European in outlook than other, national, elites (Duff 1994; Newman 1996). This assertion seems plausible in the light of reported current events, which tend to emphasize conflicts between national and European levels. On the one hand, news about the European Parliament (EP) tends to highlight incidents when legislators challenge other European or domestic institutions, as for instance when they take issue with the decisions of the domestically controlled Council of Ministers. On the other hand, the European decisions of domestic legislatures seem most likely to make headlines when national parliaments act as populist defenders of national political privileges against the encroachments of the European Union. Yet though it is plausible that these conflicts are rooted in institutionally systematic differences between individual legislators' attitudes, with those sitting in the European assembly being more generally favourable towards the European project than their national counterparts, there have been few attempts to test the extent to which this is the case. Moreover, even if evidence shows this assumption to be correct, the origins of these attitudinal differences are by no means obvious.

There are three possible sources of differences in the way that national and European representatives regard European institution-building. These are electoral bias, the self-selection of candidates for the European Parliament, and the effects of holding office within the Parliament itself. Electoral bias might function in several ways. To begin with, the differences might reflect voters' differing concerns in national and European elections. In other words, it might be the case that individual voters are more likely to support parties with more pro-European candidates in European rather than in national races. Alternately, or additionally, voter self-selection may be systematically biased in a way that reinforces this effect. Thus, if pro-European voters are more motivated than others to participate in the generally low-turn-out European contests, pro-European candidates will be relatively advantaged. According to these explanations, differences between European and domestic legislatures could be understood as the product of citizens' preferences. While this would be an encouraging interpretation for those interested in the legitimacy of the European body, the explanation seems highly implausible in light of what we know about individual decision-making in European elections.

Evidence from studies of voting behaviour in the European elections of 1979 to 1994 (Reif and Schmitt 1980; Reif 1984; van der Eijk and Franklin 1996) makes it clear that European voters do not have different objectives and concerns when voting in European elections than they do when voting in national elections. Rather, European elections function as surrogate national elections. The context presented to voters is that of their national political system and the issues are those currently on the national political agenda. This seems to be because party leaders take care not to allow European matters to impinge on the electoral process. In short, what we know about voters suggests that if there is evidence of a pro-European bias among Members of the European Parliament (MEPs), it is probably not the result of voters' deliberate choices. On the other hand, parties' internal processes for allocating winnable seats and safe list places could tend to favour more pro-European candidates when the office contested is a European one. Both of these mechanisms would yield more pro-European attitudes among winning candidates than among losing candidates. If there is no evidence of any such effect, then we will have to look to self-selection or experiences in the European Parliament itself to explain discrepancies between national and European representatives.

The self-selection argument holds that those who choose to participate in building the new institutions of a united Europe are more likely than others to regard the European project in a positive light. Accumulated experience with direct elections to the European Parliament may reinforce this self-selection bias, giving Members and prospective candidates increasing reasons to view election to the European Parliament as a prelude to a career in the European, not the domestic, arena (Scarrow 1997).

Finally, it may be that the European Parliament itself influences the attitudes of those who work within it. This process may have two aspects, long-term socialization, and the more immediate adoption of institutional interests. In the first place, it has been well-understood for many years that legislatures have a socializing effect on their members (see, for example, Matthews 1960), leading them to adopt over time the norms and behaviours sometimes called "folkways," after the title of the original socialization study (Sumner 1907). In addition, it is often assumed that "where you stand depends upon where you sit"—in other words, that upon election career-minded politicians immediately acquire a personal stake in the institution within which they serve, particularly if they hope to be re-elected (Schlesinger 1966).

Haas (1958) long ago suggested that this intertwining of personal and institutional interests might take a specific form in European bodies, where we could expect that members would develop loyalties that would predispose them to favour the integration process. Haas argued that such a process had occurred in the European Coal and Steel Community (ECSC) Common Assembly of the 1950s. Though many members entered this body as committed Europeans, once in the Assembly, "the pressures generated by ECSC institutions and the prior commitments of the parliamentarians ... combined to make the bulk of the members outgrow the boundaries of the national state as referents of legislative action" (Haas 1958: 438). Immediately before the advent of European elections, Marquand and others argued that direct elections of MEPs would intensify this process, because Members who wished to be re-elected would want to persuade voters (and themselves) of the importance of the European Parliament (Marquand 1979: 71-4; also Lodge and Hermann 1982: 280ff). More recently and more specifically, Corbett, Jacobs, and Shackleton have argued that such pro-European socialization has occurred within the directly-elected European Parliament, affecting even some legislators who initially were elected on an anti-European platform (1995: 300).

The earliest attempt to test the relative influence of socialization and self-selection in the European parliamentary context (Kerr 1973) found little evidence that parliamentary service generated pro-European attitudes. However, it did confirm that MEPs held more pro-European attitudes than members of the national parliaments from which they were then drawn.[1] These results led Kerr to conclude that Members of the European Parliament were more pro-European than national legislators as a result of self-selection, not socialization (76-7). This matched the findings of an earlier study which also concluded that self-selection, not institutional learning, accounted for the more pro-European attitudes of Scandinavian legislators who attended transnational assemblies (the Nordic Council or the Consultative Assembly of the Council of Europe) (Bonham 1970). However, later studies of the European Parliament (eg. Cotta 1984) have treated Kerr's finding cautiously. Not only was it based on a small number of interviews with British and German MEPs; also, and more importantly, the study was conducted before the advent of direct elections to the European body, when MEPs were chosen by governments from among members of the national parliaments. In another survey of MEPs, this time conducted after the advent of direct elections, Bowler and Farrell could find evidence of only very limited socialization of a different kind, the transmission of behavioural norms. However, their results do not touch directly on the transmission of pro-European attitudes or behaviours (Bowler and Farrell 1993). Elsewhere, a recent paper by Scully (1997) has attempted to ascertain the extent of pro-European socialization using roll-call data, asking whether those with the longest service records have a greater propensity to vote in ways that increase the powers of the European Union or the European Parliament. While Scully finds no evidence of pro-European socialization, the test is problematic (as he acknowledges), given that behaviour on single votes provides no insights into intensity of preferences, and seldom can be used to test whether individuals change their views over time.

In this chapter we are able for the first time to take a more direct approach to the question of self-selection versus socialization, because we are able to use survey data to investigate the nature and sources of representatives' attitudes towards Europe. These data were collected between 1994 and 1996 in connection with the European Parliament Representation Study, described elsewhere in this volume. In that period, interviews were conducted with candidates for the European Parliament prior to the 1994 election, with Members of the European Parliament (including re-interviews of some of the candidates) following the election, and with members of national parliaments after the 1994 election. (The latter were elected at various times, but all were members of domestic legislatures in the same period.) This set of surveys enables us, for the first time since the 1979 inauguration of direct elections to the European Parliament, systematically to study the attitudinal effects of parliamentary membership—without needing to infer attitudes from roll call votes or legislative speeches. Because the datasets were created for other purposes, the overlap between them is not as great as it might be; and the small sample size available for certain comparisons means that some findings may not be definitive. Nevertheless, analysis of these unique data should at least shed new light on the primary questions at issue: 1) How different are MEPs from members of the national parliaments of EU countries in terms of their attitudes towards European integration and European policy-making? 2) To what extent are these differences due to socializing processes in the European Parliament as opposed to self-selection in favour of pro-European candidates in European Parliament elections? As will be seen, comparison of these surveys sheds unexpected light not only on the socializing effects of the European parliament, but also on the nature of the difference between national and European parliamentarians

DATA AND METHODS

The data at our disposal derive from interviews with three interlocking sets of individuals:
(1) a study of 1212 candidates in the European Parliamentary elections of 1994 (Marsh and Norris 1997), 320 of whom were successful in gaining election, among whom 44 were (later still) re-interviewed as part of a study that set out to compare the attitudes of Members of the European Parliament with those of national parliamentarians;
(2) 314 Members of the European Parliament interviewed in connection with this MEP-MNP study; and
(3) 1367 members of national parliaments interviewed in connection with the same study.
These data interlock in three different ways. First, among the candidates we can distinguish those who were elected from those who were not, in case electoral effects prove important in selecting the more pro-European among candidates. Second, respondents to the MEP and national MP studies were asked many identical questions. Third, the candidates and MEPs interlock because of the happenstance that forty-

three of those interviewed in both studies were identifiable as the same individuals, thus permitting the creation of a panel encompassing both datasets. Such links are available for only forty-three candidate-MEP pairs elected from the Netherlands and Germany. This small number of individuals will only yield suggestive findings except for effects that prove to be very powerful indeed.

A deficiency of lesser moment is the absence of relevant data from several of the national parliaments. Of greatest regret is the fact that because no interviews of national parliamentarians were conducted in Britain or Denmark, it is not possible to use these data to investigate possible differences in attitudes between national and European MPs in two of the most Euro-sceptical countries of the Union (Denmark and the United Kingdom).[2] Nevertheless, while this lessens the number of cases and may reduce the variance in our dependent variables, we would not expect the effects we investigate to be specific to particular countries.

As indicators of pro-European attitudes we chose from among questions asked in identical terms of both candidates and MEPS, using only those that bear upon the question of how pro-European either of these groups is (and hence whether electoral effects or experience in the parliament led to any change in the extent of their pro-European outlook). Fortunately, the available items do encompass a number of topics of concern both to national and European members of parliament which bear upon the process of European integration. Of these, the most useful for our purposes are those that enquire about the following:
(1) Respondent's satisfaction with the way democracy works in the EU;[3]
(2) Respondent's opinion on whether specific policy areas should be decided at mostly the European, or mostly the domestic level;[4]
(3) Respondent's opinion on whether progress should continue in two particular aspects of European integration (creating a common currency and reducing national border controls).[5]

The first of these topics is important because it bears upon the learning process that MEPs must go through whatever their prior orientations towards Europe. On taking their seats in the European Parliament we would expect them to be socialized into a general belief that the EP does a good job of representing citizens' interests. This is the only variable available in similar terms in all three surveys that bears (if only indirectly) on the functions and performance of the European Parliament. The final two topics relate specifically to the MEPs' orientation, pro-European or otherwise, in regards to specific policy questions. The Parliament may have socializing effects in regard to general satisfaction with democracy without having any socializing effects which affect specific policy preferences, as Kerr (1973) determined was the case for the unelected Parliament.

These data enable us to address our research questions in four stages. In the first stage we can inquire as to the differences between members of national parliaments and members of the European Parliament. In the second stage we can look to see if electoral effects account for such differences as we observe, whether because voters choose the more pro-European candidates, or because intra-party selection processes tend to favour them. In the third stage we can look at the effect of short-term forces by evaluating the immediate impact of EP membership on candidates who were elected for the first time in 1994, and then were re-interviewed two years later in connection with the MEP-MNP study. Finally, in the fourth stage we can inquire whether such differences as we find between national MPs and MEPs arise as a result of long-term socializing forces. If so, members re-elected in 1994 should show significant differences from members returned for the first time at that election. It would be satisfying if the three different sources of different orientations that we examine in stages 2-4 could account for the total differences observed in the first stage, between MEPs and MNPs.

Of course, comparisons conducted in the second, third and final stages must take account of a variety of possibly contaminating forces. Members of national parliaments may have different attitudes from members of the European Parliament because of other differences in background and circumstance. Similarly, those elected in 1994 may have different attitudes than those who were not elected because those who were successful electorally differ in background or other characteristics from those who were not. Finally, the more recently elected MEPs may have different attitudes because their characteristics differ from those elected earlier. In addition to obvious attitudinal differences to be expected of members of different parties, a variety of demographic characteristics have been linked to differences in attitudes towards European policies and institutions among the general population. For instance, Inglehart (1967, 1977) posited that support for European integration would be higher among younger cohorts, though

subsequent research has failed to find much support for this argument
(Janssen 1991; Handley 1981). Greater education levels, too, have been
associated with higher support for European integration (B. Wessels
1995). We thus need to be aware that party, education, and age are
factors that may also account for differences in the attitudes of political
elites. In the sections that follow, therefore, we look at the effects of
our primary independent variables in the context of models that fully
specify the effects of suspected contaminants,[6] with the single exception of our analysis of short-term socializing forces. In that investigation no controls are needed since we have a panel of individuals interviewed on two separate occasions. The characteristics of the
individuals being compared are thus identical because they are the
same individuals. Because all dependent variables are interval in nature
we employ OLS regression as our method for estimating the effects of
independent variables.

ARE MEPS MORE PRO-EUROPEAN THAN THEIR
NATIONAL COUNTERPARTS?

Table 3.1 shows the effect of being a Member of the European Parliament rather than a member of a national parliament on the various
attitudes that constitute our dependent variables, controlling for other
influences. Some of the results in this table are rather surprising. First,
the final column of the table shows that Members of the European
Parliament do not have significantly more pro-European attitudes on
European integration than do members of national parliaments. Second,
while the first two columns of the table do show differences between
MEPs and national MPs that are in the expected direction—MEPs are
more satisfied with democracy in the European Union, and they are
more likely to favour decision-making at the European rather than the
national level—in neither case is the effect large, and only in the latter
case is it statistically significant at conventional levels. So it seems that
our expectations regarding differences in need of explanation were
mistaken. MEPs are barely more pro-European than national MPs, and
certainly much less than would have been expected given many of the
assertions made casually on this topic. However, the findings, though
counter-intuitive, are actually in line with past research and suggest the

TABLE 3.1. Difference Between MEPs and MNPs Regarding Attitudes to
Europe (all dependent variables are 10-point scales)

Independent variables	Dependent variables		
	Democracy	Level decided	EU integration
(Constant)	3.59 (.303)**	6.10 (.219)**	5.91 (.209)**
MEP/MNP	0.26 (.156)*	0.72 (.112)**	0.00 (.106)
Control variables:			
Education	0.11 (.068)	-0.18 (.048)**	0.00 (.047)
Age groups	0.01 (.081)	-0.01 (.058)	0.00 (.055)
1979-84 cohorts	0.01 (.150)	-0.11 (.107)	0.00 (.103)
1989 cohort	-0.21 (.143)	0.00 (.103)	0.19 (.098)*
ELDR	1.14 (.294)**	0.32 (.213)	0.52 (.203)**
PPE	1.82 (.271)**	0.35 (.197)*	0.22 (.186)
PSE	0.78 (.267)**	0.20 (.195)	-0.32 (.184)*
UPE	1.24 (.302)**	-0.12 (.219)	0.47 (.208)**
GUE	-2.07 (.372)**	-1.19 (.270)**	-1.31 (.260)**
VERDE	-1.46 (.370)**	-0.68 (.268)**	-0.63 (.258)**
R^2 (adjusted)	0.155	0.077	0.081
N	1557	1460	1518

** Significant at $p < 0.05$
* Significant at $p < 0.10$.
Note: Standard errors in parentheses.

health of European democracy rather than otherwise. We will return to
expand upon this point below.

Since the findings in Table 3.1 are both unexpected and substantively important, it is appropriate to stress two methodological caveats
that may help to account for them. First, only a small number of issues
(10 distributed over three variables) could be examined in determining
the extent of pro-European attitudes. Second, because of missing data
about national representatives, four countries are omitted from this
analysis, including two of the most Euro-sceptical countries in the EU
(Britain and Denmark). However, this latter omission should not matter
if socialization effects are uniform and linear, meaning that they should
affect all MEPs equally, regardless of the climate of opinion in the
country from which they are elected. These caveats do not seem to
undermine the conclusion that there is only a small amount of difference to be explained by either socialization or self-selection of Euro-

pean delegates. There is no particular reason to suppose that things would be different in the countries for which we have no data.

WHY ARE MEPS MORE PRO-EUROPEAN?

Despite the small extent of differences to be explained, we will still take the next steps, and see whether such differences as do exist between members of national and European parliaments can be attributed to electoral effects, or to long-term or short-term socializing forces. To the extent that none of these factors account for the differences we observe, we will assume, along with Kerr, that they are the product of self-selection by candidates.

Table 3.2 presents evidence germane to the question of whether successful candidates are more pro-European than candidates who fail to gain election. This table, constructed in much the same way as Table 3.1 (differing only in the removal of the age cohort variables and the substitution of success at the polls for the MEP/MNP variable) shows

TABLE 3.2. Difference Between Successful and Unsuccessful Candidates Regarding Attitudes to Europe (scales as in Table 3.1)

Independent variables	Dependent variables		
	Democracy	Level decided	EU integration
(Constant)	0.81 (.170)**	7.20 (.411)**	5.71 (.393)**
Elected	0.00 (.070)	0.33 (.168)*	0.31 (.162)*
Control variables:			
Education	0.00 (.028)	-0.19 (.068)**	-0.11 (.065)*
Age groups	0.00 (.019)	0.00 (.048)*	0.00 (.045)
ELDR	0.27 (.077)**	1.37 (.187)**	0.77 (.181)**
PPE	0.52 (.059)**	1.19 (.144)**	0.14 (.138)
PSE	0.39 (.068)**	1.65 (.165)**	-0.14 (.158)
VERDE	0.00 (.083)	1.10 (.210)**	-0.34 (.195)*
R^2 (adjusted)	0.093	0.183	0.033
N	942	837	904

** Significant at $p < 0.05$
* Significant at $p < 0.10$.
Note: Standard errors in parentheses.

results that are suggestive of very slight electoral effects. However, these do not meet conventional levels of statistical significance, and in any case are inconsistent with the findings reported in Table 3.1. There we saw significant differences only for opinions about the level at which policy decisions should be decided, whereas Table 3.2 shows electoral effects that would have been just as important for attitudes about EU integration. So we are forced to conclude that these effects are just happenstances of sampling variance with no substantive meaning. This still leaves the possibility that differences between MEPs and national MPs are due to socializing effects.

Table 3.3 presents evidence pertaining to the question of whether length of service in the EP is associated with a strengthening of pro-European attitudes. Again, this table is constructed in much the same way as Table 3.1 (differing only through the removal of the MEP/MNP variable). It shows no evidence of long-term socialization. Such effects might have been seen in significant coefficients on the two cohort variables, which in this table become the independent variables of interest. But these variables show no effects that meet conventional levels of

TABLE 3.3. Difference Between MEPs of Different Generations Regarding Attitudes to Europe (scales as for Table 3.1)

Independent variables	Dependent variables		
	Democracy	Level decided	EU integration
(Constant)	2.29 (.696)**	5.57 (.503)**	6.24 (.413)**
1979-84 cohorts	-0.27 (.430)	-0.19 (.297)	-0.01 (.255)
1989 cohort	0.11 (.381)	0.00 (.265)	0.42 (.227)*
Control variables			
Education	0.41 (.223)	-0.80 (.150)	0.14 (.131)
Age groups	0.21 (.208)	0.00 (.144)	-0.20 (.122)*
ELDR	1.75 (.632)**	0.47 (.460)	0.14 (.344)
PPE	2.82 (.561)**	0.91 (.416)**	0.12 (.505)
PSE	1.63 (.566)**	0.94 (.420)**	-0.57 (.337)*
UPE	2.54 (.744)**	0.90 (.527)*	0.59 (.440)
VERDE	-0.17 (.853)	-0.63 (.596)	-1.06 (.503)**
Variance explained	0.209	0.084	0.074
N	246	229	242

** Significant at $p < 0.05$
* Significant at $p < 0.01$.
Note: Standard errors in parentheses.

statistical significance, and the largest effect is on EU policies, which was not an area that saw any differences between national MPs and MEPs in Table 3.1.

So the small differences found between members of national parliaments and members of the European Parliament in regard to satisfaction with democracy and ideas about policy competencies cannot be ascribed to long-term socializing forces any more than to electoral effects. If it is the experience of sitting in the European Parliament that gives rise to these differences, then that experience must exercise its effect very quickly: during the period immediately after new members take their seats.

The unique advantage of our overlapping datasets is that they allow us to test for this possibility by comparing the responses of MEPs who have served for two years with those they gave two years earlier, when they were only candidates for the European body. We can conduct this test only for the small number of individuals for whom we have pre-election (Candidate) and post-election (MEP) surveys, and even these have to be further reduced by dividing them into returning MEPs and newly-elected MEPs. Yet though the sample is small, the findings are suggestive.

Table 3.4 shows the differences between the attitudes of the same individuals when interviewed first as candidates and then, two years later, as MEPs. Positive coefficients indicate changes towards a more pro-European outlook on each of the dependent variables in turn. Those first elected in 1994 are indeed seen to have undergone changes of up to half a point (on a ten-point scale) in the direction of more pro-

TABLE 3.4. Difference Between Candidates and MEPs Regarding Attitudes to Europe (difference of means)

Independent variables		Dependent variables		
	N	Democracy	Level decided	EU integration
First elected earlier	23	0.00 (1.74)	-0.40 (1.56)	0.14 (1.35)
First elected in 1994	20	0.50 (2.48)	0.37 (1.08)	0.38 (1.32)
N		43	38	42

** Significant at p < 0.05
* Significant at p < 0.01
Note: Standard deviations in parentheses.

European attitudes, while those elected earlier (and whose short-term socialization can thus be considered to have been already complete) show no such changes. The differences might have been thought to help account for differences between national MPs and MEPs seen in Table 3.1, except that one of the effects is twice as great as required while another equally large effect corresponds to a zero coefficient in Table 3.1. However, if we focus on the one effect in Table 3.1 that reached conventional levels of significance—the effect corresponding to the difference between national MPs and MEPs in terms of the level at which decisions should be made—it is possible to argue that this effect is completely accounted for on the basis of short-term socializing forces. This is plausible if we assume that the negative coefficient in the top row of Table 3.4 was due to a period effect involving both new and established MEPs.[7] In that case, socializing forces would have had to yield a difference of 0.77 of a point in order to account for the difference between established and new MEPs. Such an effect would be very close to the 0.73 that we have to account for in terms of differences between national MPs and MEPs according to Table 3.1. So our findings are consistent with the possibility that the small differences between national MPs and MEPs in terms of pro-European outlook are indeed due to the socializing effects of membership in the European Parliament—effects that occur very quickly upon entry into that body.

But the strongest implication of all the tables presented here is that effects of socialization, if any, are very small (at most three quarters of a point on a ten-point scale) and make virtually no difference to the pro- or anti-European stance of those who enter the European Parliament. Our most striking finding is how closely MEPs resemble the members of national parliaments in terms of pro- or anti-European outlook.

DISCUSSION

This study has found surprisingly small differences between members of national parliaments and Members of the European Parliament in terms of their attitudes towards Europe. Those who have in the past attributed to European institutions the ability to socialize their members into pro-European attitudes would doubtless be surprised by the small magnitude of the effects we have found. These small effects may not in fact reflect reality, since they are based on a very small number of attitudes measured for a somewhat unrepresentative sample of national and European legislators. However, if our findings are confirmed, they provide a new perspective on the conflicts between national and European legislators that receive so much publicity. Our findings do not support the common interpretation that these conflicts are exacerbated by fundamental differences in pro- or anti-European attitudes linked to institutional location.

At the same time, our findings provide suggestive support for the notion that the European Parliament exercises a rapid, though gentle, socializing effect on its new members. Even if real world differences between national and European MPs are greater than those found in this study, our findings provide support for those scholars who assume that any differences must be the consequence of institutional socializing forces.

This would also mean that, by deduction, the reason for MNP/MEP differences is not to be found in self-selection on the part of candidates for the European Parliament any more than in electoral effects or the consequences of long-term dedication to the European project. MEPs are very like national MPs, and to the extent that they differ it is uniquely because members of the European Parliament feel themselves competent to legislate in more areas than national MPs think they should. Such a difference would be a very natural manifestation of the "where you stand is where you sit" syndrome.

In any case, the implication that flows from our study is that such socializing forces, to the extent that they exist, are very short-term in nature. MEPs undergo a change of attitude towards Europe—if they do—within only a couple of years of taking their seats in the European Parliament. There do not appear to be additional socializing forces visible over a longer time-span. Studies of the socializing effects of EP membership have in the past focussed on long-term forces, and our findings confirm the absence of such forces. But this lack of long-term forces does not mean that the EP fails to socialize its members—a conclusion that would have been implausible in the light of findings from studies of other legislatures. To the contrary, the lack of socializing forces found in previous studies appears to have been due to the fact that such forces are small, and take effect very quickly. So they will not in general be evident in comparisons between MEPs elected at different European elections.

The lack of important differences between national MPs and MEPs is a paradoxical indication of the health of EU democracy. Since European elections respond to national political forces, it follows that members of the European Parliament should look much like members of national parliaments. If they did not look similar then something other than the will of the voters would have had to be responsible, and this might have led us to fear the effects of undemocratic forces. Our findings indicate no such forces at work. Identical (or near-identical) political processes apparently lead to identical (or near-identical) representatives, at least in terms of the variables studied in this chapter.[8] We might wish that these political processes had in fact been different, with European parliamentarians being elected as the outcome of campaigns that looked very different from national election campaigns, and stressed very different issues—perhaps along with a context shaped by a new focus on electing a European president.[9] In that case we would expect differences in the political complexions of representatives elected through this different process. We do not see this. What we do see are processes that have explicable consequences, giving us hope that reforms of these processes can be designed with predictable results. This will be encouraging to those who see the European project as a work in progress, for it suggests that this work can yet be revised to yield a more representative and accountable political process for governing the European Union.

NOTES

1   Kerr also found that membership in the European Parliament increased MEPs' knowledge about European affairs, even if it did not affect their fundamental orientation towards Europe.

2   Because of the lack of data about national parliamentarians in Denmark and the United Kingdom, respondents from these countries who were MEPs were excluded from all comparisons of national and European parliamentarians.

3   Originally this variable was measured on a three-point scale, but we
     recoded these points to 0, 5 and 10 (with higher values indicating greater
     satisfaction) in order to achieve comparability with the other two depend-
     ent variables (see below).

4   These matters encompassed security and defence, protection of the envi-
     ronment, monetary policy, health and social welfare, education, media
     policies, scientific and technological research, foreign policy, and co-op-
     eration with third world countries. Each of the questions relating to these
     matters solicited responses on a seven-point scale on which higher values
     were more EU-oriented. Our measure of pro-European orientation was
     derived from summing these nine scores and then reducing the result to a
     ten-point scale by normalizing.

5   These were both ten-point scales with larger values being more pro-Euro-
     pean. Our measure was again derived from summing the scores and then
     normalizing to a maximum of ten.

6   Some of these controls are problematic. It was not possible to control for
     age as such, since the original age variable was deleted from the dataset in
     order to maintain the anonymity of respondents. The control we employed
     is one that places respondents in three age groups. This might have biased
     our analysis towards finding a spurious cohort effect, but we will see that
     this is not a problem. The other major problem arises with party affilia-
     tion. It would be impossible to introduce dummy variables for every
     national party, especially since some of these would totally identify par-
     ticular individuals in the sample. So we have used EP party group as our
     control variable, even for members of national parliaments, ascribing to
     them the party group that they would have belonged to had they been
     MEPs with the same party affiliation.

7   Arguably, any effect on returning MEPs must be the result of something
     that happened during the period between the two interviews, and any such
     event would affect all MEPs, even new ones. On this basis, in the absence
     of socializing forces, all MEPs would have shifted four tenths of a point
     away from pro-European attitudes.

8   By 'near-identical political processes' we here imply similar campaign
     efforts in the context of similar political parties stressing similar political
     issues, even though electoral laws may be different in European than in
     national elections.

9   See van der Eijk and Franklin (1996: Chapter 21) for a discussion of, and
     elaboration on, these points.

4

Role Orientations in Parliaments

RICHARD S. KATZ

THE job of a Member of the European Parliament (MEP) is a complex one. MEPs are subject to demands and pressures from the voters they were elected to represent, from their colleagues in the parliament, from their parties at local, national, and European levels, from interest groups and journalists, from their own sense of duty and ambition. The volume of these demands and pressures, combined with limitations of time and energy force a kind of freedom on MEPs. Given the manifest impossibility of being all things to all people, each MEP is forced to choose, whether consciously or not, which aspects of the job to emphasize, and which to assign lesser priority. This problem of constructing an appropriate role within the parliament is also faced by members of national parliaments (MNPs), as well as many subnational assemblies. In these contexts, the causes, consequences, and varieties of legislative role definitions have been subjects of significant bodies of theory and research, much of which may be relevant to the European Parliament (EP) as well.

The unsettled debates about the proper nature (inter-national, trans-national, proto-national) and structure (federal or confederal, quasi-presidential or parliamentary) of the European Union add a second level to the problem of role definition for both MEPs and MNPs from member states that generally has not been an issue in the context of national political systems. When thinking about European level politics, MPs at both levels must confront not only the question of their individual roles within their institutions, but also the question of the role of the EP and the national parliaments as institutions within the broader European political system.

As in any organization, the mix of roles adopted by the individuals who occupy positions within them is influential in determining how the organization actually functions. These choices of role are particularly important in new or rapidly evolving institutions, where the absence of established practices gives current incumbents greater freedom to shape the ways in which their institution will work and relate to its environment. This is, of course, precisely the situation of the European Parliament, which has less than 20 years existence as a directly elected assembly, and whose position and powers within the European Union have yet to be finally determined. The way in which MPs define their personal roles in and with reference to the EP and the EU more generally is, therefore, likely to be quite important to the evolution of European integration.

DELEGATE OR TRUSTEE?

One of the earliest distinctions in the analysis of the role orientations of legislators is between the "delegate" and the "trustee" (Wahlke et al. 1962). The delegate is the direct agent of her constituents, trying to act as they would if they could be present in their own persons. The trustee, on the other hand, acts for her constituents in the sense of using her own judgement to advance their interests. The normal democratic expectation is that these two orientations will not come into conflict; presumably the representative was elected in large measure *because* her own views and those of her constituents coincide. Nonetheless, given differences of information and experience, among the many differences that distinguish representatives from their constituents, one must expect that conflicts will arise, forcing the representative to decide whether to defer to public opinion or to regard her own judgement as superior to it.

The simple distinction between delegate and trustee was developed in the United States, in the context of notoriously weak parties and a cultural expectation that the voter is choosing among candidates as individuals and that a representative should be particularly responsive to her own, local, constituency. In the European context of parliamentary government, with strong parties and the cultural understanding that a voter's decision should be and is based more on his preference for one national party over the others than it is on his preference for one local candidate over the others, a third role orientation must be considered, that of partisan. Again the normal expectation is that the positions of party organization, voters, and the representative herself will coincide, but from this perspective, in cases of conflict the representative's primary responsibility is to support the positions taken by her party as an organization.

MPs were asked their orientation on this matter. "In many cases people have different views concerning matters that the [European Parliament/National Parliament] must decide upon. On which one of the following would you be most inclined to base your decision in such cases?" The choices offered were "your own judgement," "the view of the voters of your party,"[1] and "the view of your national party;" MEPs also were offered the choice of "the view of your EP group." Respondents were asked to rank these alternatives (identify first, second, and (for the MEPs) third choices). Each respondent was classified according to her first choice(s), as indicated in Figure 4.1. For the purposes of this analysis, the two party organizational choices offered the MEPs were combined. Unfortunately, a significant number of respondents put more than one of the choices in first place, resulting in the intermediate categories shown in the figure.

As the figure indicates, there clearly was a "correct" answer to this question; 224 of the 300 (weighted) MEPs (74.7%) and 503 of 701

Own Opinion First	
MEP	MNP
198	405
66.8%	57.8%

Own Opinion & Party Voters First				All Three Equal				Own Opinion & Party	
MEP	MNP							MEP	MNP
10	38			MEP	MNP			11	39
3.3%	5.4%			5	21			3.7%	5.6%
				1.7%	3.0%				

Party Voters First				Party & Party Voters				Party First	
MEP	MNP			MEP	MNP			MEP	MNP
14	63			2	12			60	123
4.7%	9.0%			0.7%	1.7%			20.0%	17.5%

FIG 4.1. Decision Priorities MEPs and MNPs

MNPs (71.8%) responding ranked their own judgement in first place, either alone or tied with at least one of the other alternatives. That there was such a strong tendency among MPs to give priority to their own judgement is a rather surprising finding when contrasted with the requisites of coherent party government or stable cabinets, which could hardly exist if members of parliaments regularly acted as independent agents rather than reliable supporters of their party leaders/organizations. Beyond the possibility that many respondents are giving what they believe to be the socially approved answer regardless of their true opinions, one possible explanation is that, as suggested above, the situation does not arise frequently, so that when it does members can indulge their consciences or judgement without seriously damaging overall party unity. While it is hard to translate directly from survey responses about hypothetical policy questions to preferred action on the real issues confronting parliament, there is sufficient within-party variation on the questions posed in our survey to make it unlikely that MPs and their parties only rarely "have different views concerning matters that the [parliament] must decide upon."

If one were looking at the MEP data in isolation, one might be tempted to explain this result by observing that since the European Parliament is not an example of party government, nor is there a European executive whose stability depends on its ability to command a parliamentary majority, party loyalty simply does not matter as much as it might in a "normal" European parliament. While this may account for the somewhat greater tendency of MEPs rather than MNPs to give first priority to their own opinions, it is inadequate as an explanation of the more general finding. On one hand, it cannot account for the high proportion of MNPs who also report giving primary weight to their own judgement over the views of their parties' voters and their party organizations. And, on the other hand, party unity in the European Parliament is, in fact, quite high (Attinà 1990).

This then suggests a third explanation—that in forming their own judgements, MPs consider strategy as well as preference, and that this rather than raw agreement accounts for the infrequency of defections even as MPs truthfully claim to be following their own judgement in preference to the views of their parties (see Laver and Shepsle forthcoming).

Given the large number of MPs who report unambiguously that they would give first priority to their own opinions, it is interesting to see what those who do so ranked in second place. Of the 147 MEPs for whom this distinction could be made, 40 (37.4%) put their party's voters in second place; the corresponding figure for the MNPs is 106 of 226 (46.9%). When these data are taken with the data in Figure 4.1, it is clear that when given a choice between deferring to their party's positions as reflected in the views of the party's voters or to the party's position as reflected in their national party or EP group, MPs at both levels disproportionately report that they would give priority to party (organization) or group over the views of the voters.

When the priority given to the MP's own judgement is ignored, so that the question is only whether priority is given to the party or to its voters, then MNPs appear to be more inclined than MEPs to give priority to the voters. One possible explanation of this difference is that it reflects the different democratic contexts which the MPs confront. It may be that more MNPs see voters' preferences as the proper basis for decisions by their parties and themselves as representatives in a system of party government because they (accurately) believe that more voters have informed views on matters confronting the national parliament, and that a significant danger confronting national democracy is that party leaders will become divorced from the base they claim to represent. For MEPs, however, party becomes more important in articulating and interpreting the interests of the citizens, for whom there is less reason to believe that they have either the information or the inclination to recognize and express their interests on their own.

DEFINING CONSTITUENCIES

Alternatively, one can look at the MP's constituency functionally. To what extent does she interact with, or give weight to the views of, ordinary citizens and organized groups? And to the extent that MPs do interact with groups, are there differences between MEPs and MNPs with regard to the level (national or European) of the groups and with regard to the types of groups?

Respondents were asked how often they were in contact with a variety of types of people, institutions, and groups. Table 4.1 shows the percentages of MNPs and MEPs from the 10 countries for which MNP samples are available who report meeting at least once a month with

TABLE 4.1. Proportion of MPs Having at least One Contact per Month
with Various Groups

	MEPs	MNPs	eta
Ordinary citizens	96.4	97.3	.029
Organized groups	85.1	90.3	.068
Lobbyists	58.3	45.6	.103
Journalists	83.2	83.8	.007
Leaders of your EP group	83.0		
<COUNTRY> MEPs of other parties	84.2		
European civil servants	77.5	8.9	.659
European Commission	60.6	4.8	.612
European Council	24.0	4.2	.290
Economic and Social Committee	6.8	1.7	.127
European Court of Justice	0	0.3	.025
Committee of Permanent representatives (COREPER)	13.5	1.2	.260
National party leaders/ Leaders of your party	59.5	89.6	.328
National MPs/ <COUNTRY> MEPs	72.9	47.9	.203
National ministers/ Ministers	35.6	73.5	.322
National civil servants/ Civil servants at the national level	39.7	79.7	.357
National Interest Groups			
Consumer associations	25.8	19.7	.061
Environmental organizations	30.8	24.3	.059
Trade unions	34.7	49.1	.118
Professional associations	39.8	45.1	.043
National economic interest groups of:	30.0	24.9	.047
Agriculture and fishing			
Industry	31.0	37.7	.056
Transport	26.0	17.1	.091
Trade and commerce	25.3	28.9	.032
Banking and insurance	20.2	20.3	.001
European Interest groups			
Consumers associations (e.g. EUROCOOP)	21.5	0.9	.377
Environmental organizations (e.g. EEB)	19.3	2.5	.286
European trade unions (e.g. ETUC)	19.4	2.4	.293
Professional organizations (e.g. SEPLIS)	17.9	2.2	.280
European economic interest groups of:			
Agriculture and fishing (e.g. COPA)	16.0	3.6	.208
Industry (e.g. UNICE)	18.0	2.4	.273
Transport (e.g. LC/IRU	14.9	1.3	.278
Trade and commerce (e.g. FIPMEC)	12.5	2.0	.213
Banking and insurance (e.g. GCECEE)	7.4	1.7	.140

each type of people, institution, or group. Looking first at the top panel, it is no surprise to find that MEPs report far more frequent contacts with the institutions of the EU than do MNPs, and that the converse is true for national institutions. The much greater frequency of contacts between MEPs and national institutions than between MNPs and the corresponding EU institutions, however, suggests on the one hand that MEPs remain closely connected to their national political systems, but on the other hand that the European level is of only marginal concern to most MNPs (and that they are of only marginal concern to it). MNPs also report slightly more frequent contact with ordinary citizens, organized groups, and journalists—probably reflecting their greater geographic proximity—while MEPs report more frequent contact with lobbyists.

The question of group contacts is addressed more fully in the lower panel, in which groups are divided both functionally (i.e., consumer, labour, etc.) and geographically (national or European). Again it is not surprising to find that MEPs have significantly more frequent contact than do MNPs with European level interest organizations. What is surprising is that MEPs also report more frequent contact with a range of *national* level organizations. Additionally, MEPs report more frequent contact with *national* level interest organizations than they do with the corresponding European level of interest organization across the entire range of organizations about which inquiries were made.

Two reasons may be suggested for this anomalous pattern. First, many national groups are likely to have better access to the real seats of power and decision in the government, bureaucracy, and central party organizations at the national level than they do at the European level; with less of this kind of access at the European level, MEPs become a relatively more attractive point of access. Second, whereas ties between groups and parties often limit the contacts between those groups and MNPs of opposing parties, groups can approach MEPs as national advocates rather than as sectoral advocates. For example, a German environmental group can approach any German MEP, regardless of party, and frame its interests as the protection of the German environment against French pollution, in contrast to the national level where the issue would more likely be framed as environment versus industry.

Having contact with various groups and interests is one aspect of representation; according them influence is another. Respondents also were asked how much they take the opinions of the groups addressed in

the top panel of Table 4.1 into account when making political decisions. The average responses to these questions (asked using a seven
point scale with 1 as the high point) is shown in Table 4.2. It is clear
that party is more significant for MNPs than for MEPs; both national
party leaders and party group (EP for the MEPs and national party for
the MNPs) leaders are reported to be more influential by the MNPs,
while MEPs report slightly greater cross-party influence.

The public appears to be more influential at the national level, lend-
ing some credence to claims that governments that are closer to the
people are more democratic. MNPs report giving greater weight than
do MEPs to ordinary citizens, organized groups, public opinion, and
the media. On the other hand, MEPs report giving greater influence to
lobbyists. Consistent with the suggestion above regarding the relative
priority accorded to the views of party and the views of party voters,
the implication here as well is that MEPs require intermediaries
between their (distant) constituents and themselves, whereas MNPs can
interact with their constituents more directly.

The picture that emerges is one in which the distinction between
MNPs and MEPs lies not in whom they represent, but in the nature of

TABLE 4.2. Average Influence Attributed to Opinions of Various Groups

	MEPs	MNPs	eta
Ordinary citizens	2.59	2.36	.062
Organized groups	3.18	2.88	.087
Lobbyists	4.80	4.91	.028
Public opinion	3.47	3.25	.058
The media	4.32	4.25	.018
Leaders of your EP group	3.04	2.43	.186
<COUNTRY> MEPs of other parties	4.61	4.71	.028
European civil servants	4.58		
European Commission	4.04		
European Council	4.49		
Economic and Social Committee	5.22		
European Court of Justice	4.73		
Committee of Permanent representatives (COREPER)	5.00		
National party leaders/ Leaders of your party	3.62	2.52	.301
National MPs/ <COUNTRY> MEPs	3.83	4.29	.117
National ministers/ Ministers	4.13	4.06	.014
National civil servants/ Civil servants at the national level	4.85	4.64	.052

the connection between representative and represented, and perhaps as well in the framework by means of which the character of the represented is interpreted. On one hand, MNPs appear more likely to interact directly with their constituents, whereas MEPs are more likely to interact with lobbyists. Whether this is because distance makes MEPs less directly accessible, or because intermediaries like lobbyists have better access to more potent points of decision at the national than the European level cannot be answered here.

On the other hand, one can infer that the represented are more likely to be defined by their representatives in partisan and functional terms at the national level, but more likely to be defined in national terms at the European level. In this respect the ideal that the EP would represent the people (singular) of Europe in partisan or ideological terms, rather than representing (as one might argue the Council properly does) the peoples (plural) of Europe in national terms, still appears far from realization.

ROLE ORIENTATIONS

Rather than asking whom an MP represents, one can instead ask how she goes about the task of being a representative. MEPs responding to our survey were asked to rate the importance of the six aspects of their work and the importance of representing the five categories of people[2] listed in the first column of Table 4.3. MNPs were asked to make the same ratings, except that they were not asked about "all people in Europe" or "your EP group." In order to identify underlying role orientations, a principal components factor analysis was performed on these eleven responses, using pairwise deletion of missing data in order to include both MNPs and MEPs in a single analysis. This analysis yielded three factors with eigenvalues greater than 1.20, collectively accounting for 53.7% of the overall variance in the eleven input variables. Rather than assuming that the underlying role orientations must be independent of one another, the original component matrix was subjected to an oblique (oblimin) rotation, yielding the pattern matrix reproduced in the table (except that the signs have been reversed for the third component in the interest of easier exposition). Factor scores then were computed for all cases for which no more than four of the 11

TABLE 4.3. Pattern Matrix of Role Orientations

	Legislator	Partisan	Communitarian
Important: Taking part in legislation	.620	-.205	.250
Important: Parliamentary oversight	.697	-.089	.110
Important: Articulation of societal needs	.673	.096	-.118
Important: Development of political strategies	.585	.127	.065
Important: Mediation between interests	.619	.042	-.091
Important: Representation of individuals	.351	.134	-.373
Represent: All people in Europe	.329	.020	.733
Represent: All people in <COUNTRY>	-.010	.208	.779
Represent: All party voters	-.023	.845	.094
Represent: Your national party	-.005	.849	-.170
Represent: Your EP group	.055	.718	.236

input variables were missing data, substituting the mean of the variable for those remaining missing data cases (and dividing by the observed standard deviation to correct for the fact that this method of substitution constrains the variance of the factors scores for the MNPs to be smaller than the variance for the MEPs).

The first role orientation (dimension) revealed by the factor analysis reflects the priority given to the professional/parliamentary aspects of the job of MP. Those with high scores on this factor generally report giving great importance to taking part in legislation, exercising parliamentary oversight, articulating societal needs and interests and mediating between different interests in society. Those with high scores on this "legislator" factor are also more likely than others to say that the development of political strategies is an important part of their work. Significantly, however, scores on the "legislator" factor are virtually unrelated to orientation toward party—those with high scores are essentially no more (or less) prone to report giving high importance to representing their party's voters, their national party, or their EP group.

The complementary orientation is reflected in the second dimension, identified in the table as "partisan." This factor is defined primarily by the weight given by respondents to representing their national party and their party's voters, as well as, to a slightly lesser degree, their EP group. The strength of the intercorrelations among these variables is further evidence that MPs do not in general see any conflict between representation of party and representation of party voters. Those scoring toward the partisan end of this dimension are somewhat less likely than others to attribute great importance to taking part in legislation, perhaps reflecting the fact that the highly partisan, party government, model of government generally shifts legislative initiative from the ordinary members of parliament to their party leaders and to the executive.

The third orientation represents a non-conflictual or "communitarian" orientation. Those who score at the communitarian end of this dimension apparently believe that it is possible to represent everyone at once. In detail, this might have any of three meanings. First, it could refer primarily to the representation of individual citizens in their personal dealings with national or European authorities. If this were the sense in which respondents were reacting to the stimuli one would expect a high correlation of the score on this dimension with responses to the stimulus represent "all the people in your constituency." While the corresponding variable was not included in the factor analysis for the reasons suggested above (see note 2), its correlation with the score on this factor was virtually zero (0.010). One also would expect a significant correlation with giving importance to "representation of individuals," but this correlation, while quite high, is negative (-.439). A second sense of representing all people would cast the representative as a conciliator. In this case, however, one would expect a significant relationship between the factor score and the perceived importance of mediation between different groups in society, but again the correlation is low, and in the wrong direction (-.153). The remaining possibility is that respondents who score highly on this factor perceive there to be an overarching common interest that they can represent, if not on all issues, then on sufficiently many issues that doing so can define a major component of their role orientations.

It is important to remember that although these dimensions are not unrelated (as a result of the use of an oblique rotation), neither are they alternatives. The highest correlation between factor scores is only .194 (between the factor indicating the "legislator" role and that indicating the "partisan" role), indicating that at the individual level it is quite possible for an MP to score highly on several dimensions simultaneously. These role orientations also are largely independent of the decision priorities of MPs. As one would expect, there is a negative correlation between the partisan role orientation and tendency to give high priority to one's own judgement (either as the sole first priority, or as one of the priorities tied for first place), but the two correlations are

only -.169 and -.153. None of the other correlations between the decision priority variables and the factor-defined role orientations has an
absolute value above .093.

WHO IS ORIENTATED HOW?

The first question one might ask about role orientations is who is oriented how? In particular, are there significant differences in the distribution of role orientations and decision priorities between MEPs and
MNPs and among national and partisan groups, and what background
or experiential factors are associated with which role orientations and
decision priorities?

The first answer is that there are essentially no aggregate differences
between MEPs and MNPs with regard to their role orientations.[3]
Although the statistically necessary grand mean of approximately 0 for
each of the factor scores could have been achieved by balancing positive against negative means in the two samples, even when attention is
restricted to the 10 countries for which both MNP and MEP data were
gathered, all six sample means are within .10 of zero; the highest value
of eta between the two samples is .054 (for the partisan factor) indicating that less than one-third of one percent of the individual variance is
explained by the level of parliament of the respondent. Similarly, the
difference in the proportions of MEPs and MNPs who include their
own opinion among the top influences on their decisions is under 3
percent, with an eta of only .027.

Differences among parties are statistically significant, but substantively quite weak, explaining between 2.3 and 3.6 percent of the individual level variance in role orientation scores. MPs of the parties of
the left (PSE, GUE and V) tended to score more highly on the legislator factor than did MPs of parties of the right (PPE, ELDR, EDN, UPE
and especially ARE). There is no simple left-right relationship with the
other two factor scores, with MPs of GUE and EDN scoring particularly high (mean greater than 0.20) and those of ARE scoring particularly low on the partisan dimension, while MPs of UPE and EDN
scored particularly high and MPs of GUE, V and ARE scored particularly low on the communitarian dimension.

One might expect the reported propensity to include one's own opinion among the top decision priorities to be related to party grouping—the independence of the MP was a central part of the ideology of the 19th century Radicals and Liberals (now the parties of the right) while party discipline and the primacy of the party organization are central tenets of the mass party or socialist models of party organization and democracy (see Katz and Mair 1995). In fact, party explains only 3.5 percent of the individual level variance in this aspect of role orientation, and even that is not consistently related to the left-right orientation of the parties. The two partisan groups most likely to report putting their own opinion in first place (alone or with other influences) are ARE (right, 100 percent) and V (left, 86 percent), while those least likely to do so are EDN (right, 58 percent) and GUE (left, 45 percent). The range among the averages for the big parties (PSE, PPE, ELDR) is less than 3 percent.

On the other hand, national differences are much more substantial, explaining between 7.1 and 14.6 percent of the variance in role orientation scores and 13.4 percent of the variance in decision priority for the MEPs and between 6.4 and 14.5 percent of the variance in factor scores and 27.4 percent of the variance in decision priority for the MNPs, (between 4.8 and 12.4 percent and 23.1 percent, respectively, with the samples combined). As Table 4.4 shows, the national patterns are basically consistent across the two offices with regard to the partisan and communitarian factor scores and the decision priority measure. (The correlations between the mean scores for the two offices are .40, .55. and .53, respectively.) For the legislator factor, however, there is virtually no correspondence (r = .05), which reinforces the inference suggested by the relatively low values of eta squared that nationality, and variables relating to characteristics of the national political systems or experiences, are far less significant as explanations of this aspect of MPs' role orientations.

These results suggest two routes for further analysis. On one hand, given the strength of the national differences, one would like to specify what it is about nationality that explains the differences. Two obvious sets of variables concern national political institutions and national parliamentary "culture" as reflected in the practices and procedures of the national parliaments. On the other hand, even nationality and party taken together explain only between 11.2 percent and 20.4 percent of the variance in factor scores, and 31.1 percent of the variance in deci-

TABLE 4.4. Factor Scores by Nation and Office

	Legislator		Partisan		Communitarian		Own Opinion Among 1st Priorities	
	MEP	MNP	MEP	MNP	MEP	MNP	MEP	MNP
Belgium	-.589	-.151	.223	.500	-.404	-.470	67.4	56.9
Germany	.303	.137	-.287	-.277	-.025	-.042	92.5	97.8
Greece	-.182	.255	.282	.240	.793	.188	83.7	75.3
Ireland	.194	.150	.733	.280	-.299	-.701	39.0	80.0
Italy	-.212	-.309	-.048	-.586	.472	.518	79.4	72.8
Luxembourg	-.317	-.355	-.731	.221	-1.640	-.043	80.0	76.8
Netherlands	-.118	.190	.289	.273	.162	-.167	72.8	64.4
Portugal	.171	-.322	-.303	-.108	-.113	-.104	72.0	55.9
Spain	-.117	.122	.583	.227	.187	.162	48.0	24.6
Sweden	-.325	.614	.217	.580	-.601	-.822	71.2	
Total	-.044	.016	.068	-.067	.098	.034	74.7	71.8
eta squared	.071	.064	.113	.145	.146	.130	.134	.274

sion priorities, suggesting that individual level factors play a major role in explaining individual level differences in role orientations. While the list of potential influences is virtually endless, it seems reasonable to suppose that the MP's previous political experiences will play a major role here.

NATIONAL DIFFERENCES

In attempting to account for the cross-national differences in role orientations, the appropriate dependent variable is the national group (in this case, national group within level of parliament, n = 18 after deletions of missing data) rather than the individual MP; once one has a handle on these factors, they can be combined with individual level factors to produce an account of individual role orientations. For the purpose of this initial analysis, four classes of institutional factors were considered. The first is two variables relating to the electoral system: L.MAG (the natural logarithm of the average magnitude of national parliamentary districts) and PREF (the possibility of an intraparty preference vote). The second class concerns the organization of the national parliament. The specific variables are: level of government control over the plenary agenda (AGENDA); the number of standing committees (NCTTEE); and the level of autonomy enjoyed by committees in the drafting of legislation (C.DRAFT). The third class concerns ministerial recruitment, and consists of the percentage of ministers with backgrounds in local or regional politics, the percentage of specialist ministers, and the percentage of ministers recruited from parliament (LOCMIN, SPECMIN, and PARMIN, respectively). The fourth class concerns the role of parties in parliament and in national politics.

These variables are: the power of party whips (WHIPS); the level of partisanship in the recruitment of parliamentary presidents (PRES); reutilization and intensity of interest group contacts (GROUP); the partyness of interest group contacts (P.GROUP); the degree to which committee members influence their party's positions (C.INFL); proportional allocation of committee chairs among all parties (CHAIR); the average number of days required to form a government (FORM); and a classification of national institutions and practices as majoritarian, mixed, or consensual (LIJ). With the exception of the electoral system variables, and LIJ (from LeDuc 1996: 347; Lijphart 1984, 1989), all of these variables are taken from Döring (1995b). Naturally, not all of these variables are expected to influence each of the role orientation variables.

One would expect the legislator role orientation to be most common where partisanship is relatively low and separation of parliament and executive relatively high—that is where a professional and parliamentary rather than a partisan and governmental orientation is most appropriate. As shown in the first equation in Table 4.5, which reports the result of regression analyses with backward deletion of variables, these expectations are generally supported by the data. The legislator orientation is associated with high values of C.DRAFT and low values of P.GROUP, PARMIN, and C.INFL. Somewhat surprisingly, it is also associated with a more majoritarian orientation, although not significantly so in a statistical sense. As the table shows, the overall adjusted R^2 is .420, which is just under the conventional level for statistical significance.

The first expectation for the partisan role orientation is that it should be reflective of a partisan orientation in the organization of national politics. One might also expect it to be related to patterns of ministerial recruitment, with MPs from countries in which local politics or specialized expertise are alternative (to party politics) routes to the cabinet to be less partisan in their role orientations. As the second equation shows, the first of these expectations is at best weakly supported by the data. Although the coefficient is not statistically significant, a consensual rather than a majoritarian score on LIJ is associated with high partisan factor scores. On the other hand, if interest group activity is understood to be an alternative to partisan activity, then the significant negative coeeficient for GRP supports this expectation. The evidence for the second expectation is somewhat stronger. The coefficient for SPECMIN is negative (and statistically significant) as expected; had LOCMIN been included in the equation, the sign of its coefficient would have been negative as well. The significant negative coefficient for PARMIN is less clear in its import. One plausible explanation, however, is that once specialist knowledge, local political experience, and parliamentary experience are removed as avenues for cabinet recruitment, what is left is an explicitly partisan

TABLE 4.5. Regression Equations Relating Role Orientation to Characteristics of National Parliaments

		Constant	C.DRAFT	SPECMIN	PARMIN	PRES
Legislator	B	.181	.204		-.106	
	se	.614	.113		.005	
Partisan	B	1.719	.122	-.0106	-.0149	
	se	.488	.049	.005	.005	
Communitarian	B	-1.123	-.200	.005	.004	.086
	se	.398	.070	.004	.003	.020
Own opinion among						
1st priorities	B	1.203	-.085	.0049		
	se		.050	.002		

		P.GROUP	C.INFL	GRP	LIJ	adjusted R^2
Legislator	B	-.718	-.121		-.109	.420
	se	.301	.101		.098	p<.057
Partisan	B		-.161	-.178	.115	.642
	se		.085	.055	.074	p<.015
Communitarian	B	.238	.337		-.130	.871
	se	.180	.060		.059	p<.001
Own opinion among						
1st priorities	B	.306	.089		-.171	.536
	se	.127	.044		.044	p<..029

base. Finally, the significant positive coefficient for C.DRAFT suggests that when parliamentary committees have considerable autonomy, not only are MPs encouraged to behave as legislators, but also that they are encouraged to do so in a partisan fashion. Overall, the adjusted R^2 is .642.

The mean communitarian factors scores are extremely well explained by these institutional variables (adjusted $R^2 = .871$), but the signs of the coefficients are, for the most part, the opposite of what one might have expected. Perhaps most surprisingly, the communitarian role orientation appears to be more common among MPs from majoritarian countries. It also is associated with low committee drafting autonomy (perhaps less surprising in light of the finding that C.DRAFT is positively associated with the partisan role orientation) and with higher values of P.GROUP. It is also associated with higher partisanship in the selection of the parliamentary president, perhaps ironically indicating that when parliamentary role orientations are divisive rather than communitarian, it is more important that the presiding officer be perceived as neutral rather than partisan.

Previous research (B. Wessels 1999) suggests that electoral system should play a role in determining the propensity of MPs to rank their own opinion among their top decision priorities. In particular, one would expect high district magnitudes, which would lower the individual visibility of an MP and the plausibility of a claim to an individual mandate would be associated with lower scores on this variable, while the existence of an intraparty preference vote, by raising individual visibility and the possibility of a personal mandate would be associated with increased scores (Katz 1986a). One also would expect giving high priority to one's own views to be associated with a decentralized parliamentary regime, with ministerial recruitment on the basis of specialist expertise or local governmental experience (i.e., personal rather than partisan qualifications) and less party-oriented practices and norms. Again, while the post-dictive power of the relevant equation in Table 4.5 is moderately high (adjusted $R^2 = .536$) many of the signs are the opposite of those expected. While the electoral system variables drop out of the multiple regression equation, the sign of the correlation for L.MAG is as expected, while that for PREF is the opposite of expectation.

INDIVIDUAL DIFFERENCES

While these regressions "explain" quite a large proportion of the variance among the nation-by-parliament group means, they explain only between 2.0 percent (legislator role orientation) and 15.5 percent (communitarian role orientation) of the individual level variance.[4] What then can be said about the impact of individual background as an explanation of role orientations?

This question is addressed in Table 4.6, which shows the partial correlations between the role orientation variables and individual background characteristics, in each case controlling for the predicted role orientation based on national variables. Four aspects of background are considered here. The first is demography, in particular gender and age. The second aspect of individual background is education. The third aspect of MPs' backgrounds is their experience in politics: whether they hold or have held public office at the local or regional levels; at the national level (for the MEPs) or European level (for the MNPs); and whether they have held subnational or national party offices. The fourth set of background variables concerns the MPs' experience as officials of groups in civil society: whether they are or have been officers of "new left" (women's or environmental) groups; of economic interest groups (trade unions, business, or professional associations); or of religious groups.

As the table shows, there are a few significant correlations. Women are more likely than men to have high scores as legislators, while older MPs are a bit more likely to have high scores as communitarians; MEPs with experience in national office (either public or party) are less likely than others to have high legislator scores; MPs who have been officers of women's or environmental groups tend to score more highly as legislators; MNPs who have experience in local or regional public office are a bit less likely to put their own opinions among their first ranked decision priorities. Nonetheless, the overwhelming impression given by the table is one of weak or no relationship. At least once the differences in national institutional contexts are controlled, men and women, young and old, those drawn from "new left" organizations and those drawn from old economic groups, appear to have very much the same role orientations once they get to parliament.

TABLE 4.6. Partial Correlations of Role Orientations and Individual Background Characteristics, Controlling for National Characteristics

	Legislator		Partisan		Communitarian		Own opinion among 1st priorities	
	MEP	MNP	MEP	MNP	MEP	MNP	MEP	MNP
Age	.009	.045	-.051	-.011	.123	.074	.041	.091
Gender	.204	.158	.015	.080	-.061	-.061	-.051	.049
Education	-.111	.015	.040	.003	-.025	-.043	.009	.044
Held local or regional public office	-.047	.039	-.041	.051	-.034	-.037	-.009	.013
Held national/European office	-.136	.033	.055	.044	.044	.035	.052	-.019
Held local or regional party office	.050	-.012	-.051	.056	-.065	.069	-.066	-.114
Held national party office	-.216	.034	.009	.026	.047	-.012	-.006	-.065
Held office in women's or environmental group	.165	.092	.038	.046	.100	-.057	.001	.064
Held office in trade union, business, or professional association	.072	.025	.031	-.016	-.005	.003	-.072	-.092
Held office in religious organization	-.069	.009	.057	-.013	.045	-.009	.012	.030

Notwithstanding the attention often given to demographics and to the nature of recruitment pools in the explanation of the attitudes and behaviour of politicians, this should, perhaps, not be terribly surprising. While it is possible to talk in vague terms about the general orientation of "new left" groups, for example, there is nothing particularly feminine or tied to the interests of women or the environment, or anything requiring or derived from extensive education, or connected to particular groups that dictates a partisan or a professional or a communitarian orientation to politics. Moreover, all of the organizations about which respondents were asked are likely to require a variety of specialization's and role orientations among their leaders.

WHO THINKS WHAT?

The second "big" question about role orientations and decision priorities is whether they are related to attitudes about the European Union and opinions about its institutional development. This question is addressed in Table 4.7.

The first conclusion is that the relative priority that MPs give to their own opinions is essentially unrelated to opinions about the extent and possible shape of further European integration. There are, however, a few exceptions. MPs at both levels who give priority to their own opinions tend to favour the selection of EP candidates by European parties. They also tend to oppose the idea that national ministers should follow the instructions of their national parliaments in the Council. In both cases, that is, they favour the position that implies lower influence for the national parties. Also among those giving priority to their own opinions, MEPs tend to favour dual mandates, while MNPs tend to be opposed.

MEPs who score highly as legislators tend to be st1rongly pro-European in their orientations. They favour shifting policy responsibilities to the European level and they evaluate more positively than others the EU policies already in place. They are more likely than other MEPs to believe that the democratic legitimacy of the EU must flow from EP elections, and to be confident that EU decisions are in the interest of their own countries. They favour strong powers for the EP and selection of the Commission by the EP, and they are opposed to having

TABLE 4.7. Correlations of Role Orientations with Attitudes About the European Union

	Legislator		Partisan		Communitarian		Own opinion among 1st priorities	
	MEP	MNP	MEP	MNP	MEP	MNP	MEP	MNP
Ave. level for policy decisions (hi = Eur.)	.242[1]	-.071[2]	-.129[2]	-.115[1]	.296[1]	.110[1]	.058	-.058
Ave. eval. of EU policies (hi = bad)	-.220[1]	-.049	.014	-.029	-.041	.001	-.090	.079[2]
Confidence EU-decisions in the interest of your country?	-.282[1]	-.009	.099	.086[2]	-.202	-.035	-.049	.021
Basis of democratic legitimation of EU	-.288[1]	.076[2]	.117[2]	.170[1]	-.282	-.046	-.018	.019
Joint committee of MEPs and MPs	-.028	-.080	-.165[1]	.009	.027	-.034	.036	.105[1]
Commission chosen by EP	-.202[2]	.060	.139[2]	.101[1]	-.179	-.053	-.068	-.039
European parties choose cand. for the EP	-.106	.017	.100	.159[1]	-.258	-.070	-.120	-.080[2]
Meetings between EP and nat. cttees	-.098	-.078	-.150	-.084[2]	-.020	-.001	.029	.104
Nat.gov.: Cabinet min. for Euro. affairs	-.168[1]	-.059	.059	-.042	-.123	-.051	.058	.059
Debates/council of ministers/matter of public record	-.221[1]	-.068	.077	.030	.012	.086[2]	-.044	-.157[1]
Ministers/council follow instructions nat.parl.	.020	-.118	-.097	-.063	.208[1]	.088[2]	.116[2]	.089[2]
More MEPs should also be MPs	.230[1]	.028	-.199[1]	-.052	.047	.044	-.126	.118[1]
Stronger links between Comm./MPs	.038	-.076	-.155[1]	.017	.002	-.123[1]	-.040	.082[2]
Same electoral system in Euro. elections	-.223[1]	-.058	.040	.067	-.238	-.064	-.072	-.045
Compulsory voting in EP elections	-.244[1]	-.019	-.115[2]	-.026	-.110	.002	.103	-.040
Desired influence: EP	.341[1]	.056	-.020	-.003	.313[1]	.057	-.021	.022
Desired influence: Europ. Commission	.263[1]	.015	-.063	.054	.274[1]	.068	.094	-.058
Desired influence: council of ministers	.088	.015	.196[1]	.095[1]	.090	.057	.015	-.110[1]
Desired influence: Europ. court of justice	.210[1]	.103[1]	-.034	.065	.135[2]	-.004	-.040	-.026
Desired influence: COREPER	.073	.032	.139[2]	.074[2]	.151[1]	-.014	.087	-.060
Desired influence: economic/social comm.	.191[1]	.113[1]	.038	.100[1]	.194[1]	-.065	-.032	-.035
Desired influence: nat.governments	-.012	.071	.191[1]	.149[1]	-.148	-.042	-.029	-.070
Desired influence: nat.parliaments	-.010	.078[2]	.183[1]	.125[1]	-.168	-.027	-.046	-.043

1 p < .01
2 p < .05

more MEPs also be members of their national parliaments. They are more likely than other MEPs to favour strong powers for the other "European" institutions of the EU (the Commission, the Court of Justice, the Economic and Social Committee), but are no different from other MEPs in their views regarding the powers of the "national" institutions (the Council, COREPER, the national governments and the national parliaments). Many of the same relationships hold for the MNPs, albeit in much attenuated form. (The relative weakness of the correlations observed in the MNP sample undoubtedly reflects the lower salience of European questions for MNPs.) In cases in which the question suggests a trade-off between European and national powers however (level of decision, basis of legitimacy, influence of the national governments and parliaments), MNP legislators tend to favour the national level where MEP legislators favour the European level, and hence the signs of these correlations are reversed.

While the magnitudes of the correlations with the partisan role orientation variable observed for the MEPs are somewhat lower than those observed with regard to the legislator role orientation, and those observed for the MNPs are generally somewhat higher, the primary point is consistency. Partisans at both levels of parliament tend to favour the national over the European level. They are more inclined to have policies decided at the national level and to see the legitimacy of the EU as derivative from the legitimacy of the national governments. They favour greater involvement of the national parliaments (more dual mandates, more joint meetings) and more power for the EU bodies directly representing the national governments (Council, COREPER), and, of course, for the national governments and parliaments themselves.

The mix of positive and negative correlates is about the same for the communitarian role orientation as it is for the legislator orientation. The relative magnitudes of the correlations, however, often are quite different. One way to characterize the difference is to observe that the pro-European orientation of those with high scores on the communitarian dimension seems to be more concerned with form, while the pro-European orientation of those with high scores on the legislator dimension seems to be more concerned with substance. One might infer, for example, that legislators favour making decisions at the European level because they approve of the results. For the communitarians on the other hand, although the correlation of role orientation with belief that decisions should be made at the European level is even stronger than it is for the legislators, those scoring as communitarians are *not* more likely than others to give a positive evaluation of EU policies, and their tendency to believe that EU decisions have been in the interest of their country is weaker than the corresponding tendency among the legislators.

CONCLUSION

No parliament, or other complex organization, can survive without members who play a variety of roles: some leaders and some followers; some technicians and some facilitators; some experts on details and some who see the big picture. The process by which an individual comes to hold one role orientation rather than another is complex. Formative experiences in childhood, education and professional development, cultural milieu, institutional circumstances, and opportunities all interact and contribute to determining how an individual will act, and how he will think he should act in any particular position. Given all this, it is not surprising that data from a closed-ended-question interview project offers only limited purchase in identifying MPs' role orientations and in explaining which MPs define their role in which ways.

At the same time, it is obvious that the mix of role orientations present in the membership of a parliament will have a significant impact on the way in which that parliament works internally, and in the way in meshes with the other institutions of the political system of which it is a part. In detail, parliamentary oversight is only likely to be effective if there are a critical mass of MPs who perceive it to be their jobs to "[go] about persecuting civil servants" (Chubb 1963). More generally, party government is more likely to result when the parliament is heavily populated by partisans, and technocratic government may be more likely to result when it is not.

It is important to remember that, as in any analysis of factor scores, the variables indicate greater or lesser "presence" of the attribute defining each factor *relative to other respondents in the survey*. Thus those at the low end of the "partisan" dimension are not necessarily nonpartisan in their orientation to their work as MPs, they are only less partisan than those who score highly; similarly, those who score highly

on the legislator dimension are not necessarily parliamentary worka-
holics or policy wonks, they are only more highly orientated in this
direction than those with lower scores. Nonetheless, the findings concerning the correlations between the role orientation measures and
MPs' attitudes about the institutional development of the EU present an
intriguing and potentially serious irony.

According to many analysts, one of the principal problems confronting the EU is the "democratic deficit." The cause of this deficit is
the failure of the EU in general, and the institutional location and internal operation of the EP in particular, to conform to the dominant, party
government, model of European democracy. The cure for the deficit is
to increase both the powers and the partisan nature of the EP. It is here
that the irony lies. For while this analysis reveals a significant "partisan" dimension in the role orientations of MPs, particularly the MEPs
who are the most "partisan" in their orientation—that is, those of whom
one would presumably need more in order to make the internal behaviour of the EP conform better to the requirements of party government
at the European level—are the ones who are less supportive of
increasing the intensity of powers and the breadth of responsibilities of
the EU and its institutions in the first place. On the other hand, the
MEPs who are the most European in their outlook, and who do favour
increased authority for the European Parliament and other EU institutions as well as greater separation between those institutions and the
institutions of the national governments—that is, those with the general
attitudes and specific institutional preferences of whom one would
presumably need more to further the development of the EU as an
autonomous political system—are the ones whose role orientations are
more indicative of a technocratic rather than a party-democratic
Europe. The problem to be solved in staffing a European Parliament
consistent with the development of a European polity that is democratically legitimate is not simply to get more "partisan legislators." Rather
it is to alter the mix of "partisan" attitudes among "legislators" and the
mix of "legislator" attitudes among "partisans" to create a body of
party-democratic European legislators.

NOTES

1   Identifying "the voters" specifically with the voters of the MEPs own party somewhat alters the original American understanding of the delegate idea, which referred more generally to all the voters of the representative's district. Even in the American situation, one might suppose that the representative should be particularly responsive to the desires of her own party, which presumably embodies the majority of the constituency. In the normal European context of proportional representation, however, it seems particularly appropriate to identify the MEP's "constituents" with those who voted for her party.

2   In addition to the five categories listed in the table, respondents also were asked about the importance of representing "All the people in your constituency." This variable was eliminated from the analysis because of the uncertain and variable referent of "your constituency" between countries in which MPs are elected from several districts and those in which all MPs are elected from a single national district, between countries electing their MPs using some form of PR and the UK (using the single-member, winner-take-all, system), and between countries in which there is some form of personal voting and those in which voters can only choose a party list as a unit. An open-ended category ("A specific group in society. Which one?") also was dropped, both because of a very low response rate and because of the variable referents.

3   The analysis in this section is based on the respondents from countries for which both MEP and MNP samples were collected. The data are weighted to reflect partisan balance within the respective sampling universe (country within parliament).

4   These figures are the squared correlation coefficients between the role orientation variables and predicted values computed by using the equations shown in Table 4.5 with individual level data.

5

Recruitment into the European Parliament

PIPPA NORRIS

EVER since its inception, many have expressed concern that the European Parliament is essentially a weak institution which, despite changes in its powers, is fundamentally flawed in its core functions of decision-making, linkage and legitimation (Jacobs and Corbett 1990; Hayward 1995; Andersen and Eliassen 1996a). The question of who gets recruited and elected into the European Parliament may have important consequences for the effectiveness of the body. The institutional structure and role of the parliament, and its relationship to the European Commission and Council of Ministers, determine much of its influence. Nevertheless, as the first chapter suggests, the functioning of political institutions is not simply a matter of their formal rules and legal regulations. Parliament is also the sum of the abilities, skills and experiences of its individual members.

Theories suggest that the process of recruitment, determining who becomes an MEP, is likely to shape the decision-making and legitimation functions of the European Parliament in at least two important regards. First, theories of professionalization suggest that the recruitment of experienced career politicians to the European Parliament is essential to produce an effective and cohesive body which can act as a counterweight to the expertise of Brussels bureaucrats and national ministers. The first section of this chapter therefore considers whether career pathways within the European Parliament are more or less professionalized than in equivalent national bodies. Moreover, theories of social representation claim that parliamentary elites drawn from groups which reflect the salient political cleavages in the European electorate will tend to be perceived as more legitimate representative bodies. The second section goes on to examine how far the European Parliament meets these standards, again in comparison to the composition of national legislative elites. The conclusion considers the implications of the findings for understanding the institutional effectiveness and legitimacy of the European Parliament.

THEORIES OF PROFESSIONALIZATION

Theories of professionalization suggest that the European Parliament would be a more cohesive and effective body if it recruits, retains and promotes party politicians with full-time careers within the institution. Max Weber (1958) first drew the classic distinction between "amateurs" living for, and "professionals" living from, politics. Professionals—whether in medicine, architecture, or the law—share certain characteristics in terms of similar educational backgrounds, common standards regulating, qualifying and restricting members for entry, and recognized hierarchical pathways for career promotion. As a result there is a shared professional community so that members can easily recognize who does, and does not, belong (Norris 1997b). The boundaries for semi-professions like journalists and career politicians are less easily defined but nevertheless they share many similar characteristics.

Legislative bodies vary considerably in their degree of professionalization, ranging from those like school boards or parish councils composed of unpaid "citizen-legislators" meeting infrequently up to highly institutionalized organizations with well-established structures of rewards and status, and many full-time career politicians, like the U.S. Senate and German Bundestag. As Aberbach, Putnam, and Rockman argue (1981: 1), during the 20th century the steadily growing power of career politicians and the decline of the "citizen-legislator" has been one of the most significant developments in most established democracies.

"Guild" systems of recruitment require long apprenticeship within parties and public life as a prerequisite for admission into higher office. Professional politicians enter this career-track relatively young and may expect to devote most of their lives to public service. Guild systems produce seasoned legislators well-versed in the rules of the political game, and a shared institutional culture from many years in parliament, maximizing internal cohesion. In contrast, citizen legislators are the result of "entrepreneurial" systems characterized by a high degree of lateral entry into the elite from outside careers and institutions. This offers opportunities for those like Berlusconi or Perot who enter parliament in middle-age or later after a lifetime's experience within the world of business and industry, entertainment, or the media. Life peers in the British House of Lords can be seen to exemplify this tradition. Entrepreneurial systems bring new blood into the parliamentary elite, along with exposure to knowledge of other institutions in the private sector, thereby maximizing linkage with society.

In this chapter career politicians are defined in terms of three primary characteristics: their political experience, occupational background, and future career ambitions. Career politicians are commonly drawn from "brokerage occupations" which combine policy expertise and technical skills useful in public life with professional autonomy, financial security, extensive contact networks, prestigious social status, and flexible career paths (Norris and Lovenduski 1995). Given the contingencies of elected office, those like lawyers and journalists can move relatively smoothly and costlessly in the revolving door from the public to private sector, and vice versa. Parliamentarians are most commonly drawn from the professions of law, education and the media, as well as from full-time paid party officials, political researchers, and public sector administrators. Brokerage occupations are those most compatible with the demands of elected office. Moreover career politicians usually enter parliament after serving a lengthy political apprenticeship, being active within parties in branch and constituency meetings, and then gaining experience of elected office in local and regional government. Lastly, we would expect career politicians to be ambitious for advancement within their own institution, rather than using this body as a stepping stone to other posts like directorships in the private sector.

The causes and consequences of the growth of career politicians have been widely discussed (see Copeland and Patterson 1994). In an early study Polsby described the process by which the U.S. House of Representatives gradually became more complex, structured, and coherent, increasing its relative power and prominence in the political system, thereby changing the roles and careers of members (Polsby 1968). When first founded, service in Congress was not a stable career path for politicians, internal committee structures were poorly organized, leadership roles were weak, politics was a part-time activity, and institutional norms and routines had barely been established. This contrasts sharply with Congress today (Davidson and Oleszek 1994).

Evidence suggests that a similar process of professionalization has gradually transformed several western European national parliaments, to a greater or lesser extent, including Britain (Buck 1963; King 1981; Riddell 1993), Germany (B. Wessels 1997a), Scandinavia (Damgaard 1992), Spain and Portugal. In contrast the picture seems more mixed, as we would expect, in the newer parliaments in Central and Eastern Europe, where many new members were suddenly launched into public life, sometimes with no wish nor expectation of being elected (Ágh 1994: 42).

After the first direct elections to the European Parliament, Lodge and Hermann (1982) and Holland (1986) suggested that candidates often lacked political experience, and there was the suspicion that MEPs treated the institution as only a temporary stepping stone to their real ambitions, which involved a career in domestic politics. Yet this proposition was never clearly established and it deserves to be reexamined today since it remains unclear how far the institutionalization of the European Parliament during the last two decades means that MEPs now pursue a full-time career in European politics as their lifelong ambition.

PARTY APPRENTICESHIPS

So what is the evidence concerning the degree of professionalization in the European Parliament, compared with national legislatures? First, in terms of political experience, who gets selected, and elected, into the European Parliament? Professional legislatures in countries with strong mass-branch party organization, such as Germany, Britain and Australia, tend to be drawn from politicians who have spent many years working within their party as grassroots activists, officeholders in local branches, and officials in the regional or national party organization (Norris 1997a). In European democracies professional legislatures are usually characterized by those who have invested many years in party service. Studies suggest that in many countries selectors often regard this as an essential qualification when picking party candidates (McAllister 1997; B. Wessels 1997a; Norris and Lovenduski 1995), although in some other countries like the Netherlands and Finland the importance of this may have waned in recent years (Leijenaar and Niemoller 1997; Helander 1997). What is the pattern at the European level?

We can compare three groups: candidates for the European Parliament, Members of the European Parliament (MEPs), and members of national parliaments (MNPs), in the eleven countries where we have comparable MEP and MNP data.[1] As shown in Table 5.1, we found no significant difference between MEPs and MNPs in terms of their length of party membership: the groups divided roughly equally between those who had been party members for up to 15 years, for 16-25 years, and for longer periods. The major contrast was between elected politicians at both national and European levels and the candidates for the European Parliament who usually had less extensive party service: two-thirds of EP candidates had been party members for 15 years or less. Yet there were some differences between MEPs and MNPs in terms of other forms of party apprenticeship, with MEPs having slightly greater experience of national party office, such as positions on the national executive. Overall the overwhelming majority of all politicians had come up through this traditional party route with many years of service. In the United States, the rise of the "entrepreneurial" candidate running in primaries means that politicians can often by-pass party organizations (Ehrenhalt 1992; Fowler and McClure 1989; Kazee 1994), but in Europe this is rarely the case.

TABLE 5.1. Party Apprenticeship

	EP Cand	MEPs	MNPs	Diff Sig MEPs : MNPs
Years Party Membership				
0-15	65	35	39	5
16-25[1]	} 35	36	33	-3
26+		29	28	-2
Held local/regional party office	67	86	90	5*
Held national party office	31	81	66	-15**
N.	1231	249	1378	

Sig. p. ** >.01, * > .05
1   The EP Candidate survey coded up to, and more than, 16 years party membership
Source: European Representation Study, 1994 N.1726 (Weighted All EU)

PRIOR EXPERIENCE OF ELECTED OFFICE

The next step for career politicians is to stand for elected office at local and regional levels. Table 5.2 shows the experience of these groups in elected office. In this regard, both groups had commonly served on a local representative body, and this was particularly common for MNPs, three-quarters of whom had done this. In addition, almost half of all MNPs had held local government office, compared with about a third of all MEPs. At regional and national level of government there was no difference between these groups. MNPs were more likely to have served on a national representative body but very few of them (5%) had ever been an MEP.

Interestingly, if we compare the number of years which members have served in each parliament, differences between national and European bodies now seem to have disappeared. About one fifth of national MNPs (19%) had been in parliament for 11 years or longer, and this was true for about the same proportion (15%) of MEPs. If national parliaments once held more seasoned veterans than the relatively new European Parliament, this is no longer the case.

Pathways to power, providing organizational skills and useful networks of political contacts, also commonly include activism within associations. Trade union affiliations and work in new social movements can be particularly important among parties of the left. Table 5.2 shows that national and European politicians were equally likely to have held office in a range of professional, trade union, and group associations, with MEPs slightly more likely to be found in women's organizations, as reflects the composition of the European and national parliaments. What the comparison of party and elected office shows is that the overall level of political experience, taken as one important indication of professionalization, is about the same in the European and national parliaments. The main contrast to emerge where we have comparable items is, as we would expect, that candidates for the European Parliament generally had the least experience of all the groups. Since candidates are often in the early stages of establishing their political careers, it is not surprising that many have been less active in public life, and similar patterns have been found when comparing parliamentary candidates and elected MPs elsewhere (Norris and Lovenduski 1995).

TABLE 5.2. Political Apprenticeship in Elected Office

Please tick if you have ever ...	EP Cand	MEPs	MNPs	Diff. Sig MEPs : MNPs
HELD ELECTED OFFICE ...				
A local representative body	27	61	76	15**
A member of your local government	38	30	47	17**
A regional representative body		38	36	-2
A member of your regional government		14	19	5
A national representative body	20	44	71	27**
A member of your national government	6	16	14	-2
A Member of the European Parliament	9	100	5	-95**
Years in Parliament				
0-5		61	58	-3
6-10		24	24	0
11+		15	19	4
HELD ORGANIZATIONAL OFFICE ...				
In a Professional Association	23	43	45	2
In a Trade Union	19	43	42	-1
In a Business Organization	23	13	17	4
In a Women's Organization	11	17	12	-5*
In an Environmental Group		23	21	-2
In a Religious Organization		20	27	7
N.	1231	249	1412	

Sig. p. ** > .01, * > .05
Note: For MEPs and MNPs whether now or ever held office. The significance of the difference between MEPs and MNPs is measured by chi-square.
Source: European Representation Study, 1994 N. 1661 (Weighted All EU)

BROKERAGE OCCUPATIONS

The occupational background of members before they enter full-time political careers can also be expected to be important in distinguishing career politicians. "Amateur" legislatures tend to be characterized by more newcomers to public life, who may be drawn from non-traditional routes such as high-profile stars from sports or entertainment, entrepreneurs (like Berlusconi) direct from the private sector, or citizens action groups which have not usually provided a springboard into public office. Career politicians are more likely to choose brokerage occupations which facilitate a full-time political career, providing flexible hours and suitable skills, such as the legal profession, the media, and full-time party office. Highly institutionalized legislatures often recruit from a narrower and more predictable sector of the labour market while "citizen-legislators" come from more diverse backgrounds. To examine this pattern we can compare the occupation of EP candidates with that of MEPs and MNPs prior to their first election to parliament. The precise dividing line between brokerage and other occupations is never water-tight but we can distinguiysh between pro-

TABLE 5.3. The Occupational Background of MEPs and MPs

	MEPs	MNPs	EP cand
BROKERAGE OCCUPATIONS			
Legal profession	10.0	14.7	8.7
Media profession	9.0	5.5	8.4
Legislative official	9.0	1.8	n/a
Party Official	8.0	5.5	8.0
Government official	7.7	3.3	14.4
Political Scientist	4.3	3.6	n/a
Interest Organization official	3.7	3.5	1.5
OTHER OCCUPATIONS			
Educational profession	14.0	13.6	21.8
Business employer	7.3	8.2	15.6
Physician	5.3	7.8	3.7
Economist	5.3	5.2	n/a
Farm Manager/Employee	2.7	4.1	3.0
Engineer, architect	3.7	6.6	4.2
Service Manager/Employee	2.0	4.8	4.1
Administrative official	3.7	6.9	n/a
Clerical Manager/Employee	1.3	.5	2.8
Sales Manager/Employee	.7	.8	n/a
Production Manager/Employee	.7	2.1	2.7
Armed services	.3	.4	1.1
Home Worker	1.3	1.0	
Professionally-related jobs	51.7	38.0	41.0
Other occupations	48.3	62.0	59.0
N.	249	1412	1232

Sig. p. ** > .01, * > .05
Source: European Representation Study, 1994 (Weighted All EU)

fessionally-related and other occupations. As shown in Table 5.3, the results are quite striking: about half of the MEPs are drawn from pro-fessionally-related careers, notably the legal profession, the media, and legislative, party and government officials. This indicates a higher level of professionalization than the national parliaments, where about 38 percent of MNPs come from similar occupations. As other studies have commonly found, MEPs are also drawn disproportionately from educational professions, while manual occupations were greatly under-represented.

CAREER AMBITIONS

Another important defining feature of professional legislatures is not where members come from, but where they go. Career politicians see their primary ambitions within the institution, or related higher offices. In national parliaments the hierarchical ladder usually rises from being a backbench member towards chairing parliamentary groups or com-mittees, then moving into higher levels of cabinet office. In contrast citizen-legislators may well experience a more diverse and erratic pathway, perhaps treating the European Parliament as only a stepping stone to national office or the private sector.

To explore political ambitions politicians were asked where they would like to be ten years from now, given a multiple-choice list of national and European posts. The results in Table 5.4 show a striking and significant difference in how groups saw their future careers. Many MEPs saw their future within Europe, either by remaining a member of the European Parliament, or chairing an EP committee, or joining the Commission. Yet many MEPs were also attracted to careers within national parliaments and governments. In contrast members of national parliaments were far more likely to see their future only within the arena of domestic politics, either remaining as a backbencher or mov-ing into government office. Few MNPs (only 14 percent) expressed ambitions to enter the European Parliament.

The evidence considered so far therefore strongly suggests that if the European Parliament was once regarded as the province of citizen-legislators, this is no longer the case. The pattern that we have established suggests that in terms of the political experience of mem-

TABLE 5.4. Political Ambitions

Ten years from now...	MEPs	MNPs	Diff Sig.
Member of national parliament	20	44	-24**
Member of national government	21	25	-5
Chair of national parliamentary committee	3	16	-13**
Leader of a national organization	11	8	3
Chair of national parliamentary group	2	6	-4*
No national office	56	32	24**
Member of the European Parliament	49	14	35**
A member of the European Commission	18	6	12**
Chair of an EP committee	15	3	12**
Leader of a European organization	8	4	5*
Chair of party group in the EP	3	2	2
No European office	27	77	-50**

Sig. p. ** > .01, * > .05
Note: Q "Where would you like to be ten years from now? Please tick as many as appropriate."
Source: European Representation Study, 1994 (Weighted All EU)

bers, their prior occupational backgrounds, and their political ambitions, compared with national parliaments most of the evidence points towards a highly professionalized institution today. In most regards MEPs now have a similar profile to MNPs, with the qualification that MEPs were slightly more likely to see their future career in terms of European and domestic politics, while MNPs are more likely to see their ambitions only within the national arena. This may reflect some important residual differentials in terms of the perceived status and power of European and national parliaments. But if professionalization does produce more effective and coherent decision-making institutions, maximizing continuity over time, as proponents argue, then the consequences are likely to strengthen the European Parliament.

THE SOCIAL BACKGROUND OF MEPS

Yet the effectiveness of legislatures in terms of decision-making is only one function, and arguable not necessarily the most important one, in most countries. The other central function of parliament is to act as a linkage mechanism, connecting citizens and the state, and legitimating decisions made by governments. In this regard social representation may be critical. How far does the European Parliament look like a microcosm of European society?

The core functions of the European Parliament are legitimation and linkage, as well as decision-making. In this regard the European Parliament is the only directly elected body in the European Union which can claim to speak for all the people of Europe. Theories of social representation suggests that a parliament which recruits politicians reflecting the broad diversity of European society,—including the critical cleavages of social class, gender, age and religion,—is more likely to be perceived as legitimate, to bring diverse experiences to the decision-making table, and to be able to articulate the concerns of all groups of citizens, than one which recruits from only a narrow section of the political elite.

There have long been concerns expressed about the over-representation of privileged class interests, and the lack of working class members, in parliamentary elites (Putnam 1976; Loewenberg and Patterson 1979; Gallagher and Marsh 1988). Research on elites throughout established democracies has found most tend to attract highly educated and high status professionals and managers. Recent decades have seen stronger demands for the greater diversity in terms of the inclusion of more women in parliament, as well as ethnic minorities and younger members (Lovenduski and Norris 1993; Lovenduski 1986; Norris 1997a). A growing body of evidence suggests that this may have more than symbolic significance, since female politicians have been found to bring a distinctive range of concerns to the policy-making process (Thomas 1994; Vallance and Davies 1986; Vallance 1988; Karvonen and Selle 1995; Phillips 1993; Dahlerup 1988; Norris 1996).

CLASS AND EDUCATIONAL STATUS

The class biases in the European Parliament have already been discussed when comparing the occupational profiles of members. As already noted there are few members drawn from manual backgrounds, but in this regard the European Parliament is far from unique. The institution remains dominated by brokerage occupations which are professionally related, rather than a broader range of members who could bring the voice of direct experience on matters like farming, industrial production, or military service into the chamber. Turning to the demographic profile of members, one of the most striking long-term trends in many parliaments is the gradual rise in university-educated members, whether in Germany (B. Wessels 1997a), Britain (Norris and Lovenduski 1995) or elsewhere (Putnam 1976). As shown in Table 5.5, over three-quarters of all MEPs were university graduates, a slightly higher proportion than among MNPs (71 percent) and EP candidates (62 percent). MEPs were also slightly more likely to express a religious affiliation and to attend church regularly than national MPs, although there was a similar profile by type of religious denomination.

AGE

Turning to the age profile of members, MEPs proved to be marginally older than national MPs: one fifth of MEPs, but a quarter of MNPs, were in their mid-forties or younger, while this was true of over half of the EP candidates. The age profile of MEPs could be significant if, as Inglehart suggests, the younger generation bring distinctive values and priorities to public life (Inglehart 1977b, 1991). Moreover, this may prove important for political careers since early entry into legislative life facilitates life-time service, stronger institutional socialization, and internal promotion within the body.

GENDER

Lastly, the representation of women in the European Parliament has gradually grown during the last four decades. The Common Assembly (1952-58) included one woman out of 78 representatives, or 1.3 percent of the total. This increased marginally to 3 percent of members in the Parliament of the Six (1958-1972), then 5.5 percent in 1978 (European Commission 1979). Originally MEPs were nominated by

TABLE 5.5. The Social Background of EP Candidates, MEPs and MNPs

	EP cand	MEPs	MNPs	Diff Sig. MEPs : MNPs
EDUCATION				
University graduates	62	78	71	7*
Other higher education	23	14	18	-4
No higher education	16	8	11	-3
MARITAL STATUS				
Married	69	86	87	-1
Non married	31	14	13	1
AGE GROUP				
44 or less	51	19	26	-7**
45-54	32	44	42	2
55+	17	37	33	4*
RELIGION				
Protestant	38	13	16	-3
Catholic	25	51	55	-4
Other	3	4	5	-1
None	34	32	24	8**
RELIGIOSITY				
Attend church weekly	17	21	20	1
Attend church monthly	16	17	27	-10**
Attend church once a year	33	29	31	-2
Never attend	34	33	23	10**
GENDER				
Men	73	75	85	-10**
Women	27	25	16	10**
N.	1231	249	1412	

Sig. p. ** > .01, * > .05
Source: European Representation Study, 1994

national legislatures, and responsibility for the low representation of women rested squarely with the parliamentary parties. The major breakthrough came in the first direct elections in 1979, resulting in 69 women out of 410 representatives, or 16.8 percent. The proportion increased, with some fluctuations, during the next decade until by 1994 one-quarter of all MEPs are women. This compares with women constituting about a fifth (16 percent) of members in equivalent national legislatures. Based on trends since the first direct elections, we can estimate that women will achieve parity in the European Parliament in the year 2044.

Although members are being elected to a common body, female representation varies substantially across member states (see Table 5.6). In 1994, women were 8 percent of representatives in Portugal compared with 44 percent in Denmark. Women represent over a third of the members in six other countries. Women's representation in the European Parliament lags behind other member states most clearly in the UK, Greece, Italy and Portugal, often by a large margin. The comparison reveals a strong link between the proportion of women elected in each country to the European and national parliaments ($r = .63$ $p > .05$), as well as a strong correlation between the proportion of women MEPs and women members of national cabinets ($r = .73$ $p > .05$). This pattern strongly suggests that systematic patterns affect women's recruitment across these levels. Nevertheless countries such as France and Belgium have a far higher proportion of women in the European than national parliaments, while the reverse is true in the Netherlands and Denmark.

TABLE 5.6. Women Elected in European Elections, 1979-94 (%)

	1979	1984	1989	1994
Belgium	8	21	17	32
Denmark	31	38	38	44
Germany	15	20	31	35
France	22	21	23	31
Ireland	13	13	7	26
Italy	14	10	10	10
Luxembourg	33	17	33	33
Netherland	24	28	28	32
UK	14	15	13	18
All Nine	19	20	22	29
Greece		8	4	16
Portugal		4	13	8
Spain		10	15	33
All Twelve		16	19	25

Sig. p. ** > .01, * > .05
Source: *The Times Guide to the European Parliament* successive volumes (Times Publications).

CONCLUSIONS AND IMPLICATIONS

The evidence presented in this chapter focuses on only two aspects of recruitment, in terms of its possible effects on the professionalization and the social representation of the European Parliament. Nevertheless these are important aspects of legislative institutions which may have significant implications for the policy-making process.

In terms of social representation we can conclude that the profile of members of the European Parliament closely reflects that of members of national parliaments, being disproportionately male, middle-aged and middle class. The EP contains slightly more women than at national level, but also slightly more older members. Nevertheless the general pattern of social representation in the European Parliament reflects the well-known social biases evident throughout political elites. The most plausible explanation for the recruitment process, developed elsewhere (Norris 1997a), draws upon the supply and demand model which suggests that three sets of factors are important:

(i)   The *systemic context* of recruitment, including the effects of the electoral system, the political culture, and the party system on the competition for candidacies for the parliament;

(ii) *Supply*-factors, including the experience and motivation of the candidates who come forward; and,

(iii) *Demand*-factors, which includes the preferences and attitudes of the selectorate.

These factors can be expected to shape who comes forward, and who succeeds, in entering the European Parliament.

In terms of career politicians, we can conclude that the European Parliament is now as highly professionalized as national parliaments, in terms of the political experience which MEPs bring to office, their prior occupational backgrounds, and their political ambitions. If the European Parliament was ever once an amateur body, as early studies suggest, this evidence suggests that it is no longer so.

The consequences of this development, however, remain open to debate. Arguments about the pros and cons of the growth of career politicians often revolve around different perceptions about the most appropriate role of parliamentarians. On the one hand proponents of professionalization argues that it brings a new level of expertise to the complex process of European policymaking. Career politicians who regard the European Parliament as their full-time vocation are probably more likely to draw on a lifetime's experience of the policy process to strengthen their work in Strasbourg, Luxembourg and Brussels. If the European Parliament moves further down this road, this may help it to counterbalance the expertise provided by the Commission and by national governments. This is particularly important for mastering the Byzantine complexities of the European policy-making process. If there is a clear and well-established vertical career ladder within the European Parliament, we would also anticipate that talented and ambitious politicians would work to be promoted within this body, rather than seeing the organization as a stepping stone to national politics or the private sector. Again this should promote continuity, stability and cohesion in policy-making within the European Parliament. In contrast if the European Parliament remains weakly institutionalized we might expect it to prove less effective in decision-making, lacking continuity and legislative expertise compared with members of the Commission or national governments.

Yet on the other hand critics charge that the growth of career politicians may have negative consequences. This development may make politicians increasingly out of touch with the concerns of the European public, and may make entry into European politics more difficult for all but a narrow elite who have spent a lifetime in politics but who lack experience of other institutions. Critics deplore the tendency towards professional politicians, arguing that this produces a narrower, technocratic elite, out of touch with the real world of the electorate, who are also averse to taking risky independent positions which threaten their career (Riddell 1993). The popular term limits movement in the U.S. is a call to revert to the older tradition of "citizen legislators," undermining incumbents. The consequences of a highly professionalized European Parliament therefore remains open to alternative interpretations and only time will tell whether this phenomenon will contribute towards, or serve to mitigate, problems of the democratic deficit and the gap between European citizens and their political leaders.

NOTES

1   Note that throughout, to compare like with like, the study excluded all countries where we lacked equivalent data for national and European elites. The 11 countries included are Belgium, France, Germany, Greece, Ireland, Italy, Luxembourg, Netherlands, Portugal, Spain and Sweden.

PART II

Linkages

6

European Parliament and Interest Groups

BERNHARD WESSELS

THE 'NUMBER PROBLEM OF REPRESENTATION' AND INTEREST GROUPS

THE political procedures of liberal democracy are designed to ensure the responsiveness of the elected to the electors. Voting rights, freedom of speech and association, equality of information, and the predominance of the electoral decision over intervening decisions are designed to ensure that elected representatives in fact carry out public desires. That is, all conceptions of democratic government hinge upon some form of control of leaders by non-leaders (Dahl 1975). Although this idea may be simple, the practice of political representation is complex. Given the complexity and multiplicity of interests in modern societies, it is impossible for representatives to recognize public desires and demands by relying solely on individual citizens or the electoral process. That is why social groups are so important in political life in general and political representation in particular. Without the aggregation of individuals' interests into collective demands, interests are not visible enough or not structured enough or not simple enough to be recognized correctly by political actors and to elicit the necessary degree of responsiveness. The importance of (organized) groups has long been highlighted in interest group research (Bentley 1967 (1908); Truman 1951; Rokkan 1966).

In contrast, the focus on interest groups in the discourse about European integration has been primarily concerned with the contribution of interest groups to the integration process. This strand of discussion and research has been inspired by neo-functionalist theory. It was argued that groups could play an important role in the integration process by producing and inducing a spill-over effect into national structures and interests (Haas 1964: 111). Interest group development at the European level has been interpreted as an indicator of integration (Kirchner 1978). And indeed, the number of Euro interest groups has increased tremendously from some 300 in 1970 to more than 600 in the mid-1980s, or from roughly 400 in 1980 to more than 500 in 1990, depending on one's source (Greenwood, Grote, and Ronit 1992: 1-2).

In recent years, the focus slowly has shifted to the question of representation, and the influence of interest groups at the European level (Kohler-Koch 1997: 2). The shift of focus was a result not only of difficulties with the neo-functionalist spill-over hypothesis and the doubts raised about the implied simplicity of the integration process (Greenwood, Grote, and Ronit 1992: 4) but also of the deepening integration of the EU and the question of how democratic representation will be possible in the emerging polity. And indeed, the EU does face serious problems of representation, identified with the so-called "democratic deficit." One might call this problem the *"number problem of political representation."*

Political representation is already quite complex at the national level. But at the European level it is even more so. Numbers make interest groups even more necessary than at the national level. At the national level, the ratio of elected to electors is 1:67,668 in the worst case (Germany) and 1:3,734 in the best (Luxembourg). On average, one member of a European national parliament has to serve 54,844 electors. For the EP, the worst ratio is one representative per 610,848 electors (Germany), and the best is 1:37,339 (Luxembourg). On average, 429,729 electors are represented by one member of parliament at the European level. The sheer number of people represented by a single member of the EP has important implications for political representation. Larger numbers include a larger variety of interests and a higher complexity of problems. They also mean, given the fact that a day has only 24 hours, that the density of contacts as measured with respect to the electorate cannot be as high as in the national contexts. This could mean that the flows of communication and information are not sufficient to transmit the whole complexity and variety of interests, demands, and problems. Or it could mean that—since individual representation is not feasible—collective representation and channels of communication with collective actors are of greater relevance. In fact, collective linkages probably are the only solution to the linkage problem in the European Union, given the numbers just reported. It has been explicitly argued that interest groups might compensate for the lack of direct contacts between EC institutions and the citizens of member states (Haas 1964; see also Schmitter 1996a: 133f.). Thus, the "second circuit" of the "machinery of the democratic representative polity" (Offe 1981: 141), or the "two-tier-system" of political representation with votes constituting "only one among many different power resources in ... bargaining processes" of which associations are a part (Rokkan 1966: 105), seems to be even more important at the European level than at the national level. It might be therefore that *functional representation* as well as *territorial representation* must play an important role in the the future of the European polity. Schmitter, for example, has construed ideal-types of possible outcomes of the formation of the European polity, in which functional representation plays a major role (Schmitter 1996a: 133-36).

Many aspects of the question of interest groups and the EU have been discussed, ranging from huge questions like whether a convergent system of European interest intermediation will emerge (Schmitter and Streeck 1991) and the question of corporatism at the European level (Schmitter and Grote 1997) to more concrete questions like the functional differentiation of interest group arenas, and the access of and responsiveness to interest groups. This chapter is an attempt to pick up some central points of discussion and research on the structure and channels of functional representatives, i.e. interest groups, within the European polity and the EP in its centre. In particular, it addresses questions along the following dimensions: access and responsiveness, functional differentiation, and linkages. All three aspects are clearly interrelated. However, they are disentangled into the following questions:

1. What is the access of interest groups to the EP and how responsive are its members?
2. Are there any indications of an emerging European system of interest mediation? In empirical terms this means an investigation of the functional differentiation of contact arenas of organized interests.
3. Is there a trend from national corporatism to transnational pluralism or has corporatism a chance at the European level?

4. Do patterns of cleavage, expressed in party group-interest group alliances well known from the national level reappear at the European level?
5. What are the linkage patterns with respect to the functional differentiation of interest groups and the functionally specialized committees of the EP?
6. What is the scope of access of interest groups to institutions other than the EP that might connect them to European policy-making?

EP AS A VETO PLAYER? ACCESS TO AND RESPONSIVENESS OF THE EP TO INTEREST GROUPS

The EU has accumulated a considerable degree of institutional competence and policy-making capacity. This is obviously a reason for interest groups to be engaged in Euro-lobbying and to try to have a voice at the transnational level. Despite the peculiarities of the transnational level, the institutionalization of an intermediary system at the European level appears to have much in common with the development of interest groups at the national level. The formation of supranational interest groups can be regarded as a correlate of the growing competence of the "European state." Most authors on European interest groups agree that "the development of the power of the European Economic Community has given rise to reaction from those interests, which are most directly affected." (Sidjanski 1972: 401). Kirchner, for example, (1978: 4) detected a simplified model of "co-evolution" in the process of European interest group formation that he called "the circle of institutionalization." In this respect, it is not so important whether community policies directly influence a group's exercise of demand and pressure or whether organizational strength of one actor provokes another set of interests to counter this influence (Kirchner and Schwaiger 1981: 5). The growing competence of the European level and growing competition between interests on the European scene are two sides of the same coin—the growing competence of the (supranational) state. Sidjanski (1972) separates several phases of interest group formation at the continental level, each caused by the emergence of a new centre of political decision. The first wave started when the Marshall plan and the OEEC were launched. "They were mostly groupings with a very loose structure, mirroring in this sense the loose power" with which European institutions were vested. The next wave dates from 1952, with the establishment of the ECSC bringing up about ten new organizations, most of them specialized. In 1958, the EEC commission was launched and this had more profound effects; this third wave saw the birth of many European-level federations. In the beginning, and for a long time after, the targets of interest groups clearly were the commission, the council, the ESC etc. But since the European Parliament became more important, in particular with the new cooperation procedure under the terms of the SEA, the EP has become an important target for lobbying as well (Greenwood, Grote, and Ronit 1992: 26; Kohler-Koch 1997). This clearly marks a fourth wave of integration relevant for interest groups.

Although nothing can be said about change in the centrality of the EP as a target for interest groups, the figures on contacts of MEPs show that there is a tremendous amount of exchange between the EP and interest groups, be it that interest groups contact representatives or the other way round. Average MEP reports roughly 109 contacts with interest groups from the national and supranational level each year. In total this amounts to some 67,000 contacts between the EP and interest groups annually (Table 6.1). Not taking into account contacts with journalists, the relevance of this kind of linkage as compared to others is obvious. Roughly 42 percent of all contacts providing some linkages between MEPS and society are those with interest groups. About a fifth of contacts are with either national or European political institutions, another 17 percent are contacts with citizens.

Kohler-Koch (1997: 16) reports that consultants pay differential attention to the EP according to which legislative procedure is applied. It is the experience of MEPs that the codecision procedure receives the highest attention of interest groups whereas the consultation procedure is more or less neglected. This again points to the fact that the formation and action of organized interests tend to follow increases in competencies. The more the EP becomes a veto-player, the more attention it receives.

As to the question of which interest is best able to give voice at the European level, there is wide consensus that this is business. Kirchner and Schwaiger demonstrate in their study that business including agriculture shows the highest organizational development (Kirchner and Schwaiger 1981: 22-4). This view is confirmed by Greenwood and

TABLE 6.1. Contacts of Members of the EP with Interest Groups
and Citizens

Contacts with	Average number of contacts per year per representative[a]	Estimated total number of contacts of all EP members[b]
Citizens	43.76	27,394
National non-business interest groups	33.02	20,671
- Consumer associations	6.53	4,088
- Environmental organizations	8.31	5,202
- Trade unions	9.05	5,665
- Professional associations	9.13	5,715
National business interest groups[c]	36.52	22,862
European non-business interest groups	19.73	12,351
- Consumer associations	4.54	2,842
- Environmental organizations	5.77	3,612
- Trade unions	5.19	3,249
- Professional associations	4.22	2,642
European business interest groups[c]	19.33	12,101
National political institutions/actors[d]	56.59	35,425
EU-Institutions[e]	50.25	31,457
Total	259.19	162,253
Citizens contacts	16.9 %	27,394
Interest groups contacts	41.9 %	67,984
Contacts national political institutions	21.8 %	35,425
Contacts European political institutions	19.4 %	31,457

a   Average is based on the following calculation: contact "at least once a week" (counts 52), "at least once a month" (counts 12), "at least every three months" (counts 4), "at least once a year" (counts 1), and "less often", "not contact" (counts 0). This is a rough and conservative estimate. The real numbers are certainly not smaller, and probably are larger.
b   Estimate based on average contacts multiplied by number of members of parliament.
c   Included in this category are interest groups of agriculture and fishing, industry, transport, trade and commerce as well as banking and insurance.
d   Included in this category are contacts with national party leaders, national members of parliament, national ministers and national civil servants.
e   Includes European civil servants, European Commission, European Council, Economic and Social Committee, European Court of Justice and COREPER.
Source: Members of European Parliament Survey 1996.

others who state that capital "includes the most developed forms of political representation at the European level" (Greenwood, Grote, and Ronit 1992: 21). In their opinion, this is due to the degree of coherence that can arise as a result of unitary purpose, i.e. pursuit of profits (ibid.:

TABLE 6.2. Contacts with and Responsiveness to Interest Groups

	MEP with frequent contact			%-diff. respons.- non-respons.	diff. in % of non- responsive
	% of all MEP	% of non- responsive	% of responsive		
National interest groups:					
- Consumer associations	29	24	42	+18	75
- Environmental organizations	34	31	44	+13	42
- Trade unions	39	37	45	+8	22
- Professional associations	39	32	56	+24	75
- Agriculture/fishing	32	26	48	+22	85
- Industry	36	30	53	+23	77
- Transport	28	24	38	+14	58
- Trade/commerce	28	23	41	+18	78
- Banking/insurance	20	16	32	+16	100
European interest groups:					
- Consumer associations	19	15	31	+16	107
- Environmental organizations	21	15	35	+20	133
- Trade unions	22	18	32	+14	78
- Professional associations	17	11	34	+23	209
- Agriculture/fishing	17	12	29	+17	142
- Industry	19	15	29	+17	113
- Transport	14	10	24	+14	140
- Trade/commerce	13	09	22	+13	144
- Banking/insurance	09	06	16	+10	167

19). At first glance, the figures in Table 6.1 seem to support this notion. National and European business interest groups come up to about one half of the interest group contacts of MEPs. However, Schmitter and Streeck (1981) point out that business is anything but unitary. A closer look to business sectors shows that there is considerable variation by sector: agriculture being most present, followed by industry, transport, trade and commerce, with banking/insurance being least present not only among the business interests but of all interests on average. This is shown by average contact figures as well as by a count of MEPs with frequent contacts with interest groups, where frequent means at least 12 times a year (Table 6.2). The figures show that, for example, trade unions and consumer associations have frequent contact with a greater number of MEPs than businesses with the exception of agriculture.

However, contacts do not tell the story of which voice will be heard in the end. In order to have a rough estimate at least, MEPs have been classified according to whether or not they are responsive to interest groups in general.[1] Altogether, 27 percent of the MEPs indicate that they are responsive toward interest groups. But responsiveness is not equally distributed. We can estimate this from a comparison with those who report themselves not to be responsive to particular interest groups. If the difference between responsive and non-responsive among those having frequent contacts with interest groups does not vary across groups, then there would be no indication of responsiveness to particular groups. Deviations from this equal distribution assumption on the other hand can be read as an indicator of selective responsiveness. Table 6.2 provides this information in two ways: the difference in the proportion of those with frequent contacts between responsive and non-responsive, and this difference as a proportion of the non-responsive MEPs having frequent contacts. Only three interest groups stand out in percentage point differences for national interest groups (professional associations, industry, and transport) and two at the European level (environment and professional associations). Taking the same difference as a percent, the result is somewhat different but still does not provide evidence for an obvious advantage of business as a whole. Rather, the impression is that there are clear differences between different businesses with respect to the responsiveness of MEPs.

Whereas very obvious and clear patterns of differences in responsiveness across interest groups cannot be found, this is not true with respect to country differences. Kohler-Koch's report of her findings (1997: 23) suggests that the group "friendly towards lobbying" consists of Belgium, the UK, Ireland, Finland, Austria, Denmark, the Netherlands, and Sweden. The middle group holds Germany and France, the sceptical group consists of the MEPs of Luxembourg, Italy, Spain, Portugal, and Greece. Our results contrast with these findings. Whereas we find the UK, Ireland, Finland, Austria, and the Netherlands also in the group of the interest group friendly, we do not find Belgium and Sweden. Except for Portugal, in our findings the "southern" countries do not belong to the sceptics (Figure 6.1). It is difficult to say whence these differences in findings result. One possible explanation is the difference in sampling strategy and sample size (Kohler-Koch: n = 176, n = 314 in this study).

More important, however, than the classification of countries is the finding that there is a clear relationship between the frequency of contacts and responsiveness. The more responsive an MEP country group is on average, the more contacts it has. The correlation is quite high at the aggregate level (.69) and also holds at the individual level (.38) and

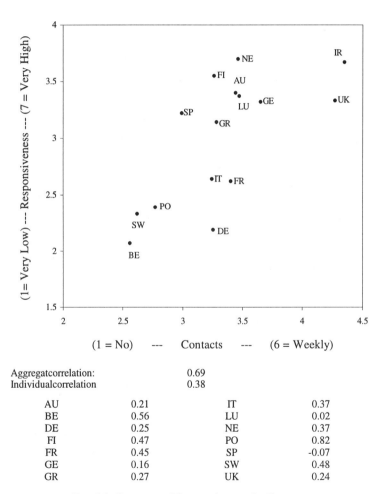

| Aggregatcorrelation: | 0.69 |
| Individualcorrelation | 0.38 |

AU	0.21	IT	0.37
BE	0.56	LU	0.02
DE	0.25	NE	0.37
FI	0.47	PO	0.82
FR	0.45	SP	-0.07
GE	0.16	SW	0.48
GR	0.27	UK	0.24

FIG. 6.1. Contacts and Responsiveness by Country

even—with the exception of Spain—at the individual level within country (Figure 6.1). To draw a causal arrow from responsiveness to frequency of contacts might appear arbitrary, but there are good theoretical reasons: rational actors first go where they are best heard (Prewitt 1968).

EMERGENCE OF A EUROPEAN SYSTEM OF INTEREST MEDIATION?

There is a long-standing discussion concerning the degree to which a European system of interest intermediation has emerged in the European union. The contact figures of members of the EP clearly show that it has become attractive for organized interests to have a voice at the supranational level. However, this does not necessarily mean that a *European* system is developing. Although there is a tremendous increase in the founding of European interest groups, partly encouraged by the European Commission, the central role of Euro interest groups in the mediation process is doubted. This has to do with the difficulty of Euro groups in finding the lowest common denominator of their members' interests (Avery 1975; Grant 1989) and the weakness of the federations of federations. Kohler-Koch (1997) and Lanzalaco (1992: 203f) even argue that due to path dependency and differing national legacies, no convergent system of European interest intermediation will emerge. Greenwood and others summarize the reasons for the survival and persistence of a national route to Europe: the EU's reliance upon member states for policy implementation; experience with the national route as tried and tested; costs of European level organization for smaller concerns; large firms' reliance on national governments; negative collective action problem; etc. (Greenwood, Grote, and Ronit 1992: 22-3). On the other hand, economic and political integration lead national systems to converge within limits and clearly the demand for a European level response in functional and political terms is strong. Thus, the pressure for organized interests to adapt is very strong. Greenwood and others therefore came to the conclusion that "the importance of the national route appears in fact to have been somewhat overstated" (ibid.: 23). Although there are good theoretical arguments and empirical evidence (Kirchner 1978) to expect a Europeanization of interest intermediation, we tend to follow the hypothesis of Kohler-Koch (1997: 3) that no convergent system of European interest intermediation will emerge.

We test this hypothesis by using the logic of the network approach in a specific way: regarding MEPs as knots in the contact network of interest groups, it is possible to map the patterns and configuration of interest groups vis-à-vis the EP. Figure 6.2 shows the result from a multidimensional scaling of a similarity matrix of contacts of MEPs with interest groups. The results suggest four distinct contact arenas defined by two dimensions: a "territorial" dimension separating the European from the national interest groups and a functional dimension separating consumer interests in a broader sense (consumer, environment, labour unions) from business interests (agriculture, industry, transport, trade and commerce, banking and insurance as well as professional associations, near the border to consumer interests). These four arenas are quite distinct as indicated by the distance between types of interest groups.

This mapping indicates that there are different routes to the EP which do not converge at the level of the contacts of individual MEPs. The individual patterns of contacts with each interest group type point in the same direction: the portion of MEPs who have contact with the national organization of the respective interest not only by far exceeds those having contacts with European level organizations, but also those serving as "brokers" between national and European level organized interests. On the other hand, the quite large portion of MEPs in frequent contact with both levels indicates that organized interests keep a plurality of channels for lobbying open. Of those who have frequent contacts with interest groups, roughly 40 percent have contacts with both levels of organization. On the other hand, the percentage of those who have contacts with the national organization level only on average is higher than fifty percent (Table 6.3).

The differences between types of interests are interesting. Contrary to the widely reported finding that business interests show the most European organizational development (Kirchner and Schwaiger 1981: 22-4; Greenwood, Grote, and Ronit 1992: 21), these results indicate that these interests are dominated by national organizations in terms of contacts. Rather, the most "Europeanized" areas of interests are those of the consumers, environmentalists, and labour. This "Alliance of the Weak" (Kohler-Koch 1997), specialized on social, consumer, and

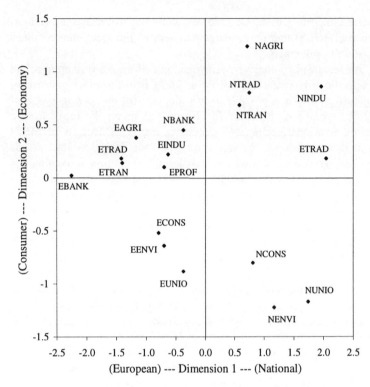

Multidimensional scaling, Euclidean model.
Stress .15; squared correlation of distances (RSQ) .90.

NCONS	Nat. Consumer	ECONS	Eur. Consumer
NENVI	Nat. Environment	EENVI	Eur. Environment
NUNIO	Nat. Trade Unions	EUNIO	Eur. Trade Unions
NPROF	Nat. Profess. Org.	EPROF	Eur. Profess. Org.
NAGRI	Nat. Agrar. Org.	EAGRI	Eur. Agrar. Org.
NINDU	Nat. Industr. Org.	EINDU	Eur. Industr. Org.
NTRAN	Nat. Transport	ETRAN	Eur. Transport
NTRAD	Nat. Trade	ETRAD	Eur. Trade
NBANK	Nat. Banks	EBANK	Eur. Banks

FIG. 6.2. Mapping the Contact Landscape of Interest Groups with the EP

environmental questions, might be so "Europeanized" in contact patterns because the EP is considered to be the natural ally of an advocacy coalition (Kohler-Koch 1997: 13). Later we will see whether this alliance also translates into party specific contact arenas in the EP.

Summing up, a European route of interest intermediation clearly is not dominant. Rather, the national route seems to be of greater importance, in particular in the business arena. Thus, the contact figures and constellations support the hypothesis that the emergence of a European system in a narrow sense is unlikely. However, it is obvious as well that a plurality of channels prevails. It is not a question of European *or* national, but a matter of European *and* national level contact. Does this also mean that there is no "Europeanization" of interest mediation? In the literature, Europeanization is defined solely in terms of European level organization. The question, however, is whether this is an adequate perspective. As Schmitter (1996a) has pointed out, it is unlikely to be productive to conceptualize the European system by drawing an analogy to what we know from national settings. Rather, the EU will be a mixture of national elements with a new character, or to use a dictum of Durkheim, more than the sum of its parts. A simple dichotomy between national and European levels of organization in order to define a national route or a European system of interest intermediation thus is not very helpful. New developments in interest group research in federal polities show that a similar dichotomy within the nation-state, i.e. local versus national, does not capture reality.

TABLE 6.3. Patterns of Frequent Contacts with Interest Groups of Members of the EP: National, European, and Acting as Broker In Between

Interest Organizations	% all respondents*			% of MEP	% respondents with contact**		
	National only	Broker	European only		National only	Broker	European only
Consumer Org.	15.3	13.4	5.7	34.4	44.4	38.9	16.7
Environmental Org.	17.2	16.9	3.8	37.9	45.4	44.5	10.1
Labor Unions	19.1	19.7	2.2	41.1	46.5	48.1	5.4
Professional Assoc.	22.9	15.9	1.3	40.1	57.1	39.7	3.2
Agriculture/Fishing	16.6	15.6	1.0	33.1	50.0	47.1	2.9
Industry	20.4	15.9	2.9	39.2	52.0	40.7	7.3
Transport	16.2	11.8	1.9	29.9	54.3	39.4	6.4
Trade/Commerce	17.2	10.5	2.2	29.9	57.4	35.1	7.4
Banking/Insurance	12.1	8.0	0.6	20.7	58.5	38.5	3.1

*   % of MEPs with frequent contact (at least 12 times a year) of all MEPs.
** % of MEPs with frequent contact in the respective organizational arena, i.e., either at the national or the European level or at both levels.

NO EUROPEAN CORPORATISM?

Closely related to the question of the emergence of a European system of interest intermediation is the question of whether something like a transnational corporatism is emerging. The positions in the debate are clearly divided. Andersen and Eliassen take the position that a more structured system with corporatist elements will evolve. Falkner (1997) stated recently that the predicted decline in neo-corporatist interest intermediation is premature and that at the national as well as at the European level encompassing negotiations between both sides of industry and the Commission as the representative of the European state are gaining ground. Whereas Schmitter obviously agrees with the argument as far as the national level is concerned (Schmitter and Grote 1997), he clearly opposes the second part concerned with the European level. Schmitter and Streeck rather have predicted a transformation from national corporatism to transnational pluralism (Schmitter and Streeck 1991). The reasons they gave are size, complexity, multiple layers of access, differing national practices etc. Since corporatism rests on two pillars, i.e. an autonomous distribution capacity and a relative equilibrium of class forces, and both qualities are missing at the transnational level, chances for corporatism are weak. Schmitter together with Grote has recently reiterated this argument.

However, some contributions in the volume of Greenwood and others (Greenwood, Grote, and Ronit 1992: 5) demonstrate that corporatism-like arrangements exist in certain domains and sectors. And incentives to implement something like corporatist structures at the European level in order to get a better grip on macro economic management are clearly stronger now than ever before. The convergence criteria may "not have presided over the initial resurgence of macro-corporatism in such countries as the Netherlands, Belgium and Ireland," but it might be one of the reasons for its re-establishment at the national level. Thus "the primary growth potential for macro-corporatist architects in the future lies in the feverish efforts of national governments to adapt to the single market directives" (Schmitter and Grote 1997: 33, 36). The question is whether it is likely that this will cause spill-over effects in an opposite direction from that normally assumed in integration theory, namely from the national to the transnational level. Thus the question is whether the route goes from national corporatism to transnational corporatism.

Looking at this question from the perspective of parliamentary corporatism, a term introduced by Lehmbruch (1982), our data allow us to contribute to this discussion. Lehmbruch defines parliamentary corporatism as the embededdness of parliaments and their members in multiple relationships mirroring macro-corporatism. That is, parliamentarians in contact with both sides of industry at the same time can be regarded as one necessary though not sufficient element of corporatist structures. Looking to the figures clearly shows that MEPs with relationships to labour unions as well as national business associations are the minority; about one quarter of MEPs have such a double contact structure (Table 6.4).

In order to check which kind of corporatist communication structure these contacts facilitate, contact structures have been differentiated into: a) the national level (frequent contact both with unions and business on the national level); b) the national-European mix (frequent contact with national labour and European business); c) the European-national mix (frequent contact with European labour and national business) and d) the European level (European labour and business). The figures show that corporatist-like contact structures are most prominent for the national level (24 percent of MEPs). For the European level the figure is only one third, and for each of the mixed types about half, of the national pattern. This becomes even more obvious looking to those having frequent contacts with at least one of the two parties of industry: 61 percent show the national corporatist contact pattern, all other types are shown by less than 30 percent.

Thus the answer to the question of whether we find national corporatism, transnational pluralism or transnational corporatism is that we find national corporatism at the transnational level. This is clearly an exaggeration: contact patterns are not proof of corporatist-like negotiations and bargaining. But assuming that parliamentary corporatism at least needs the appropriate contacts, we can conclude that the ground is laid in the European Parliament more for national corporatism at the transnational level than for a European corporatism.

CLEAVAGES AND ALLIANCES: DEJA VU

Another aspect of convergence and character of the intermediation process at the European level is the degree to which selective linkages exist between party groups and organized interests. Stinchcombe (1975) has argued that these relationships can be regarded as alliances or coalitions, depending on the point of observation, i.e. from the population or the organizational perspective. We know that typical patterns of alliances and coalitions came into existence in all Western democracies with the emergence of political cleavages. Constellations of alliances and oppositions create more or less well-structured paths of interest representation and security in expectations. Opponents know each other's interests. The more formalized the adversaries'

TABLE 6.4. Corporatist Contact Patterns in the EP

	% of all respondents*	% of all respondents with frequent contacts**
National Labour Unions – National Business[a]	23.9	60.5
National Labour Unions – European Business[b]	12.9	24.8
European Labour Unions – National Business[c]	15.0	28.5
European Labour Unions – European Business[d]	8.3	21.5
All Forms	24.8	39.0

* % MEPs with frequent contact (at least 12 times a year) of all MEPs.
** % MEPs with frequent contact in the respective organizational arena, i.e. labour unions or business organizations.
a MEPs with frequent contact with national labour unions and with at least one of the business organizations of industry, transport, or trade and commerce at the national level.
b MEPs with frequent contact with national labor unions and with at least one of the business organizations of industry, transport, or trade and commerce at the European level.
c MEPs with frequent contact with European labour unions and with at least one of the business organizations of industry, transport, or trade and commerce at the national level.
d MEPs with frequent contact with European labour unions and with at least one of the business organizations of industry, transport, or trade and commerce at the European level.

roles are, the more likely it is that intentions and behaviour will meet reciprocal expectations. At the same time, coalitions, for example between unions and left parties or between churches and religious parties, provide distinct channels of interest representation. Thus, clear-cut spheres of interest provide relative *security in expectations* as well as relatively secure *channels of representation* (B. Wessels 1994: 154-5; B. Wessels 1997b). As we know from representation studies, this pattern appears in legislatures as well. Considerable efforts have been made to assess the impact of lobbying through parties. However, little is known about the patterns and impact at the European level (Greenwood, Grote, and Ronit 1992: 27). It is not clear whether one should expect those patterns of alliances and coalitions between parties and interests that are well-known from the national level to emerge. Different cultures and legacies of interest structures as well as internal conflicts differentiate the party groups. However, given the fact that European policies are becoming more and more politicized, one can assume that some similarity in coalition patterns should already be visible, even if a European party system is missing.

Results of the mapping of party groups and interest groups according to the density of their communication indeed reproduce a pattern well known from the national level (Figure 6.3).

Results reveal a "bourgeois" alliance, indicated by dense contacts between the liberal, Christian, and conservative party groups and business interests; a labour alliance between communist and socialist party groups and unions; and an "alliance of the weak" between Greens, Radicals and environmental as well as consumer interest groups.

Despite the fact that no religious alliance can be observed due to missing information concerning contacts with churches and religious groups, the pattern is very much the same as in many European countries. In terms of political cleavage, we find the arenas of labour, capital interests, and of the so-called New Politics (Hildebrandt and Dalton 1977). Results indicate that, as at the national level, interest groups will be the organizational underpinnings of an emerging party system.

FUNCTION SPECIFIC LINKAGES

Having found politically specific linkages, a further question is whether contact patterns also translate into function specific linkages. The European Parliament is a "Working Parliament" (Weber 1921) with its committees having a strong position. Thus, it would be rational for interest groups to address those MEPs who work in areas of the substructure of parliament related to their policy interests. Altogether, the European Parliament has 20 standing committees of which at least 16 can be regarded as policy specific. The other four deal with internal affairs, budgetary control, institutional affairs, and rules of procedure. In order to examine this question, we inspect the map of closeness and distance of MEPs working in functionally specialized committees and interest groups in terms of their contacts.

The mapping reveals four larger arenas, which might be called: 1) the arena of consumer interests; 2) the arena of industry interests; 3) the arena of trade and transport interests; and 4) the arena of agricultural and fishery interests (Figure 6.4). In the consumer arena, national and European environmental and consumer interest groups are at the centre with committees on environment, culture, women, petitions, legal affairs, and citizens' rights. The industry arena is much more complex. It consists of all committees related to economic issues (economy, external economic relations, research, regional policy and development and cooperation, budget) as well as the committee on social affairs. Most prominent in terms of contact in this arena are European and national interest groups of industry and labour unions of both levels. The transport and trade arena is made up of the committee of transport, along with trade and transport interest groups of both levels as well as banks. The committees on agriculture and fisheries plus agrarian interests constitute the fourth arena.

The arenas are relatively distinct, although there is some overlap between the industry arena in the centre and the consumer and trade/transport arenas beneath. The compartmentalization observed for the Commission and their policies (Greenwood, Grote, and Ronit 1992: 17) does not exist as strongly at the level of the parliament. This observed compartmentalization is also associated with nontransparency and fragmentation and the resulting problem for a rationally functional differentiation. For the European Parliament this seems not to be valid.

Instead, a clearly structured arena of contacts evolves following lines of functional differentiation.

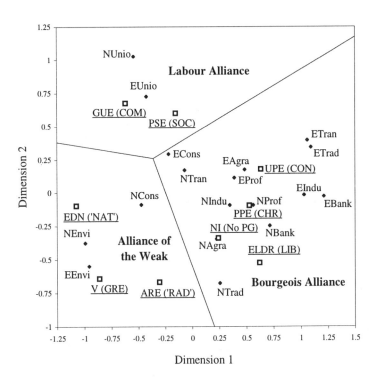

Correspondence analysis, canonical normalization.
Explained variance 71.8 % (Dim. 1: 56.6; Dim. 2: 15.3)

Ncons	Nat. Consumer	ECons	Eur. Consumer
Nenvi	Nat. Environment	EEnvi	Eur. Environment
Nunio	Nat. Trade Unions	EUnio	Eur. Trade Unions
Nprof	Nat. Profess. Org.	EProf	Eur. Profess. Org.
Nagri	Nat. Agrar. Org.	EAgri	Eur. Agrar. Org.
Nindu	Nat. Industr. Org.	Eindu	Eur. Industr. Org.
Ntran	Nat. Transport	Etran	Eur. Transport
Ntrad	Nat. Trade	Etrad	Eur. Trade
Nbank	Nat. Banks	Ebank	Eur. Banks

FIG. 6.3. Party Groups and Interest Groups Contact Patterns

124		*Linkages*

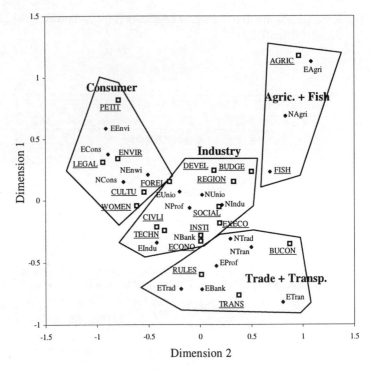

Correspondence analysis, canonical normalization.
Explained variance 55.1 % (Dim. 1: 37.1; Dim. 2: 18.0)

Ncons	Nat. Consumer	ECons	Eur. Consumer
Nenvi	Nat. Environment	EEnvi	Eur. Environment
Nunio	Nat. Trade Unions	EUnio	Eur. Trade Unions
Nprof	Nat. Profess. Org.	EProf	Eur. Profess. Org.
Nagri	Nat. Agrar. Org.	EAgri	Eur. Agrar. Org.
Nindu	Nat. Industr. Org.	EIndu	Eur. Industr. Org.
Ntran	Nat. Transport	ETran	Eur. Transport
Ntrad	Nat. Trade	ETrad	Eur. Trade
Nbank	Nat. Banks	EBank	Eur. Banks

FOREI	Committee on Foreign Affairs, Security and Defence Policy
AGRIC	Committee on Agriculture and Rural Development
BUDGE	Committee on Budgets
ECONO	Committee on Economic and Monetary Affairs and Industrial Policy
TECHN	Committee on Research, Technological Development and Energy
EXECO	Committee on External Economic Relations
LEGAL	Committee on Legal Affairs and Citizens' Rights
SOCIAL	Committee on Social Arrays and Employment
REGION	Committee on Regional Policy

Figure 6.4 continued on next page

Figure 6.4 continued

TRANS	Committee on Transport and Tourism
ENVIR	Committee on the Environment, Public Health and Consumer Protection
CULTU	Committee on Culture, Youth, Education and the Media
DEVEL	Committee Development and Cooperation
CIVLI	Committee Civil Liberties and Internal Affairs
BUCON	Committee on Budgetary Control
INSTI	Committee on Institutional Affairs
RULES	Committee on the Rules of Procedure
WOMEN	Committee on Women's Rights
FISH	Committee on Fisheries
PETIT	Committee on Petitions

FIG. 6.4. Linkage Patterns Between EP-Committees and Interest Groups via MEP-Contacts

LINKAGES BEYOND THE EUROPEAN PARLIAMENT

Having addressed the question of the access of interest groups and their configuration vis-à-vis the European Parliament from different angles, we now turn to the question of whether interest groups might have any further impact through the parliamentary channel. Kohler-Koch (1997: 11) has found that, even though it is approaching the parliament, the final target for the "alliance of the weak" is the Commission or the Council. Contacting and making alliance with the European Parliament is "an indirect strategy to cope with their limited resources." In many cases the final target of interest groups is not the European Parliament. Baker (1992) put it this way: "you don't lobby the EP—you lobby the Commission and the Council via Parliament" (cited from Kohler-Koch, ibid).

Given the complex structure of decision-making, one can think of several possibilities for this to work. One possibility is to support the EP in positions challenging Commission and Council. Another possibility is to lobby MEPs, who can prepare policies themselves through consultation with the Council or the Commission, or who are in contact with both through other channels. This implies a kind of interorganizational exchange in which MEPs are the central brokers. Thus it makes sense to make use of the network approach in an even more explicit way.

Again, we are exploring the chances of organized interests to reach a target beyond the European Parliament by lobbying the parliament.

This time we assume that MEPs could function as a bridge for indirect exchange between organized interests and European institutions. Thus they are mapped in their contact space according to their frequency of contacts with European institutions and administration on the one hand and interest groups on the other. Interestingly enough, the outcome shows a differentiation found before in this chapter: a territorial dimension separates the European and the national level, a functional dimension separates consumer from economic interests (Figure 6.5). Since this is true for institutions as well as interest groups, the outcome is that European interest groups have better access to European institutions by means of contact with MEPs, national interest groups with institutions at the national level.

Thus the question is put forward again and again whether there is a European route of interest intermediation emerging or whether the national route persists. The results support what Greenwood et al. also have found: interest groups are very flexibly accommodated to the Europeanization of politics. National routes are used in different ways as are transnational routes (Greenwood, Grote, and Ronit 1992: 246). If there is something in the network and exchange assumption made here, then the national route might be of a much greater variety than thought so far. The contact patterns would allow at least, that a) national interest groups approach national governments, governments approach MEPs, and MEPs approach the Commission or Council; or b) national interest groups approach MEPs, who approach the national governments and administrators, who in turn approach the Commission or Council. In contrast, the European route seems to be more straightforward: European interest groups contacting MEPs targeting European institutions.

CONCLUSIONS

Interest groups and lobbying at the European level seem to be much more structured than many researchers have suggested, at least with respect to the European Parliament. This, however, does not mean that a European system of interest intermediation in the narrow sense is emerging. There are clear national differences a) in the willingness to be responsive to interest groups and b) in the national interest profiles.

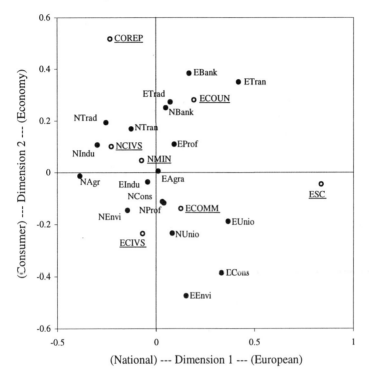

Correspondence analysis, canonical normalization.
Explained variance 74.6 % (Dim. 1: 49.5; Dim. 2: 25.1)

Ncons	Nat. Consumer	Econs	Eur. Consumer
Nenvi	Nat. Environment	Eenvi	Eur. Environment
Nunio	Nat. Trade Unions	Eunio	Eur. Trade Unions
Nprof	Nat. Profess. Org.	Eprof	Eur. Profess. Org.
Nagri	Nat. Agrar. Org.	Eagri	Eur. Agrar. Org.
Nindu	Nat. Industr. Org.	Eindu	Eur. Industr. Org.
Ntran	Nat. Transport	Etran	Eur. Transport
Ntrad	Nat. Trade	Etrad	Eur. Trade
Nbank	Nat. Banks	Ebank	Eur. Banks

ECIVS	European Civil Servants
ECOMM	European Commission
ECOUN	European Council
ESC	Economic and Social Committee
COREP	COREPER
NMIN	National Ministers
NCIVS	National Civil Servants

FIG. 6.5. Linkage Patterns Between Political Institutions and Interest Groups
via MEP-Contacts

It is also obvious that the interest group arena is segmented along a territorial dimension, separating the European and the national level, and a functional dimension. Results suggest that both the national and the transnational route to Europe will persist and that convergence or a kind of melting together will not take place—at least not in the near future. The arena of European and national interest groups is also still separated in terms of approaching different MEPs. The proportion being approached by both levels, who might act as brokers between them, is quite limited. A corporatist pattern of interest intermediation is not emerging at the European level, although national corporatism seems to have some impact at the transnational level.

Clear structures appear, however, looking to alliances between particular interest groups and party groups. Here some well-known patterns, associated with traditional and new cleavages at the national level, reappear. Lobbying is also well structured in functional terms. Function specific linkages between interest groups and MEPs seem to provide efficient policy channels into the functionally differentiated committees of the European Parliament. Linkages reaching beyond parliament seem also to be well structured, but point to the fact that national and supranational routes of interest intermediation will coexist for the near future.

NOTES

1   The classification is based on the answers to two questions about the degree to which MEPs take the opinions of a) organized groups, and b) lobbyists into account when making political decisions. Answers have been added and divided between those who take them into account much or very much and those who don't.

7

Partisan Structures in the European Parliament

JACQUES THOMASSEN AND HERMANN SCHMITT

INTRODUCTION

> Political parties at European level are important as a factor for integration within the Union. They contribute to forming a European awareness and to expressing the political will of the citizens of the Union. (article 138a Maastricht treaty)

THIS article, which was added at the very last moment to the Maastricht Treaty,[1] should, of course, not be read as a factual, but as a normative statement: as an ideal to which the European Union should aspire. As such, it is intriguing enough. Despite all pessimism[2] about the progress of the European project towards further political integration, this article can hardly be understood in a different way than as the expression of the ideal of a federalist, i.e. a supranational, Europe with a well functioning democracy in which European political parties should play an essential role.

If this is a constitutional principle of the European Union, it is a fair question to ask to what extent this principle has materialized in reality. This is the question we shall try to answer in this paper: *to what extent is there a party system at the European level capable of expressing the political will of the citizens of the Union.*

In order to put this question into the proper perspective we should first clarify what the role of political parties in a system of democratic government is, and to what extent the European Union can be considered as a system of representative government.

POLITICAL PARTIES AND DEMOCRATIC
GOVERNMENT

In theories of political representation, political parties gradually were promoted from the role of enemies of democracy, as *pars pro toto* for dividing factionalism, to the role of the key actors in a representative democracy. According to modern — or, if one prefers, elitist — democratic theory, representative democracy without political parties is close to impossible. The "will of the people," so prominent in classic democratic theory, is no more than an abstract principle as long as it is not formed and organized by political parties or functionally equivalent organizations (Schattschneider 1942).

Political parties are the intermediary between the will of the electorate and public policy. They take care of the political mobilization of the voters; they provide political recruits for the nomination process; and, they provide ideologies, programs and platforms for voters to choose from (Pedersen 1996: 15). The majority of the elected parliament forms and controls the government and therefore has a final say in the legislative and policy making process. This is the basic idea of the concept of *party government*: the majority of the people elect the majority in parliament, this majority forms and controls the government; ergo the (majority of the) people themselves are in control of the government.[3]

From the concept of party government three requirements can be deduced that refer to the *party system*, *political parties*, and the *system of government*.

1. The party system needs to be *competitive*.
2. Political parties need to be *cohesive*.
3. The government should be *formed* and *controlled* by the majority.

COMPETITIVENESS

According to Schumpeter's famous definition of democracy, the "competitive struggle for the people's vote" is the very essence of democracy (Schumpeter 1976: 269). And in his view a political party is little more than "a group whose members propose to act in concert in the competitive struggle for political power." Similarly, G. Bingham

Powell (1983: 3) considers "The competitive electoral context, with several political parties organising the alternatives that face the voters" as "the identifying property of the contemporary democratic process."[4] It can be argued that the democratic meaning of the competitiveness of the party system is quite limited unless the voters are offered a choice, not just between different political parties, but between political parties with *distinct policy proposals*.

COHESIVENESS

Competitiveness is a necessary, but not a sufficient condition for any electoral control over public policy. Political parties also must be *reliable*, i.e. must act in accordance with their party platform and campaign promises. Political parties can only be reliable when all representatives of the party act in accordance with the party line.

If individual representatives of a political party deviate from the party line or act differently, voters have no cue what the party stands for, are unable to vote rationally and therefore their vote cannot be linked to a particular policy view. Therefore, political parties need to be *cohesive*, i.e. individual representatives of a political party should take similar stands on policy issues.

THE FORMATION AND CONTROL OF GOVERNMENT

Still, the democratic effect of elections would be futile unless the elected (majority in) parliament has a say in the formation and the policy of the government. If the formation of the government and the policies adopted by the government were not derivative of the elected parliament, there would be no direct linkage between the will of the electorate and government policy. To what extent does the European political system meet these requirements?

Of course, it is easy to demonstrate that the political reality of the EU with respect to the last requirement is a far cry from the concept of party government. Despite the increased—and perhaps underestimated—powers of the European Parliament, it does not form and control a European government, for the simple reason that there is no such thing as a European government, at least not in any traditional sense of the concept of a state government, let alone a *responsible* government. Also, because there is no government to form or to support at the European level, the concept of government vs. opposition parties, so essential in any parliamentary democracy, has no meaning at the European level.

Therefore, it hardly needs to be argued that at least one important leg of the system of party government, formation and control of the government by a majority in parliament, is at best a very crippled one.

In this paper we will focus on the two remaining requirements, the *competitiveness* of the European party system and the *cohesiveness* of political parties *at the European level*.

But, of course, it only makes sense to do this if a party system at the European level exists in the first place. This is the question we will address first.

A EUROPEAN PARTY SYSTEM?

In an institutional sense the answer to this basic question is an unequivocal "yes": a European party system does exist, both as a system of extra- and intra-parliamentary parties.

The traditional European political families, socialists, Christian democrats, liberals and the green parties have organized themselves in transnational party federations. In 1999 there are four party federations in the European Union: the Party of European Socialists (PES), which until November 1992 was the Confederation of Socialist Parties of the European Community (CSP); the European People's Party; the Federation of Christian Democratic Parties of the European Community (EPP); the Federation of European Liberal, Democrat and Reform Parties (ELDR); and the European Federation of Green Parties (EFG). In addition to those major federations there are a few additional transnational party groupings, but only the PES, the EPP, the ELDR, and the EFG possess all the elements of a transnational party federation: a statute, a common program, a secretariat, an executive body, a party assembly, a hierarchical leadership structure, the ability to make decisions binding on the member parties, and the aspiration to become a fully fledged European political party (Hix 1996: 308). Still, there is little reason to overestimate the meaning of these transnational federations. Important functions of extra-parliamentary party organizations are the formation of a party program and the selection of candidates for parliaments. In both respects the importance of the transnational parties is limited. Their most significant role in the European elections is to co-ordinate transnational party manifestos. Being a compromise between different political traditions in member states, these manifestos offer little more than platitudes (Smith 1996: 278). Moreover, these manifestos hardly play a role in the elections. European elections are fought by national parties and mainly on national issues (van der Eijk and Franklin 1996). Candidates are selected, not at the European level, but at the national level by national parties.

As a consequence, the question of competitiveness can be answered easily and quickly. The function of competitiveness in the process of representative democracy refers to the *supply side* of politics, to the extra-parliamentary role of political parties. Political parties are supposed to supply different policy platforms for the voters to choose from. At the European level this does not happen. European political parties as such do not compete for the votes of a European electorate. European elections are still the arena of national political parties. This conclusion might be the end of our search. However, being interested in the European Union as a *developing* political system, we are inclined to reformulate the question of competitiveness somewhat and to see to what extent a competitive political system at the level of the European Union is at least *feasible* (cf. Thomassen and Schmitt 1997; Schmitt and Thomassen 1999).

Even though European political parties as such do not compete at the European level, the major transnational parties consist of national political parties that, with all their differences, share a common ideology with a long international tradition. Liberal, Christian democratic and socialist parties in different countries are based on common ideologies that do not change colours once they cross national borders. Therefore, even though transnational political parties as such do not compete in a European electoral arena, it is quite conceivable that the *conditions* for such a competitive system do exist. Even if political parties in different countries that are grouped together in the European Parliament do not address themselves as a group to a European electorate, but rather as national parties to a national constituency, they might still represent a European electorate on the assumption that the parties belonging to the same political group do take a similar stand on important political issues. If that is the case, there would still be quite a distance to be bridged to truly European political parties, in the sense that they would present themselves at the European level to a European electorate, but at least there would be no substantive barrier preventing this. Therefore, the reformulated question that we will address in this chapter is to what extent European political party groups take *distinctive* positions on relevant political issue dimensions. In order to answer that question we will not look into the supply side of politics, i.e. party manifestos and campaign promises, but into the positions taken *in the European Parliament*.

The function of the *cohesiveness* of political parties refers to the *reliability* of political parties. The cohesiveness of political parties is a necessary requirement for being able to stick to their promises after the elections. Cohesiveness refers to political parties as intra-parliamentary organizations. As such, the role of European political parties, or European party groups, is more substantial. Members of the European Parliament are organized in transnational rather than national party groups. Of the EP elected in 1994, 594 out of 627 members affiliated with one of the political groups. The European Parliament is clearly dominated by the PSE and the EPP. Together they occupy 397 of the total number of 626 seats. Adding the seats of the ELDR and the EFG makes 467. These party groups play the decisive role in changing the Parliament's leaders. The groups also set the parliamentary agenda, choose the rapporteurs and decide on the allocation of speaking time.

> They have their own large and growing staff, receive considerable funds from the Parliament and often have an important say in the choice of the Parliament's own top officials. The power of the Groups is also shown by the powerlessness of those non-attached members who are not in Political Groups, who are highly unlikely, for example, ever to hold a powerful post within the Parliament (Ladrech 1996: 292).

Therefore, in a formal sense a truly European party system clearly exists. However, all the indicators of the importance of party groups mentioned above refer to the power of party groups in the daily routine of the European Parliament. As such they say little about the *cohesiveness* of these groups. This cohesiveness is the second empirical question we will address in this chapter.

THE MEASUREMENT OF COMPETITIVENESS AND COHESION

The cohesiveness of political parties is an important aspect of the system of party government because it is a pre-condition for the *reliability* of parties, i.e.. the extent to which they behave according to what they promised to their voters. From this perspective one might argue that there is only one form of cohesiveness that counts: the extent to which individual members of parliament *behave* according to the party line. In the model of party government, political parties and not individual members of parliament are the principal actors. The model assumes disciplined parties. Individual members of parliament are supposed to be delegates of their parties, and to behave according to their party line. Not their opinion, but their behaviour is relevant as a measure of cohesion. Therefore, from this perspective, the best way to measure cohesiveness is by measuring the extent to which individual members *vote* according to the party line. *How* political parties reach an agreement on how to vote does not really matter. The result, the vote, is the only thing that matters in the linkage between voters on the one hand and legislation and policy making on the other. Roll call analysis seems to be the perfect way to measure the cohesiveness of parliamentary parties or groups. Roll call analyses done so far reveal a surprisingly high level of cohesiveness within the major European party groups (Brzinski 1995: 150). However, as useful as roll call analyses are to measure the cohesiveness of European party groups, they also have their drawbacks. To some extent roll call analyses tend to conceal a lack of agreement as much as they seem to unveil consensus.

Unanimity is often only reached after long preparatory committee and party group sessions have smoothed out most disagreements (Bardi 1994: 367-8). Relying on these expressions of quasi-unanimity would be most unfortunate from our perspective. As argued above, we are primarily interested in the *feasibility* of a European party system. From this perspective, knowing how much massage of diverse original positions is needed in order to reach a common stand when it comes to voting is at least as important as knowing to what extent this massage is finally successful. Therefore, in order to measure the cohesiveness of European party groups, we will rely on a measure of the agreement of the individual members of European party groups on several policy dimensions rather than on roll call analysis. These issue positions are taken from the survey among members of the European parliament in 1996.

Competitiveness in the context of the party government model refers to a political system where the electorate has a choice at regular intervals between at least two competing parties with different party platforms (Strom 1992: 31). But whether a choice between two parties is better or worse than a choice between more than two parties, and *how different* different should be, is a matter of dispute in the literature. Taking sides in this dispute is beyond the purpose of this chapter.

What seems to matter from the perspective of the party government model is the extent to which each political party represents a unique or *distinct* position on a policy or issue dimension. Above we have argued why we will rely on issue positions taken in the European parliament rather than on party manifestos. Also, for the reasons just given in the context of cohesiveness, we will rely on the measurement of attitudes of individual MEPs rather than on their behaviour in formal roll calls. The extent to which different party groups have distinct positions, as measured by the attitudes of their individual members will not only depend on the *distance* between party groups, but also on the *homogeneity* or *cohesiveness* of the groups. Party groups can be close together, and yet distinct when there is no overlap in the distribution of opinions of the members of party groups. At the same time party groups will be further apart, but less distinct, when the average positions of the members of the two groups are further apart, but the two distributions strongly overlap. Thus, *distinctiveness* and *cohesiveness* are neither conceptually nor operationally completely independent of each other. The measure of this distinctiveness is the statistic *eta*. It measures the extent to which issue positions are constrained by party group membership. This measure will be 0 when the between party groups variance is 0, i.e. when there are no differences between party groups, and it will be 1 when there is perfect homogeneity within party groups and all variance can be attributed to the differences between party groups.

COMPETITIVENESS AND COHESIVENESS:
THEORETICAL EXPECTATIONS

What expectations with respect to competitiveness and cohesion in different issue domains can be formulated in advance? Above we have argued that although European party groups are no more than the aggregate of national political parties which in the context of the European elections compete at the national level for the votes of a national electorate, this is not to say that the aggregation of these national parties and processes might not lead to a European Parliament in which the major party groups are still to a great extent *distinct* and *cohesive*. This will be the case to the extent that the national political parties that compose those European party groups share a common ideology. The logical consequence of this argument is that political party groups will be both more competitive and internally more homogeneous to the extent that issue domains are related to this shared ideology. Therefore, in order to be able to come to more refined hypotheses on the competitiveness of the European party system and the cohesion within European party groups we need to explore what this common ideology is. This, of course, is a classic question in comparative European politics. The party systems in Europe are, or used to be, a reflection of the major social cleavages at the beginning of this century (Lipset and Rokkan 1967a). The two major cleavages that have defined the structure of the party system in most European countries are *social class* and *religion*. It has been argued that the direct relationship between these social cleavages and politics has gradually diminished. Although the major political parties in most European countries still have their roots not only in the social class cleavage, but in the religious-secular dimension as well, political competition has become one-dimensional. There seems to be a general consensus that the left-right dimension has become the dominant space of competition (Sani and Sartori 1983: 330; Pedersen 1996: 19). As a consequence the ideological identity of political parties will be related to this dimension. It can be argued that the left-right dimension could become the dominant conflict dimension, because other conflict dimensions gradually diminished or were gradually absorbed by the left-right dimension. But still, this is a matter of degree. With all the nuances one can find from country to country, the left-right dimension is primarily the ideological translation of the class cleavage. Issues like social equality and the role of government are related to the heart of this dimension. Even though it might be argued that other issue dimensions have become less salient or have been absorbed by this super dimension, there is no reason to believe, even in theory, that each and every issue or issue dimension will be equally strongly related to the left-right dimension (Converse and Pierce 1986: 230). In particular, the religious-secular dimension might still be a *domain of identification* (Sani and Sartori 1983: 330). The modern legacy of this conflict dimension is reflected in the libertarian-traditional value dimension. Former research has demonstrated that this dimension, although empirically related to the left-right dimension is not completely absorbed by it.

Also, there is no reason to assume that the left-right dimension is related to issues that refer to the process of European integration. It is hard to deduce an indisputable position on European integration in general, let alone on more specific issues like a common European currency or the Schengen agreement, from the principles of socialism, liberalism or Christian democracy. Of course, parties of these families have developed positions on these issues, but it is hard to predict these positions on the basis of the general ideology alone. These positions seem to be related at least as much to national histories and circumstances as to transnational ideologies.

Also, it can be argued that on issues that refer to the development of the European Union as such it is not very likely that there will be a strong competition, or great policy differences, between party groups. The closer issues come to the constitutional framework of the Union, to its institutional make up, the more the European Parliament will tend to move to a non-party, or institutional mode, rather than an interparty mode (cf. King 1976). As long as European unification is still a process rather than the outcome of a process and as long as there is no such thing as a European government, supported by a majority in parliament and opposed by a parliamentary minority, it is most unlikely that the political arena will be dominated by interparty differences, but rather by *institutional* differences and interests: the European Parliament *as an institution* is still in a process of securing a stronger position vis-à-vis other institutions of the Union, in particular the Council of Ministers. As long as this is the case the European Parliament will be inclined to act as an institution and to downplay rather than to emphasize its possible intra-parliamentary disputes.

As a result, in general it can be expected that the more a particular issue domain is related to the socio-economic left-right dimension, the more political parties will be competitive and cohesive on this issue domain (Thomassen forthcoming). We expect that both issues on the traditional-libertarian domain and European issues will be less related to the left-right dimension and that both competition and cohesiveness will be less for these issue domains.

Therefore, we will test the following hypotheses:

Hypothesis 1. The more an issue dimension is related to the left-right dimension, the more competitive European party groups will be.

Hypothesis 2. The more an issue dimension is related to the left-right dimension, the more cohesive European party groups will be.

ISSUE DOMAINS

In order to test these hypotheses we should first explore the extent to which different issue domains are constrained by the left-right dimension. MEPs were asked to give their opinion on a great number of issues.

A factor analysis (see Table 7.1) of these issues nicely reveals three issue domains: a European, a socio-economic and a traditional-libertarian domain.

The issues in the European domain all refer to the power and competencies of the Union vs. the member states, rather than to the distribution of power between different European institutions. The second dimension consists of socio-economic issues that all refer to the classic left-right dimension: social equality, the role of the state and maintaining the welfare state vs. a free market economy. The third dimension, which can be labelled traditional-libertarian consists of a moral issue (abortion), and two issues in the domain of law and order.

The question of the extent to which these three issue domains are related to the left-right dimension can be answered in two different ways. First, it is still to be seen to what extent the three dimensions revealed by the factor analysis in table 7.1 are *independent* dimensions. If, as we have argued above, the left-right dimension has gradually absorbed other cleavage dimensions, and in particular the religious-secular dimension, it is highly unlikely that this is the case. As it turns

TABLE 7.1. Factor Structure of Issue Opinions of MEPs

Issues	European-national	Socio-economic left-right	Authoritarian-libertarian
Increase range responsibilities EU?	.87	.04	.03
Democratic legitimation EU based on EP/NP	.87	-.03	.12
EP power to pass laws that directly apply to all member states	.84	.03	.12
National/European currency	-.80	.12	.10
Decisions national/European level[1]	-.77	-.11	.18
Remove national borders/border control	.71	-.08	.26
Reduce unemployment/limit inflation	-.07	.84	.13
EU employment program vs. Concentrate on completion single market	.07	.84	.12
Reduce inequality of incomes	.06	.80	.22
Maintain levels of welfare even if tax raise	-.05	.80	.28
Government greater role in economy	-.04	.76	-.09
Tougher action against criminals	.07	-.08	-.75
Decriminalize use of marijuana	.32	.14	.73
Women free to decide on abortion	-.02	.23	.71

N = 252
The three factors, extracted by a Principal Components Analysis, together explain 67% of variance between the issues. The eigenvalues are respectively: 4.2, 3.8 and 1.5. The solution is VARIMAX rotated.
1 This index is based on a number of issues on the relationship between the national and European levels of government (v6_1 to v6_17). Cronbach's alpha = .93.

out, there is a certain correlation between the socio-economic and the traditional-libertarian dimension (r = .28), whereas the relationship between the European-national dimension and the socio-economic dimension is much less (r = .15). However, these correlations are not such that we should no longer speak of different dimensions.

A second way to answer this question is by relating the positions within these three issue domains to self-placement on a left-right scale. The results of this analysis are presented in the first column of Table 7.2. They are consistent with the outcome of the factor analysis. Left-right self-placement is strongly related to the socio-economic dimension, less so to the traditional-libertarian dimension and hardly at all to positions on the European-national dimension.

TABLE 7.2. Correlation with Left-Right Self-placement and Impact of
Party Groups and Nationality

Factors	Left-right (Pearson's R^2)	Party Groups (eta^2)[1]	Nationality (eta^2)
European-National	.03	.08	.44
Socio-economic left-right	.38	.45	.18
Authoritarian-libertarian	.20	.30	.10
Issues			
Increase range responsibilities EU	.04	.04	.31
Democratic legitimation EU based on EP/NP	.03	.06	.35
EP power to pass laws that directly apply to all member states	.06	.04	.40
National/European currency	.00	.13	.24
Decisions national/European level	.02	.04	.35
Remove national borders/border control	.06	.08	.21
Mean European issues	.04	.07	.31
Reduce unemployment/limit inflation	.21	.36	.13
EU employment program vs. Concentrate on completion single market	.31	.38	.22
Reduce inequality of incomes	.36	.34	.10
Maintain levels of welfare even if tax raise	.32	.38	.08
Government greater role in economy	.21	.30	.11
Mean socio-economic issues	.28	.35	.13
Tougher action against criminals	.15	.12	.10
Decriminalise use of marijuana	.19	.26	.10
Women free to decide on abortion	.23	.31	.11
Mean libertarian issues	.19	.23	.10

1 The analysis is limited to the four largest parties (PSE, PPE, ELDR and GUE), both
for the analysis with party groups as for the impact of nationality.

COMPETITIVENESS

Therefore, according to hypothesis 1 we should expect that the extent
to which policy positions are constrained by party group membership is
high for issues within the socio-economic domain, less so, but still sig-

nificantly, for the traditional-libertarian dimension and hardly at all for the European dimension. In column 2 of Table 7.2 the etas squared are presented, indicating the proportion of the total variance that is explained by party group membership. The differences between these figures are consistent with our predictions. Whereas close to half of the variance on the socio-economic factor is explained by party group membership, this proportion declines to a still considerable 30% for the traditional-authoritarian dimension, and falls below 10% for the European dimension. Therefore, we conclude that the major European party groups have distinct positions on the socio-economic dimension, less so on the libertarian-traditional dimension, but hardly at all on the European-national dimension.

How the party groups position themselves in relation to each other can be seen in Figure 7.1. The positions on the socio-economic and traditional-libertarian dimension reflect our finding that on these two dimensions the aggregation to the European level of more or less similar cleavage structures in the member states has been successful. The combination of the two dimensions reflect a pattern that can be found in many of the member states: not two totally independent dimensions

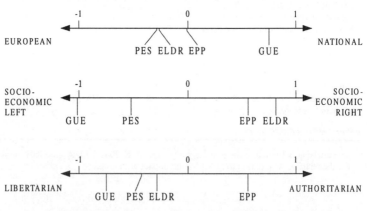

FIG. 7.1. Mean Factor Scores of Policy Dimensions by Party Group

FIG. 7.2. Left-right Self-Placement by Party Group

but a split of the socio-economic right on non-material issues, as a legacy of the religious dimension. The EPP and the ELDR change places on these two dimensions. On the libertarian-traditional dimension the liberals are closer to the socialists than to the EPP (mostly Christian democrats), whereas it is the other way around on the socio-economic dimension.

The position of the major party groups on the two dimensions can be represented schematically in the following simple matrix:

		traditional	libertarian
socio-economic	right	EPP (religious parties)	ELDR (liberal parties)
	left		PES GUE (socialist parties)

On the European dimension our findings are totally different. Here the major European party groups hardly take different positions, not because their position is indifferent but because the dominant position in all major party groups is strongly pro-European. One should not be misled by the positions of the parties on the European dimension in Figure 7.1. These are relative positions, based on the distance to the mean of the distribution. The mean position of the three major party groups on these European issues is in general strongly pro-European. More detailed information about where the party groups stand on specific issues can be found in Table 7.3, where the mean positions on the issues composing the three factors are presented. Contrary to the issues of the other two dimensions, the three major party groups are less than one scale position (on a 7- or 10-point scale) from each other on the pro-European side of each issue, whereas the European Unitary Left can be found at some distance on the anti- or at least less pro-European side of the scale.

Our main finding is that in so far as there is a European party system, it is a reflection of the dominant party system in Europe. The

TABLE 7.3. Mean and Standard Deviation by Party Groups on Issues and Factors[1]

Factors	PSE		PPE		ELDR		GUE	
European-national	-.3	(.9)	-.1	(.8)	-.2	(.5)	.8	(1.3)
Socio-economic left-right	-.6	(.6)	.7	(.9)	.8	(.8)	-1.0	(.3)
Authoritarian-libertarian	-.4	(.7)	.5	(.8)	-.3	(1.0)	-.7	(.7)
Issues								
Increase range responsibilities EU	2.4	(1.6)	2.8	(1.6)	2.3	(1.3)	3.6	(2.4)
Democratic legitimation EU based on EP/NP	2.4	(1.6)	2.8	(1.6)	2.9	(1.7)	4.0	(2.3)
EP power to pass laws that directly apply to all member states	2.5	(1.7)	2.9	(2.0)	2.8	(2.0)	4.0	(2.4)
National/European currency	9.0	(2.3)	9.2	(2.0)	9.1	(2.3)	5.9	(3.3)
Decisions national/European level	4.7	(1.0)	4.5	(.9)	4.2	(.9)	4.1	(1.3)
Remove national borders/border control	2.2	(2.0)	3.1	(2.6)	2.7	(2.6)	4.7	(3.2)
Reduce unemployment/limit inflation	2.4	(1.5)	4.5	(1.9)	4.6	(1.5)	1.2	(.7)
EU employment program vs. concentrate on completion single market	2.3	(2.3)	6.4	(3.0)	6.3	(3.3)	1.7	(1.4)
Reduce inequality of incomes	1.8	(1.1)	3.6	(1.8)	3.9	(1.7)	1.1	(.3)
Maintain levels of welfare even if tax raise	2.3	(1.3)	4.6	(1.8)	4.6	(1.3)	1.7	(1.5)
Government greater role in economy	2.7	(1.3)	4.4	(1.7)	4.9	(1.3)	2.4	(1.4)
Tougher action against criminals	3.2	(1.5)	2.3	(1.3)	3.1	(1.4)	3.7	(1.7)
Decriminalize use of marijuana	3.7	(2.2)	6.1	(1.4)	4.3	(2.4)	3.8	(2.4)
Women free to decide on abortion	1.6	(1.1)	3.9	(2.2)	2.7	(1.9)	1.0	(0.0)

1 Note that not all variables are measured on the same scale.

viability of these party groups as future political parties *at the European level*, capable of *expressing the political will of the citizens of the Union* will depend on a multitude of developments. Probably one of the most important ones will be the extent to which transnational political differences as institutionalized in the transnational parties will prevail over national differences.

An indication of the likelihood that this might happen can be found in the extent to which nationality constrains positions taken on the different policy dimensions as compared to party group. This can be seen by comparing the second column of Table 7.2 with the third column. The eta squares in the third column indicate the extent to which positions on the different policy dimensions and single issues are constrained by nationality. By comparing these figures with the figures in column 2 one can see which variable is more important, party group or nation. This comparison leaves little room for dispute. On the two traditional policy domains, party group is much more important than nation, whereas on European issues it is the other way around. Here national differences across party groups are the differences that count.

Therefore, the somewhat paradoxical conclusion is that distinct European party groups do exist as long as these parties are defined in terms of traditional conflict dimensions and not in terms of conflicts that touch upon the development of the European Union itself. Then national differences, crosscutting European party groups, are the dominant factors. As we have argued above, the future development of Europe, the strengthening both of the European institutions and of the competencies of the European Union are hardly matters of dispute within the European parliament. As far as there is a dispute and perhaps a political struggle on the future of Europe, this is not a matter of internal dispute within the European parliament, but of a dispute between the governments of the member states and between the European Parliament *as an institution* and other institutions of the European Union, in particular the Council of Ministers and the European Council. As far as there are differences of opinion within the European Parliament, they are a reflection of these national interests and positions rather than of ideological differences that can be related to transnational political cleavages.

COHESION

Above we have distinguished two requirements for an effective European party system. The second requirement, in addition to competitiveness, is internal *cohesion* or *agreement* within party groups. We have indicated that our measure of competitiveness or distinctiveness is not totally independent of internal cohesiveness. Without a certain level of internal cohesion political parties can hardly be distinct. Therefore, both hypotheses point in the same direction.

In Table 7.3 the standard deviations as a measure of cohesion have been presented. It is difficult to draw any conclusions from these figures. First, we do not have an absolute yardstick to assess what these figures mean. What should be interpreted as a high or low level of cohesion? Lacking such an absolute standard we can only look for relative standards. The most obvious one is the cohesion within national parliamentary parties. This would give us an indication of the way European party groups are developing compared to their national counterparts. This we have done elsewhere (Schmitt and Thomassen forthcoming). We found that measured on some of the same issues as used in this chapter (left-right self-placement, a European currency, removal of national borders, a European employment program), the cohesion within the major European party groups is no less than within the major political parties in most national parliaments in Europe. Other possible comparisons do not lead to clear or consistent conclusions. According to hypothesis 2 in conjunction with our findings on the dimensionality of issues, we should expect a different level of cohesion within different issue domains. The extent to which this is the case, can be learned from a comparison across rows in Table 7.3. However, no clear pattern can be observed here. There is no systematic difference in cohesion between policy dimensions. Also, a comparison across columns does not reveal a systematic difference in cohesion between the party groups, at least not between the three major party groups. The GUE is comparatively divided on the European dimension and strongly cohesive on the socio-economic dimension.

CONCLUSION

The objective of this chapter was to assess the extent to which there is a party system at the European level capable of expressing the political will of the citizens of the Union.

Following the concept of party government we distinguished three requirements that should be met in order to enable a party system to express the political will of the citizens. These requirements are:

1. The party system needs to be *competitive.*
2. Political parties need to be *cohesive.*
3. The government should be *formed* and *controlled* by the majority.

In this chapter we concentrated on the first two requirements. With respect to competitiveness we found that the European party system is to a great extent a reflection of the dominant party systems in Europe. As in these systems, the mutual positions on policy issues are most clearly defined in those issue domains that are strongly related to the left-right dimension. These are primarily issues in the socio-economic domain. Parties also differ on a second dimension, the libertarian-traditional dimension, although the mutual positions of parties on this dimension do not completely parallel the positions on the socio-economic dimension. In this sense the European party system is not different from most national party systems in Europe.

Where the major party groups hardly differ is on issues that refer to the process of European integration. On these issues there is a great pro-Europe consensus across the major party groups. As far as differences do exist between Members of the European Parliament on these issues, nationality is a much more important factor than party group.

It is hard to evaluate the cohesiveness of European party groups due to the lack of a clear criterion. However, from analyses published elsewhere (Schmitt and Thomassen forthcoming) we already know that the cohesion of European party groups is no less than of national political parties. Contrary to our expectations, there is no systematic difference in cohesion between different policy dimensions.

The lack of competition between the major European party groups on "European" political issues seems to support the point of some observers that a major aspect of the democratic deficit refers precisely to this point. However, we do not think this is the only possible conclusion. One might as well argue that a European party system based upon different views on the future of Europe would be totally paralysed when it comes to substantive policy-making. Agreement on the future of Europe might be considered as a *condition* for effective European policy-making. From this perspective, proponents of European unification might have more reason to welcome than to criticize the apparent agreement.

At the same time one should not be blinded by this consensus. As we argued above, this consensus might to a large extent be the product of the institutional circumstances. Lacking the power to form and control a truly European government, members of the European Parliament have a common institutional interest. Once the European Parliament would have acquired these powers, this common interest might at least partly yield to the representation of parochial interests. However, for the time being we have no reason to conclude that a *party system at the European level capable of expressing the political will of the citizens of the Union* would be out of reach.

NOTES

1   It was not included in the December version of the Treaty but emerged when the IGC returned to Maastricht in February 1992. By then consultations had taken place on appropriate wording (Church and Phinnemore 1994: 260).
2   Or optimism from the perspective of the opponents of further political integration.
3   Basically, this is a populist model of democracy. For the credibility of such models, and alternative views on democracy, see Riker 1982.
4   For a more extensive overview of the relevant literature, see Strom 1992.

PART III

Problems and Institutional Change

PART III

Countries and International Bodies

8

What Kind of Future; Why?[1]

PETER ESAIASSON

THE future is an important dimension of politics. Promises about a future Utopia have motivated collective actions in most known cultures across the world (e.g. Manuel and Manuel 1979). According to Western self-understanding, the notion that rationally planned policies for the future can improve the conditions of life is a key component in the modern project. Indeed, as Founding Fathers Monnet and Schumann shared a vision about a Europe to be, the institutionalized co-operation between the original member states was initiated in this spirit of rational planning.

In a shorter time-perspective, the importance of the future is evident in the continuous struggle over the agenda-building process. The competitiveness of political actors is largely decided by their capacity to determine which issues will be discussed in the politics of tomorrow. Those who control the long-term agenda-building process have clearly placed themselves in an advantageous position.

Given the general importance of the agenda-building process, representatives' policy priorities for the future are highly relevant for our understanding of the European Parliament. What policy areas are judged as the most important problems for the future by those who serve as elected representatives of the European citizens? Depending on what issues are given highest priority (be it economic development of the current member states, reformation of institutions, enlargement with new member states, or some other issue area) the European Parliament can be expected to behave differently during the years to come.

There is, however, a theoretically even more interesting reason to analyze the long-term policy priorities of European representatives. In addition to providing a preview of coming developments, individuals' views about the future may reveal central aspects of their present political thinking. Among others, adherents to *Cultural Theory* argue that probing individuals about their perceptions about future risks is an efficient way to understand their definition and portrayal of the current situation (e.g. Thompson, Ellis, and Wildavsky 1990; Grendstad and Selle 1996; Jensen forthcoming). According to this reasoning, representatives' priorities for the future are indicators of their present political views which are more subtle than standard survey questions on specific policy proposals.

In this chapter an analytical perspective similar to Cultural Theory will be utilized. On the basis of information about issue priorities for the future, a recurrent theme of this volume will be analyzed—the degree of integration among the European elite. What empirical support is there for the belief that European representatives, by the process of selection and/or by socialization, come to share a common view about the European Union?[2]

In what follows I will specify a particular idea of unified Euro-representatives and evaluate how well this specified model is supported by the data. The model argues that the European Parliament is a homogenous institution in the sense that MEPs from different countries are in close agreement about which are the most pressing problems and issues for the future. This is a pattern that would likely emerge if European representatives constitute a *truly integrated elite*.

To enhance analysis, the model of integrated elites will be pitched against an alternative. The alternative model argues that the European parliament is heterogeneous in the sense that representatives from different member states have radically different issue priorities for the future. This is a pattern that would likely emerge if European representatives were first and foremost *agents of national interests*. In the famous words of Edmund Burke, according to this model the European Parliament would function as "a congress of ambassadors from different hostile interests, which interests each must maintain, as an agent and advocate, against other agents and advocates."[3]

LOGIC AND CONCEPTS

The analysis draws upon the fact that identical questions on issue priorities for the future have been put to Members of the European Parliament (MEPs) and to their counterparts in the national parliaments (MNPs). The logic is straightforward. The larger the similarities of issue priorities between MEPs from different countries, and the larger the differences in priorities between MEPs and MNPs from the same country, the better support for the model of an integrated elite of European representatives. And correspondingly, the larger the differences between MEPs from different countries, and the greater the similarities between MEPs and MNPs from respective country, the stronger support for the alternative model of European representatives as national agents.

In addition to this analysis at the collective level of countries and institutions, support for the idea of European representatives as an integrated elite will be tested at the level of individual representatives. If European representatives constitute a homogenous elite, it can be expected that those who are personally involved in the future prospects of the European Union as a political project should have adopted similar priorities for the future. Moreover, as implied by the theory of socialization, if life in Brussels make a difference for representatives' political thinking, the relationship between involvement and priorities for the future should be stronger among MEPs than among MNPs.

Five indicators of personal involvement in the European Union as a political project have been identified. The first relate to attitudes toward the *influence of the European Parliament*.[4] Representatives who want the European Parliament to be very influential are considered to be more involved in the EU-project than those who want a less influential European Parliament. The second indicator concern representatives' *sources of information*. Representatives who rely heavily on information from official EU-sources are considered to be more involved than those who only rarely rely on official EU-sources. Indicators three and four cover *career plans of representatives*. Those who plan for a future political career on the European level, and those who do not plan for a career in national politics, are considered to be more involved in the EU than those who have the reverse plan for their future careers. Finally, the fifth indicator of involvement concerns the *number of national political offices held by representatives*. Those who have held few national political offices during their political career are considered to be more involved in the EU-project than those who have held many national offices.

These five indicators do not cover all possible aspects of representatives' personal involvement in the European Union. However, the range of indicators—attitudes, sources of information, career plans, and political experiences—is fairly broad. If representatives' personal involvement really matters for their priorities for the future—if there is support for the model of integrated elites—it seems reasonable to assume that the relationship is captured by one or more of the indicators.

Just like "involvement in European politics," priorities for the future of the European Union, our main focus of attention here, is a multifacetted phenomenon. Once more, it has been impracticable to construct a logically exhaustive taxonomy of the phenomenon under scrutiny. For the purpose of this study, representatives' priorities will be conceptualized on three different levels of abstraction. (That is, three types of dependent variables will be employed in the study.) Since the levels of abstraction are rather different, differences in empirical support for the models of integrated elites and national agents are likely to be picked up by one or more of the types of dependent variables.

The first conceptualization relates to the distinction between *procedural rules for decision-making* and *substantive policies*. This conceptualization is motivated by the unique character of the European Union. Compared to traditional nation-states, where procedures for decision-making are well-established, the European Union is an institution in constant change. In European politics, questions of *how* to make decisions are often as important as questions about *what* decisions should be made. It takes a certain degree of specialized knowledge to practice politics on the European level, and experiences from national politics may be of lesser importance. If European representatives are systematically different from national representatives—if they make up an integrated elite—we can expect them to give higher priority to procedural aspects of politics than do national representatives. Correspondingly, we can expect a positive relationship between personal involvement in the European Union and the priorities given to procedural topics.

The two remaining conceptualizations concern substantive policies. First we will focus on the rather high-flying question of the very *purpose of the European Union*. What support is there among representatives for alternative visions of the European Project? Some would argue that the European Union is mainly a vehicle for the economic development of the member states. Others would say that the main purpose of the Union is to enhance external security on the continent and, ultimately, on the global arena. Yet others would argue that an important task of the EU is to foster the formation of a common European culture; to create a shared frame of reference among citizens of the member states. A further vision is to stress that the European Union is a vehicle for the fight for environmental protection.

These four alternative visions for the European Union— economic development; external security; a common European culture; and environmental protection—can be expected to be of varying interest for national and European representatives. If there is empirical support for the model of integrated elites, European representatives' should give relatively high priority to the fostering of the EU as an international actor, and as promotor of a common European culture. Correspondingly, national representatives can be expected to emphasize issues that immediately concern nation-states (economic development, and environmental protection). Support for the alternative model of representatives as national agents should manifest itself in similar priorities of MEPs and MNPs from the same country.

The final conceptualization concerns *specific policy areas*. Thirteen detailed policy issues have been identified (jobs; economic growth; law and order; social welfare; external security; environmental policies; immigration; agriculture; regional development; taxes; energy policies; foreign aid; and equality between men and women). Depending on how representatives' priorities are structured (whether agreements are larger within countries across institutions, or within parliamentary institutions across countries), the model of national agents or unified elites is best supported by the data.

DATA

The question on representatives priorities for the future was worded as follows: "Thinking ahead about the next few years, which are the most serious problems and issues facing the European Union?" No predefined response alternatives were offered, and up to eight answers were registered. The responses were coded according to a detailed coding scheme with approximately 250 categories. These categories constitute the building blocks from which the three different types of dependent variables will be constructed (priority given to *procedural aspects of politics*; to alternative *visions of the European project*; and to *specific policy areas*).[5]

The question on priorities for the future opened the questionnaire for both MEPs and MNPs. Representatives seemed fairly interested in the topic. The average numbers of responses given by MEPs and MNPs were 3.0 and 2.7, respectively. These numbers are roughly comparable to previous studies of the Swedish case. When a similar question on priorities for future national politics was put to Swedish MPs (mail questionnaire) and voters (personal interviews) in 1988, the average numbers of responses given were 3.6 and 2.1 respectively (Esaiasson and Holmberg 1996: 173). The somewhat higher number of responses among MEPs (personal interviews) than among MNPs (mail questionnaires) may indicate a small study effect, but likely it also reflects that the future of the European Union is more salient for those who are directly engaged in European politics.[6]

Although the question was posed to all MEPs, it was included in only six surveys of national parliamentarians (covering France; Germany; Greece; Ireland; the Netherlands; and Sweden). With reference to the logic applied in this study, the following analysis will be restricted to the countries for which information is available for both MNPs and MEPs.[7]

PROCEDURAL ASPECTS OF EUROPEAN POLITICS

Firstly, we will look at representatives' propensity to give priority to procedural aspects of politics (as opposed to substantial policy issues). The concept "procedural aspects of politics" has been broadly defined. It includes response categories that belong to the core of the theoretical concept, as well as categories that are more peripheral. Examples of core-categories are "less anonymous decision making"; "more power to the European Parliament"; and "simplification of the law-making process." Examples of peripheral categories are "control of spending"; "reduction of subsidies"; "completion of the Maastricht Treaty"; and "regulation of health policies." The latter categories concern the need for the European Union to come up with well-functioning regulations, and should be understood in relation to responses that unambiguously deal with substantial policies (e.g. "development of economy"; "regional development"; "unemployment"; "social security"; "environmental protection").

Having an operational definition of "procedural aspects" which includes a broad array of responses facilitates the correlational analysis to be presented below.[8] It should be noted that other and narrower definitions give essentially the same results. However, the decision to go for a broad definition has a price. In interpreting the findings of this analysis, one should look mainly at the structure of the data, while marginal distributions are of little substantial interest.

Table 8.1 gives the basic frequency distributions of priorities along with summary measurements of homogeneity within institutions and within countries. Respondents have been classified according to a dichotomous principle—either they mention a topic related to procedural aspects of politics, or they do not.

The model of integrated elites expects MEPs from different countries (i) to have similar priorities; and (ii) to give higher priority to procedural/regulative topics than do MNPs. Indeed, this is exactly the pattern found in the data. Both summary measurements of differences within institutions (eta-values and maximum percentage differences) show greater differences among MNPs than among MEPs; and in all countries MEPs are more prone to emphasize procedural topics than are MNPs.

TABLE 8.1. Proportion of European MPs and National MPs That Give Priority to Procedural Topics (as Opposed to Policy-Oriented Topics) When Identifying Important Problems for the Future of the European Union (percent, eta-values, maximum percentage differences)

	FR	GE	NE	IR	GR	SW	Eta	Max diff
European MPs	75	87	81	78	82	67	.16	+20
National MPs	67	69	61	59	61	40	.25*	+29
diff	+8	+18	+21	+19	+20	+27		
Eta	.07	.13*	.16	.12	.19	.10		
Unweighted n	32/ 134	45/ 304	11/ 57	9/ 66	21/ 61	12/ 300		

* p ≤ .05

However, the empirical support for the model of integrated elites is not overwhelmingly strong. In most countries, differences between MEPs and MNPs are rather limited. Thus, our belief in the idea of integrated elites is strengthened, but it would be premature to declare it a winner.[9]

The second test of the empirical support for the model of integrated elites concerns representatives as individuals. Various indicators of representatives' personal involvement with the European Union should be positively related to propensity to stress procedural topics. Moreover, with reference to the process of socialization, these relationships should be stronger among European representatives than among national representatives. Table 8.2 shows the relevant correlational coefficients.

Once more the empirical data nicely support the model of integrated elites. As predicted, European representatives who would like the European Parliament to have much influence, who rely heavily on European sources of information, and who plan for a future career on the European level, are more prone to stress the importance of procedural aspects of politics than representatives with the reverse characteristics. Likewise, MEPs who plan for a career in national politics, and who have held several national political offices during their careers, are less prone than others to emphasize procedural topics. Given the small sample sizes, it is not surprising that correlation coefficients reach standard levels of statistical significance mainly among the overall group of MEPs, but more often than not (in 20 of 30 cases) coefficients show the expected sign within countries as well.

Furthermore, the positive relationships do not show up among national representatives. This is consistent with a hypothesis that the causal mechanism underlying the importance of representatives' personal involvement is socialization rather than selection of a certain breed of candidates. This would suggest that it is not until representatives are seated in the European parliament that their personal involvement in the European project makes a difference for their priorities for the future of the European Union.

Judging from the first test of the viability of the two models, the idea of European representatives as an integrated elite is better supported by the data. However, priorities given to procedural topics concern a rather abstract aspect of politics. The remaining empirical tests deal with substantive policies.

TABLE 8.2. Relationship Between Five Indicators of MPs Personal
Involvement in the European Union and Propensity to Identify Procedural
Topics as Important Problems for the Future of the European Union
(Pearson's r)

	European MPs					
	All	FR	GE	NE	IR	GR	SW
Attitude Towards More Power to the European Parliament (0-10)	.24*	.39*	.29*	-.10	-.10	-.31	-.09
Degree of Information Collected from EU-sources (0-3)	.22*	.49*	.01	.03	.48	.21	.08
Plan for Future EU-career (0-1)	.18*	.33	-.11	-.04	.19	.51*	.35
Plan for Future National Career (0-1)	-.22	-.39	.08	.16	-.36	-.39	-43
Number of National Offices Held During Career (0-4)	-.18*	-.02	-.01	.06	-.53	-.37	-.53
Average number of respondents	129	31	45	21	9	11	12

	National MPs					
	All	FR	GE	NE	IR	GR	SW
Attitude Towards More Power to the European Parliament (0-10)	.02	.07	.01	-.16	-.34	-.08	-.08
Degree of Information Collected from EU-sources (0-3)	.03	.05	.01	.23*	-.03	-.16	NA
Plan for Future EU-career (0-1)	-.00	-.00	.03	-.13	.15	-.05	-.08
Plan for Future National Career (0-1)	.02	.09	-.06	-.01	-.11	.11	.08
Number of National Offices Held During, Career (0-4)	.04	-.02	.06	-.02	-.13	-.06	.07
Average number of respondents	883	131	290	59	66	57	280

* $p \leq .05$
NA Not available
Comment: Respondents are weighted for size of country.

VISIONS ABOUT THE FUTURE EUROPEAN UNION

The second empirical test investigates the possibility that European
representatives and national representatives have different ideas about
the very purpose of the European Union. From the national perspec-

tive, it may be natural to emphasize the importance of problem areas that are of immediate concern for the nation-state. Two such areas are *economic development* and *environmental protection*. From the inside perspective of the European Parliament, it may be more relevant to give priority to policy areas that are connected to the future of the European Union itself. Two such areas are *external security* (with the possible emergence of the EU as a new powerful international actor), and the development of a *common European culture* (which might foster the emergence of a true political union).

If the model of integrated elites is supported by the data we can expect (i) that MEPs are more prone than MNPs to identify external security and the fostering of a common European culture as important problems and issues for the future; and (ii) that MEPs are more homogenous in their priorities than are MNPs (as the political context is highly variable between countries).

Operational definitions are based on the basic coding scheme. From the list of approximately 250 categories, topics that are related to economic development, environmental protection, external security, and a common European culture have been identified. Respondents who mention at least one topic within each "vision" have been coded as giving priority to the vision in question. Once more it should be stressed that marginal distributions are of little substantial interest. What matters is the structure of relationships.[10]

Table 8.3 shows the frequency distributions for the four alternative visions about the future European Union, along with two measurements of homogeneity within institutions, and within countries. This time the data do not clearly support one model. Or rather, there is support for and against both the model of integrated elites and the model of national agents. Evidence against the idea of integrated elites is that, overall, MEPs are about as likely as MNPs to emphasize the importance of economic development, environmental protection, and external security (the EU as an international actor). For instance, Irish MEPs are even more concerned about economic development than are Irish MNPs. Moreover, differences in priorities tend to be larger among MEPs than among MNPs. Supporting the model of European representatives as national agents, differences between MEPs and MNPs within countries are small in relation to differences between MEPs from different countries.

Priority given to environmental protection is a case in point. This vision of the main European project is strongly supported by Swedish representatives from both the national parliament and the European Parliament (40 and 58 percent respectively). In sharp contrast to their Swedish counterparts, French representatives from both institutions are not at all prone to stress the environmental issue (3 percent among national representatives and 0 percent among European representatives). Indeed, whereas environmental protection is top priority for Swedish MEPs, it is ranked bottom by French MEPs. Evidently, Swedish and French MEPs have different visions about the main purpose of the European Union. This is the type of empirical pattern that would emerge if European representatives acted mainly as national agents.

TABLE 8.3. Proportion of MEPs and MNPs Who Support Various Visions of the European Project (percent, eta values, maximum percentage differences)

Vision of the European Project	All	FR	GE	NE	IR	GR	SW	Eta	Diff
Economic Development									
European MPs	55	53	56	48	89	45	58	.20*	+36
National MPs	55	48	58	41	62	70	70	.16*	+29
Maximum diff	*+0*	*+5*	*-2*	*+7*	*+27*	*-25*	*-12*		
Eta	*.00*	*.04*	*.02*	*.06*	*.18*	*.19*	*.05*		
Environmental Development									
European MPs	13	0	11	19	0	9	58	.47*	+58
National MPs	15	3	18	23	8	21	40	.27*	+37
Maximum diff	*-1*	*-3*	*-5*	*-12*	*-6*	*-4*	*+18*		
Eta	*.04*	*.08*	*.04*	*.11*	*.09*	*.04*	*.08*		
Development of Common European Culture									
European MPs	68	72	69	86	44	73	42	.27*	+42
National MPs	44	50	40	49	53	39	29	.12*	+24
Maximum diff	*+24*	*+22*	*+29*	*+34*	*-9*	*+37*	*+13*		
Eta	*.19**	*.17**	*.20**	*.33**	*.06*	*.25**	*.05*		
Development of EU as an International Actor									
European MPs	12	19	9	5	0	36	8	.28*	+36
National MPs	12	8	9	26	14	16	25	.18*	+18
Maximum diff	*+0*	*+11*	*+0*	*-21*	*-14*	*+20*	*-17*		
Eta	*.01*	*.13**	*.01*	*.23**	*.14*	*.19*	*.08*		
Number of Respondents	130/	32/	45/	21/	9/	11/	12/		
	902	131	297	61	66	57	290		

* p < .10

However, views on the importance of fostering a common European culture present a different pattern. Here the data tend to suppport the model of integrated elites. As predicted by the model, MEPs are much more prone to emphasize this vision than are MNPs. Furthermore, Swedish and Irish MEPs set aside, European representatives form a homogenous group on this matter. It would appear that on a key issue, the overall group of MEPs have political priorities that are consistent with the notion of an integrated Euro-elite.

An individually oriented analysis offer a possibility to further evaluate the empirical support for the model of integrated elites. If there is to be consistent support for this model, we can expect those representatives who are personally involved in the future of the European project to be especially inclined to emphasize the vision of a common European culture. Table 8.4 gives the relevant correlation coefficients. The model of integrated elites is supported if propensity to emphasize "a common European culture" is positively related to the first three indicators of involvement, and negatively related to the two bottom indicators.

As it turns out, results from this complementary test are inconclusive. On the one hand, supporters of the idea of integrated elites can point out that overall among the MEPs the correlation coefficients show the expected signs. On the other hand, sceptics can stress that the

TABLE 8.4. Relationship between Five Indicators of MPs' Personal Involvement in the European Union and Propensity to Identify the Idea of a Common European Culture as an Important Vision for the Future of the European Union (Pearson's r)

| | European MPs | | | | | | |
	All	FR	GE	NE	IR	GR	SW
Attitude Towards More Power to the European Parliament (0-10)	.18*	.33*	.11	-.37	-.61	-.26	.34
Degree of Information Collected from EU-sourcers (0-3)	.13	.44*	-.02	.07	.10	.13	-.15
Plan for Future EU-career (0-1)	.13	.25	-.11	.04	.16	.26	.51*
Plan for Future National Career (0-1)	-.20*	-.34*	-.09	.13	-.48	-.24	-.25
Number of National Offices Held During Carrer (0-4)	-.08	-.02	.02	.00	.06	-.16	.25
Average Number of Respondents	129	31	45	21	9	11	12

Continued on next page

Table 8.4 continued

	National MPs						
	All	FR	GE	NE	IR	GR	SW
Attitude Towards More Power to the European Parliament (0-10)	-.09*	-.13	-.02	-.20	-.25*	.01	-.06
Degree of Information Collected from EU-sourcers (0-3)	.03	.06	.08	-.01	.10	-.14	NA
Plan for Future EU-career (0-1)	-.01	-.15	.10*	-.22	.20	.05	-.03
Plan for Future National Career (0-1)	-.03	.02	-.09*	.13	-.06	-.01	.05
Number of National Offices Held During Carrer (0-4)	-.04	.06	.08	-.20	-.07	-.08	.04
Average Number of Respondents	883	131	290	59	66	57	280

* p ≤ .10
Comment: MPs are weighted by size of country.

correlations are weak, that only two coefficients are at all statistically significant, and that the correlations are more or less random within countries (only 18 of 30 coefficients show the expected sign).

What seem to be clear, however, is that the evidence is consistent with a hypothesis of socialization. Among national representatives, relationships are close to zero, and coefficients are more often than not of the wrong sign. That is, national representatives who are personally involved in the future of the European Union are not systematically different from representatives who lack personal involvement. To the extent that MEPs really constitute an integrated elite, it appear as if the process of integration starts after their arrival in Brussels.

PRIORITIES OF SPECIFIC POLICY ISSUES

The third test of the viability of the model of integrated elites concern priorities on specific policy issues, rather than ideas about the purpose of the European Union. Once again the model and its competitor are evaluated on the basis of a comparison of the degree of homogeneity, on the one hand, within *institution* across countries, on the other hand, within *country* across institutions. Specifically, the model of integrated elites is supported if the data show that (i) MEPs are more homogenous in the priority given to each policy issue than are MNPs; and (ii) MEPs from different countries are in close agreement as how to rank the complete set of policy issues.

Table 8.5 shows the proportion of representatives who give priority to 13 specific policy issues. As in previous tables, the frequency

TABLE 8.5. Issue Priorities for the Future of the European Union of MEPs and MNPs (percent, eta-values, maximum percentage differences)

| Type of Issue | European MPs | | | | | | | | |
	All	FR	GE	NE	IR	GR	SW	Eta	Max diff
Jobs	47	44	47	43	78	36	50	.18	+42
Economic Growth	37	22	58	19	44	54	8	.40*	+50
Law and Order	16	16	11	29	33	0	17	.24	+33
Social Welfare	15	31	11	5	11	18	0	.30*	+31
External Security	12	19	9	5	0	36	8	.28*	.+36
Environment	12	0	11	14	0	9	58	.48*	+58
Immigration	8	9	2	24	11	0	0	.30*	+24
Agriculture	4	0	7	5	11	0	0	.19	+11
Regional Development	2	0	0	9	0	0	0	.28*	+9
Taxes	1	0	2	0	0	0	0	.12	+2
Energy	1	0	0	5	0	0	0	.21	+5
Foreign Aid	0	0	0	0	0	0	0	.00	+0
Equality	1	0	2	0	0	0	0	.12	+12
Number of Resp.	130	32	45	21	9	11	12		

| Type of Issue | National MPs | | | | | | | | |
	All	FR	GE	NE	IR	GR	SW	Eta	Max diff
Jobs	44	35	48	34	59	58	55	.16*	+25
Economic Growthl	41	14	61	30	58	56	16	.45*	+47
Law and Order	12	8	13	23	38	4	14	.17*	+34
Social Welfare	24	24	27	18	14	19	5	.13*	+22
External Security	12	8	10	25	18	18	25	.17*	+17
Environment	14	3	17	23	8	21	39	.26*	+36
Immigration	10	11	8	15	3	19	3	.12*	+12
Agriculture	4	0	5	2	9	7	17	.20*	+17
Regional Development	1	1	2	2	2	2	0	.05	+2
Taxes	3	5	2	2	2	0	0	.11*	+5
Energy	1	0	2	0	0	4	1	.10	+4
Foreign Aid	1	2	0	2	0	0	0	.09	+2
Equality	0	0	1	0	0	0	1	.06	+1
Number of respondents	902	131	297	61	66	57	290		

*   p < .10
Comment: Respondents are weighted by size of country.

distributions are complemented with two summary statistics concerning homogeneity in the priority given to respective policy issue among MEPs and MNPs.[11]

It should be noted that this time results give relevant descriptive information. In accordance with the reasoning in the introduction, issue priorities of MEPs may provide insights as what actions to expect from the European Parliament in the near future. Issues that are given high priority will likely play a greater role in measures taken than issues of low priority.

Expectations that MEPs constitute a different breed of politicians with an issue agenda of their own is rather clearly refuted by results in Table 8.5. What matters the most for European representatives is the creation of new jobs and continued economic growth (stressed by 47 percent and 37 percent, respectively). The same two issues are given highest priority by national representatives (jobs by 44 percent; economic growth by 41 percent). There is thus agreement across institutions as of what are the most important problem areas for the future of the European Union. It would appear that initiatives that deal with the economic difficulties that plague many member countries stand a good chance to be well received by the European Parliament, at least on the rhetorical level. In this respect, the supranational assembly located in Brussels and Strasbourg is no different from national assemblies located in Bonn, Paris, Athens, Dublin, Stockholm or other capitals of EU-countries.

A second group of issues that are given relatively high priority by MEPs consists of "law and order"; "social welfare"; "external security"; "environment"; and "immigration." This group of issues contain several controversial issues, not the least "immigration." The sensitive immigration problem divides MEPs. It is mainly Dutch, French, and Irish MEPs who would like the EU to deal with the issue, whereas Swedish, Greek and German representatives ascribe it low priority.

More revealing still is to look at issues that are prioritized by only a few MEPs. The group of subordinated issues consists of "agriculture"; "regional development"; "taxes"; "energy"; "foreign aid" and "gender equality." This order of priority is bad news for critics who call for reform of key sectors of European politics. To the extent that the future agenda is determined by representatives' long-term priorities, the European Parliament is not likely to press for reform of farming policies, or policies for regional development. Likewise, it is not likely that initiatives will be taken towards policies for enhanced equality between the sexes, or for a change in policies for foreign aid.

As regard support for the two competing models, the two summary statistics for homogeneity within institutions show consistent results. On not a single issue are MEPs from different countries in stronger agreement over priorities than are MNPs from different countries. If anything, MNPs tend to be more homogenous than their European counterparts. In other words, the data do not support the model of European representatives as an integrated elite.

This empirical pattern is even more evident when we compute the full rank order of issue priorities. Table 8.6 shows coefficients for the rank-order correlation between issue priorities of MEPs and MNPs from the same country, along with the average rank-order correlation for MEPs of respective country with MEPs from other countries, and the corresponding average rank-order correlation among MNPs.

In all countries MEPs and MNPs are in close agreement over prioritization of policy issues (Spearman's rho varies between a high of .83, and a low of .66, all coefficients are statistically significant at the .05-level). And for all cases, agreement between MEPs of a given country and MEPs from other countries are lower than agreement between MEPs and MNPs from the same country. To take a specific example: When defining the most important problems and issues for the future of the European Union, German MEPs have more in common with German MNPs than with MEPs from France, Greece, or other member countries.

TABLE 8.6. Relationship Between MPs Ranking of Specific Policy Issues as Important Problems for the Future of the European Union (Spearman's Rho)

	MEPs and MNPs	Average between MEPs and Other MEPs	Average between MNPs and Other MNPs
France	.83	.61	.68
Germany	.83	.67	.85
The Netherlands	.70	.55	.77
Ireland	.66	.48	.83
Greece	.78	.60	.84
Sweden	.78	.57	.72

Comment: Unit of Analysis are priority given to an individual issue area by MPs as shown in Table 8.5.

A TEST OF THE NATIONAL AGENT-MODEL

So far the analysis of representatives' priorities of specific policy areas suggests that the model of national agents is best supported by the data. However, the evidence is mainly of a negative character (i.e., that the model of integrated elites is not particularly viable). Our belief in the national-agent model would certainly be stronger if we could muster more positive support. The final step in this analysis will be to evaluate whether the model of national agents is still viable when subjected to a direct test.

The test starts from the assumption that each member state has a national agenda for the future of the European Union, which may be more or less accepted by its elected representatives. If European representatives can justifiably be characterized as national agents, we should be able to predict their issue priorities from this national agenda. If, however, knowledge of national priorities does not help us in predicting the content of representatives' agenda, our belief in the model of national agents is weakened.

Social scientists have not agreed upon an operational definition of the concept "national agenda." It seems reasonable, however, to assign the role of interpreter of national interests to the government of each member country. In the following, "national agenda" is taken to mean the priority given to policy issues by the government of a each country.

Unfortunately there is no easy way to estimate the priorities of a government at a given point in time. The most valid estimate would probably result from a combination of in-depth interviews with government ministers, and careful documentary analysis. In the absence of data of this kind, I have opted for the more immediately accessible method of collecting *expert judgements*.

Specifically, two leading Swedish journalists specializing on European affairs, and one high-ranking official from the Swedish Foreign Office with insight into governmental deliberations, were asked to give their best estimate of the national agenda of each member state.[12] These experts were asked to rank the importance given by national governments to each of the 13 policy issues described above. As was the case in the corresponding survey question, the time frame was defined as "during the next few years." Five response alternatives were offered, reaching from "low priority" (coded as "1") to "high priority" (coded as "5").

Although a larger and more diversified group of experts would have been desirable, there is reason to accept expert judgments as an indicator of true national agendas. From a statistical point of view, at least, judgments provide acceptable information.[13] For instance, there is no strong tendency to classify some governments as more "eager" than others (in the sense that every issue is highly prioritized by this government). The average rate of importance ascribed to a policy issue varies marginally between countries, with a low of 3.2 (the Irish national agenda), and a high of 3.6 (German and French national agendas). Moreover, the average correlation between the judgments of the journalists and the Foreign Office official is a fairly high .55 (Pearson's r). The experts were most in agreement on the French national agenda (Pearson's r = .73), and least in agreement on the Dutch national agenda (Pearson's r = .20).

The test examines how well the priority given to each specific policy issue by national governments (according to expert judgments) predicts the priority given by representatives' to the same policy issues. In technical term, one frequency distribution (e.g. Irish MEPs' prioritization of respective policy issue as shown in Table 8.5) was regressed on the variable for priorities ascribed by their national government (e.g. the Irish government) to the same policy issues.[14] Large positive coefficients which are statistically significant indicate that representatives' issue priorities can be predicted from our measurments of national agendas. Table 8.7 summarizes the results.

The results are quite consistent. In most cases (in seven of twelve cases, counting both MEPs and MNPs) coefficients for national agendas are positive, fairly large, and reach a standard level of significance. We are thus quite successful in predicting the priorities of representatives from our measurement of national priorities.[15] When deciding what issues to identify as important problems for the future, it would seem that representatives take a lead from their national government.

There is however, a dividing line among representatives. The difference is not between, on the one hand, European representatives, and on the other hand, national representatives. Rather, representatives of the small nation-states differ from representatives from the dominating forces of Germany and France. The tendency to fulfil the role of

TABLE 8.7. Issue Priorities of National Governments Predicts Issue Priorities of Representatives (unstandardized regression coefficients, OLS-estimates)

	MEPs	MNPs
France	$.36^{.25}$	$.58^{.17}$
Germany	$.51^{.41}$	$.55^{.35}$
The Netherlands	$.89^{.07}$	$.90^{.03}$
Ireland	$.98^{.05}$	$1.06^{.06}$
Greece	$1.23^{.02}$	$.69^{.26}$
Sweden	$1.22^{.01}$	$1.46^{.01}$

Comment: Unit of analysis are priority given to a specific policy issue.

national agents is present mainly among representatives of small countries and not among representatives of the big member countries. Thus, with important qualifications, it is accurate to characterize European representatives as national agents as regard priorities of specific policy issues.

CONCLUDING REMARKS

Dr Euro-Elite and Mr National Agent—the analysis of the viability of the two competing models of integrated elites and national agents has painted a rather complex picture of the European Parliament. In some respects European representatives are best characterized as an integrated Euro-elite (as regards propensity to stress procedural aspects of politics, and the need foster a common European culture), and in other respects they are best characterized as national agents (as regards priority given to specific policy issues). Moreover, findings indicate that size of member states is sometimes a relevant factor. It might be that representatives from small member states are more prone than representatives from large member states to be ambassadors of national interests. The analysis thus speaks for a broad understanding of the institution under scrutiny; the European Parliament is not to be captured by easy formulas.

This analysis is helpful for the evaluation of seemingly contradictory findings about the nature of the European Parliament. Broadly speaking, studies that focus on matters that are of immediate concern for the

European Union will likely find that European representatives tend to distance themselves from the traditional nation-state.

In a corresponding way, studies that focus on matters that immediately concern nation-states will likely find that European representatives are not substiantally different from national representatives. MEPs are just as likely as MNPs to ascribe importance to the fundamental materialistic factors of continuous economic growth and the creation of new jobs.

In other specific matters where national priorities differ, European and national representatives from the same country tend to share a common view about desired actions of the European Union.

To sum up, centuries ago, in a speech before the electors who had just chosen him to be their representative in the House of Commons, Edmund Burke forcefully advocated the idea that representatives should act independently from the immediate interests of constitutents. Burke would probably find the functioning of the European Parliament to be partly agreeable. But only partly.

NOTES

1   I would like to thank Martin Brothén and Staffan Kumlin for their help in preparing the data for this analysis.
2   The relevant literature on this topic is cited in the contribution to this volume by Franklin and Scarrow.
3   Of course, Burke's reasoning fails to acknowledge that his own ideal parliament—"a deliberative assembly of one nation, with one interest, that of the whole"—runs the risk of neglecting the responsiveness of elected representatives.
4   Coding details are given in the Appendix.
5   The highest number of responses offered by any respondent was six. The basic coding scheme was developed by Bernhard Wessels and his colleagues at the Wissenschaftszentrum Berlin. Participants in the project were encouraged to fill in complementary categories. Coding details are available upon request.
6   The question on priorities for the future of national politics has been put to Swedish MPs in both personal interviews (in 1968) and mail question-

naires (in 1985 and 1988). The number of responses offered were somewhat higher in the 1968 study based on personal interviews (4.2 responses as compared to 3.2 responses in 1985 and 3.6 in 1988) (Holmberg and Esaiasson 1988: 207).

7 Information about MEPs from other countries will be used occasionally though. The question was also included in the survey of Belgian MNPs. However, the question seems to have worked differently in the Belgian case. The internal refusal rate in the Belgian study was 61 percent compared to an average of 6 percent for the other studies.

8 This is so because the distribution of the broadly defined variable is less skewed than the narrowly defined variable.

9 The data indicate that complementary causal factors may be at work. In particular, Swedish representatives constitute something of a deviant case. For instance, French and German MNPs are equally prone to stress procedural topics as are Swedish MEPs. This result would seem to suggest that newcomers to the EU are different, that it takes time to catch up with the established member states. However, this conclusion is not consistent with information from the full set of member states. British MEPs are not more prone to emphasize procedural topics than are Swedish MEPs. Moreover, differences between Swedish MEPs and MEPs from other countries disappear when a more restrictive definition of "procedural aspects of politics" is applied.

10 Coding details are given in the Appendix.

11 Definitions of specific policy issues tend to vary between studies; to this day, social scientists have not agreed upon a standard list of relevant policy issues. The definitions applied here follow a standard that has been developed within the framework of the Swedish National Election Studies program (cf. Holmberg 1994). In addition to the 13 policy issues reported in Table 8.5, the original list of policy issues included six more categories (defence; media; transportation; trade; education; job standards). However, these six policy issues were mentioned by few if any respondent.

12 The journalists are Ingrid Hedström of *Dagens Nyheter*, and Rolf Gustavsson of *Svenska Dagbladet*. The official from the Foreign Service Department has asked to remain anonymous. The data were collected during the spring of 1998.

13 A data set was constructed on the basis of expert judgments. The basic data set has 13 observations (equal to the number of specific policy issues), and 18 variables (three experts who give their best estimates on the national agenda of six countries). For instance, the high ranking official's judgment on the national agenda of Germany constitutes one variable, and the journalist Ingrid Hedström's judgment on the Irish national agenda constitute an other variable.

14 I took as the measurement of national agendas an average of, on the one hand, the journalists' judgments, on the other hand, the Foreign Office official's judgment. This index variable was multiplied by ten to constitute

a variable that ranges from 0 to 40. On this kind of analysis, see Geer (1989, 1993); Esaiasson and Holmberg (1996: 181-4).

15   The unit of analysis is the specific policy issues. The number of observations is 13, which is equal to the number of specific policy issues as shown in Table 8.5. Results should be read as follows: An increase of one point in priority given to a specific policy issue by the French national government (on a scale from 0 to 40), increases the predicted priority given to the same issue by French MEPs by .36 percentage points. Note that the regression coefficient for French national priorities does not reach a standard level of statistical significance.

APPENDIX
CODING OF VARIABLES

Personal involvement in the European Union

Attitude Toward Influence of the European Parliament:
"Could you say how much influence the following institutions and organs ought to have concerning decision-making in the European Union?" Respondents were offered an eleven-point scale reaching from 1 (very influential) to 11 (very much influence).

Sources of information:
Additive index (0-3) based on the following question: "For your personally, which of the following are important sources of information about the European Union. Please tick as many as appropriate." Out of eleven alternatives, the following three were selected: "European information office"; "European civil servants"; "MEPs from respondent's country."

Career Plans:
"After your present term of office, would you like to stay in politics on the national level, would you prefer a political position on the European level, or would you prefer something else?"
European Career:
Coded 1 if "Be active within European politics", else 0.

National Career:
Coded 1 if "Be active within national politics", else 0.

Number of National Political Offices Held:
Additive index (0-4) based on the following question: "Are you now, or have you ever been, a member of any of the following bodies?" Out of seven bodies, the following two were selected: "National representative body"; "Member of national government." The following response alternatives were offered: "No, never" (coded 0); "Yes, in the past" (coded 1); "Yes, at the moment" (coded 2).

9

Which Political Competencies for
Which Political Level?

BERNHARD WESSELS AND ACHIM KIELHORN

INTRODUCTION

EUROPEAN integration was—for a long time—primarily the integration of markets. This process of economic integration led to positive performance of the national economies and contributed considerably to the economic well-being and relative wealth of the peoples of the member states. The EEC Treaty in 1957 had set out the future rules for trade rather clearly, but only guiding principles were laid down for social and agricultural policy (Nugent 1989: 38). Only with the signing of the Single European Act (SEA) in February 1986 were the first steps formally taken to incorporate constitutional provisions for policy competencies at the European level. The main inclusions were foreign policy cooperation, environment, research, technological and regional development. Since then, the political integration of the European Communities has become more and more relevant, as further decision and policy competencies have been shifted to the European level. According to Schmitter, in 1950 competence rested at the national level in all of the 28 policy areas he investigated. Competence shifted to the European level fastest in the economic area. In 1968 competence rested solely with the nation-state in two-thirds of the economic policy areas, in 1992 in roughly 50 percent, and in 2001 the figure will be no more than 7 percent. In the area of welfare state policies, constitutional issues and foreign policy including defence, the process of shifting authority was much slower and did not have its real take-off before the 1990s (Schmitter 1996a, calculated from Table 6.1, p. 125). This development clearly indicates progress in political integration, although it is mainly taking place in the area of economic issues. But why has economic integration been followed by political integration, including these tremendous shifts of authority from the nation-state to the European level? What have been the driving forces in, and reasons for, this process of shifting competencies and what are the factors of resistance against it?

The explanations considered in the following argue from a rationalistic and institutional perspective rather than from an idealistic one. Right from the beginning, the two camps concerning European integration have been the realists and the idealists. Although idealistic arguments point mainly to the public goods an integrated Europe can provide, it might be doubted that such ideals as community, peace, wealth, and the like are the driving forces motivating political actors in the process of integration. Two features of globalization—an elusive term, but useful in this context—can rather be regarded as the driving force behind political integration. One has to do with the nature of policy problems. The other is regime competition, which is, to a certain extent, self-produced by the process of economic integration. On the other hand, forces of resistance against a further shifting of authority can be found in variations of the national institutional settings. These are closely related to the problem of legitimacy as well as to the problem of being the winner or loser of further political integration.

In this chapter, an attempt will be made to investigate three aspects of shifting competencies: 1) How does support for higher authority for the European level differ between policy areas and why? 2) How does general support for more competencies at the European level differ between countries and why? 3) How does support by members of national parliaments for more competencies at the European level differ between polities and why?

Answers to these three questions will be sought by setting out specific hypotheses. With respect to differences in support for shifting competencies between policies, it will be argued that the degree to which problems can be regarded as globalized is of crucial importance (*globalization of problems hypothesis*). With respect to differences between countries, it will be argued that they are on the one hand due to the differences between countries with respect to their embeddedness in and dependence on a globalized economy (*globalization of the economy hypothesis*), and on the other hand on the degree to which vested interests place an institutional constraint on political flexibility (*vested interests hypothesis*). Thirdly, it will be argued that national institutional settings account for the differences in support for shifting competencies between members of national parliaments (*national institutional setting hypothesis*).

The chapter starts with the exploration of the problem globalization hypothesis for the members of the European Parliament and national parliaments, going on to the globalization of the economy hypothesis and then to the vested interest resistance hypothesis. In the fifth section, all four aspects will be explored in a common explanatory model. After this, particular attention will be turned to MNPs and the national institutional setting hypothesis.

THE GLOBALIZATION OF PROBLEMS

The process of European integration since the 1980s is often regarded as an answer to and a product of a process of societal and economic globalization starting in the mid-1970s. Some authors even argue that states are steadily dissolving, leaving their societies increasingly exposed to the cultural, economic, and human dynamics of the whole continent (Buzan 1994: 13). In other words, problems are globalizing. One expression of globalization is the convergence of problem agendas across countries. Convergence is discussed as one of the major outcomes of globalization (e.g., Berger and Dore 1996). A second and more direct expression of globalization arises from the nature of some issues, which penetrate or transcend national borders. Sinnott calls them a case for *endogenous internationalization of policies* (Sinnott 1995: 247f.).

Thus there are two features of globalization: 1) the convergence of problem loads across countries, i.e., that countries face the same problems to a similar extent, and 2) the emergence of problems like environmental pollution which by their nature cross borders.

One solution to globalized problems is to increase or to regain the initiative and steering capacity of politics and the state by establishing adequate international and supranational institutions (Zürn 1995). But there is clearly a difference between problem areas where the problem load has converged and those where the problems themselves are of a border-crossing scope. Sinnott (1995: 248) distinguishes supra-national measures taken to cope with the problems as *endogenous internationalization* of governance in the latter case and *exogenous internationalization* in the former. The reason is obvious: a converged problem load does not necessarily mean that the nation-state is not able to handle the problem. It might just be more effective to do it in a common effort. A global problem scope by definition means that problem solving within national borders is not possible because the problem itself crosses those borders. There are two reasons for a global problem scope. In the first case, the problem naturally crosses borders, as for example air or water pollution. In the second case, lowering or eliminating point-of-entry barriers to the flow of economic transactions and the encouragement of market forces by governments have inadvertently undermined the efficacy of the nation-state's standard policy tools (Ruggie 1994: 8), or the internationalization of governance has already been so successful that problems can be handled only at the supranational level (Zürn 1995: 8).

As Sinnott has already noted in his attempt to classify problems and policies as endogenous or exogenous, an operationalization of such concepts is not easy (Sinnott 1995: 262). However, in order to explain why policy competencies should be shifted to the European level or authority should stay with the nation-state, such an approach has a central position at least in theoretical terms. Theoretically, it seems to be quite realistic that the globalization of problems is the main source of the internationalization of governance in the European Union. The following interrelated hypotheses can be drawn from such an approach:

1. *The larger the global problem scope, i.e., the more problems are border-crossing by their nature (or by already achieved levels of internationalized governance), the more likely it is that elected representatives want to shift (even more) authority to the European level.*
2. *The more global the problem load, i.e., the more converged across countries, the more likely it is that elected representatives want to shift authority to the European level.*
3. *Global problem scope is more conducive to the support of internationalized governance than global problem load.*

In order to investigate these three hypotheses empirically, it is necessary to classify problem or policy areas according to the two dimensions of "load" and "scope." To start with easy and typical cases in such a typology, environmental problems are obviously border-crossing, i.e., the problem scope is high and the problem load is also quite high across countries. An opposite case is education. Neither is it a border-crossing problem nor is it a problem across countries. It ranges low on both dimensions. An example of a high cross-country problem load is unemployment, but this is not a border-crossing problem. It could in principle be managed by the nation-state although it is not independent of the management of economic problems in an economically interdependent world. Monetary policy is obviously of an international scope, but there is not a cross-national problem load. Two further problem areas that fall into the category of high load and high scope are agriculture, because of its early international institutionalization as well as the sharp subsidy problems, and immigration, because of its border-crossing nature as well as its obvious load. In addition to education, health and taxation can be regarded as low in load and scope. Other policy fields fall into middle categories either of problem load or scope or both. The classification of 17 policy fields can be seen in Figure 9.1.

Regional development and social policy show some importance across countries, particularly regarding the problems of the welfare state and the unequal development of regions in many EU countries. Fighting crime is also of medium relevance considering load and, with a liberal border-crossing regime, medium in scope as well. Given the interdependence of economic development and competitiveness, economic and research policies show a medium problem load in the cur-

Cross-country Problem Load				
High	Unemployment		Agriculture Environment Immigrants	
Medium	Region. Devel. Social Policy	Crime Economy Research	Defence Devel. Countries Foreign Policy	
Low	Health Education Tax	Media	Money	
	Low	Medium	High	Cross-border Problem Scope

FIG. 9.1. Classification of Policy Areas According to Cross-country Problem Load and Cross-border Problem Scope

rent situation of the EU economies and can only partly be handled by the nation-states alone. Defence, policies for developing countries, and foreign policy are so interdependent and the EU is regarded as a unitary actor to such a high degree that a nation-state's ability to act independently is very limited in such policy areas (with respect to war and defence, see Hirst and Thompson 1995). Media policies, in particular rules for broadcasting systems, show a low problem load but, given the capacity of stations to cross borders with their programs, they are at least of medium scope. This classification depends very much on the current problem agenda across nations as well as on the current degree of interdependence and international institutionalization. If one of the conditions changes, the classification of policies changes as well.

As questionable as this classification of policy areas may be, in this section of the paper it will serve as the independent variable to estimate the position of elected representatives, both at the national and the European level, towards a shift of authority to the European level.

A first inspection of the empirical results for members of the European Parliament and eight national parliaments does not contradict the general hypotheses that problem load and problem scope have an impact on the support for internationalized governance (Figures 9.2 and 9.3).

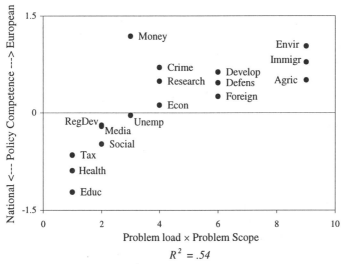

FIG. 9.2. Competence Level and Problem Character,
Members of the European Parliament

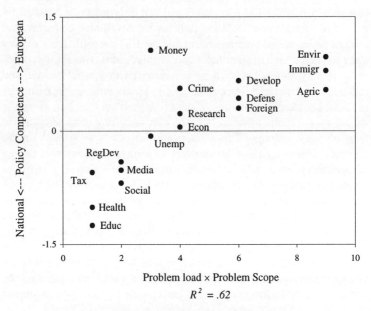

FIG. 9.3. Competence Level and Problem Character,
Members of Eleven National Parliaments

Exploring the hypotheses set out above in more detail, regression analyses have been performed, introducing problem load and problem scope as separate determinants of the average support for shifting authority to the European level. An aggregate analysis has been performed for each of the 26 country groups of MEPs or MNPs, each with 17 cases, i.e., 17 policy areas. We expect problem scope, and to a lesser extent problem load, to have a positive impact on preferences for shifting authority from the national to the European level.

The average R^2 from these regressions is quite high (.62). It is on average somewhat higher for the groups of MEPs than for the groups of MNPs from eleven countries (see Table 9.1). The mean regression coefficient for problem load is about one third of that for problem scope. Scope is somewhat more important in the case of MEPs. Results are quite stable across groups. This is confirmed by individual group regressions (see Table 9.2).

The hypotheses are obviously supported. The coefficients for problem load are sometimes quite low, indicating that problem scope, i.e.,

TABLE 9.1. Summary Table of 23 Regressions of Policy Competencies
Attribution to the European Level on Problem Load and Problem Scope

Groups/Regressions	R^2	x (Load)	x (Scope)
Mean all	0.62	0.19	0.62
Mean MEPs	0.63	0.20	0.66
Mean MNPs	0.60	0.18	0.57
Cross-country regression	0.34***	0.19**	0.62***

Aggregate regression of mean competence score for 17 policy areas for 15 groups of country MEPs and 11 groups of MNPs (n=17 for each regression); cross country regression n = 442. Results for MEP and MNP by country are given in Table 9.2.
* sign. at .05.
** sign. at .01.
*** sign at .001.

being a globalized problem and by its very nature crossing borders, is much more important for support of internationalized governance. Thus, the whole set of the three related hypotheses can be regarded as confirmed.

Testing the hypotheses in a regression that combines all 26 groups confirms the difference in impact of problem load and problem scope but the portion of explained variance is much lower than the average for the individual group regressions (see Table 9.1, last row). This points to the fact that although load and scope are quite good predictors of the differences in support for shifting authority between levels of governance, there must be substantial differences in the level of support between countries. We thus turn now to the question of what might account for the differences between countries, namely the globalization of the economy hypothesis.

GLOBALIZATION OF THE ECONOMY AND ECONOMIC INTERDEPENDENCE

As already mentioned, European integration started with the liberalization of economic markets, i.e., the integration of the economy. In the context of this discussion particular emphasis lies on the relationship between European integration and economic globalization and the

TABLE 9.2. Regression of Policy Competencies Attribution to the European
Level on Problem Load and Problem Scope

Country MEPs and MNPs	R^2	x (Load)	x (Scope)
MEPs (or MNPs where noted):			
- AU	0.53***	-0.09	0.61***
- BE	0.74***	0.04	0.98***
MNP BE	0.53**	-0.13	0.65**
- DE	0.77***	0.29	0.93***
- FI	0.47**	0.21	0.60**
- FR	0.66***	0.13	0.51***
MNP FR	0.63***	0.29	0.49**
- GE	0.84***	-0.03	0.86***
MNP GE	0.80***	0.08	0.83***
- GR	0.61**	0.34	0.50**
MNP GR	0.33	0.24	0.39
- IR	0.33	0.31	0.26
MNP IR	0.45**	0.37	0.34
- IT	0.64***	0.07	0.52***
MNP IT	0.72***	0.10	0.57***
- LU	0.75***	0.39*	1.31***
MNP LU	0.56**	0.05	0.75**
- NE	0.83***	0.22	1.00***
MNP NE	0.80***	0.13	0.81***
- PO	0.55**	0.08	0.48**
MNP PO	0.40*	0.27	0.35
- SP	0.71***	0.19	0.52***
MNP SP	0.72***	0.08	0.59***
- SW	0.42*	0.39	0.31
MNP SW	0.64***	0.48*	0.45*
- GB	0.61***	0.39*	0.46**

Aggregate regression of mean competence score for 17 policy areas for 15 groups of
country MEPs and 11 groups of MNPs from (n=17 for each regression).
*   sign. at .05.
**   sign. at .01.
***   sign at .001.

increasing interdependencies between economies. It is argued that the
internationalization of the economy was *too* successful. Nation-states
are now feeling that their capacity to handle the impact of economic
globalization has decreased on almost all matters of relevance, in particular economic matters but also social and cultural. The only possibility to erect shields against the unintended and disliked consequences

of the economic market on all sectors of society, it is argued, is to strengthen the state. That is, the geographic range of state authority should be made a match for the geographic range of the economy (see for example Zürn 1995: 8f). This obviously means the internationalization of governance. It can be argued, however, that nation-states and their societies are affected by the globalization of the economy to different degrees. Given a nation with a strong domestic market and a range of production in which neither importing nor exporting goods is actually necessary, there would be little impact from globalized markets. On the other hand, a nation which has a very small domestic market and whose range of production is too narrow to meet its demands for goods clearly depends on other economies since it must import the missing goods and pay for them through exports.

There are huge differences between the different schools of economic thought concerning what external economic dependency means (see the contributions in Berger and Dore 1996). It is most common to measure economic interdependence through the external trade rate. However, this is a largely mercantilist understanding of the role of trade. A classical economist like Ricardo or John Stuart Mill would argue that the purpose of trade is imports, not exports. As Krugman has put it, "exports are costs—something we must produce because our import suppliers are crass enough to demand payment. Or to put it differently, an export is an indirect way to produce an import, which is worth doing because it is more efficient than producing our imports ourselves." (Krugman 1996: 18).

In this sense, the question of economic interdependence takes its starting point from the question of how much imports are necessary in order to have an efficient and satisfying allocation of goods in a country not able to produce everything by itself. Imports then are a burden to the extent that they must be paid for by exports. Dependency then is the strength of the pressure for exports in order to balance imports. A measure that takes this consideration into account thus must relate imports to exports, asking how good the balance of payments is in respect to the imports, i.e., if the amount of imports is matched by a corresponding export figure. A standardized measure for this is the amount of imports minus the amount of exports as a percentage of the GDP. This measure takes into account the extent to which a country is dependent on the international division of production of goods and whether it is economically able to compensate for such a dependency.

The globalization of the economy hypothesis thus assumes that the higher the dependency on international trade, division of labour, and global competition, the more countries favour shifting policy authority to the European level in order to have the same conditions of market participation with respect to the structure of regulation, incentives, and the like.

Empirical results support the economic dependency hypothesis to a certain degree. Those countries that are exposed to the international economy in a negative way, i.e., their exports do not meet their need for imports, show stronger overall support for greater competencies at the European level. In particular, these are Greece, Belgium, Portugal, Spain and Austria. Countries that profit from the structure of the international division in the production of goods in the sense that the demand for their products exceeds their own needs favour the internationalization of governance to a lesser degree (see Figure 9.4).

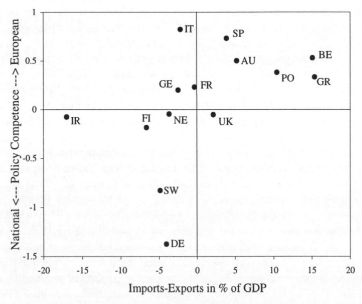

Correlations for Overall Competence Score: MEP and MNP (24 cases; Luxembourg missing): 0.46[*]; MEP only (14 cases): 0.49; MNP only (10 cases): 0.48.
* sign. at .05.

FIG. 9.4. Economic Interdependency and Overall Support for Shifting Policy Competencies to the European Level

However, the correlations are not strong. Thus, other factors have to be taken into account to explain the differences between countries in support for internationalized governance.

RESISTANCE BY VESTED INTERESTS?

Organized interests play an important role in policy-making in many national settings. The debate about corporatism in Western democracies is one important indication of this. Research shows many cases in which the integration of organized interests into the policy-making process produces positive outcomes, particularly in the areas of economic performance and social policies, compared with nations where corporatism is not as strong. Corporatist countries seem to manage unemployment better, have on average higher growth rates, and so on. While the integration of organized interests in policy-making plays an important role, the political composition of governments and how this corresponds with the institutionalization of participation of organized interests also plays an important role (Alvarez, Garrett, and Lange 1991). But the structure and integration of organized interests in the policy process is of crucial importance. If interest groups gain some advantage from being embedded in the structure of policy-making, they might hesitate to give up such a setting. In other words, interest groups that benefit from the national setting of interest intermediation are likely to oppose changes to it. Thus, one can assume that the existence of a strong corporatist arena constitutes some institutional constraint on the shift in policy competencies to the European level. However, this general assumption has to be differentiated a little bit more.

Since their particular interests are specifically related to policy areas in the corporatist circuit, one can assume that vested interests put a constraint on these policy areas and are rather indifferent to any competence shift in others. The vested interest hypothesis thus reads as follows:

1. *The more interest intermediation is of a corporatist kind and the stronger organized interests are, the stronger the resistance of a country to change to the national setting of policy- and decision-making.*

2. *Resistance exists in particular with respect to the shift of those competencies that directly affect the corporatist arena, namely economic and social/welfare policies.*

In order to test these hypotheses, measures are needed for the degree of corporatism and the strength of national interest groups in the corporatist arena. Data on the strength of corporatism are provided by many experts. Lijphart and Crepaz have created a synthetic measure from many expert judgements that is quite reliable (Lijphart and Crepaz 1991). However, it is available for only 11 of the 15 countries under investigation here. Sometimes union density is used as a surrogate measure for corporatism, although this is obviously problematic (see Golden 1993; B. Wessels 1996). Union density is an indicator of the strength only of one party to the corporatist circuit. Another measure, which to a certain extent is a bridge between corporatism and strength of unions, is a measure of the legal regulation and legal privilege of unions developed by Armingeon (1992). These three measures serve as surrogate measures for the degree to which the participation of organized interests in the corporatist arena is institutionalized.

Aggregate correlations between these three measures and the mean overall competence score across countries are all negative, and with respect to union density also significant even with the small number of cases investigated. The strength and embededdness of vested interests in the national policy-making arena indeed make a difference. Vested interests are an institutional constraint on support for shifting authority (Table 9.3).

TABLE 9.3. Vested Interests and Resistance to Shift in Policy Competencies to the European Level

	Corporatism Score	Union Density 1970-1990	Legal Regulation of Union Systems
	(Correlation with Overall Competence Score)		
All	-0.43	-0.57[**]	-0.46[*]
	(n = 18)	(n = 26)	(n = 24)
MEP	-0.35	-0.64[**]	-0.46
	(n = 11)	(n = 14)	(n = 14)
MNP only	-0.72	-0.43	-0.48
	(n = 7)	(n = 11)	(n = 10)

*   sign. at .05.
**   sign. at .01.

Exploring the hypothesis that this constraint exists particularly for policies in the corporatist arena, policy fields have been divided between those related to corporatism and others. The first are policies concerning the social or equality dimension, namely social policy, health, unemployment, taxation, and education (see Roller 1991 for a similar classification of policies). In order to avoid losing too many cases, the corporatism score is dropped. Instead, union density, legal regulation and privileges of unions are included in two regressions, one referring to all non-social non-equality related policies and one to those related to social policy and equality.

Results across policy fields and across countries show the following. Firstly, resistance to a shift in authority to the European level covaries much more strongly with the strength of vested interests in social policy and equality areas than in others. The proportion of explained variance is about 50 percent higher, which means 25 percent for social and equality issues and 17 percent for others altogether. Secondly, the effect of legal regulation in the regression is only significant in the case of social policy and equality issues (Table 9.4).

The results of these analyses clearly support the vested interest hypotheses. In countries where vested interests are strong, this is an institutional barrier against a change in the distribution of policy competencies between the nation-state and the European level. Furthermore, it is in particular in the area of social policy and equality issues where the strength of corporatism constrains the institutional flexibility of the national setting.

TABLE 9.4. Regression of Competence Shift for Non-Social Policy and Social Policy Issues on the Strength of Vested Interests

	R^2	Beta (Union Density)	Beta (Legal Regul.)
Non-Social Policy Issues	0.17^{***}	-0.40^{***}	-0.01
Social Policy and Equality Issues	0.25^{***}	-0.25^{**}	-0.30^{**}

Aggregate regression across policy fields and countries.
Number of cases: non-social policy issues 288; social policy and equality issues (social policy, health, unemployment, taxation, and education) 120.

A MODEL OF CROSS-POLICY CROSS-COUNTRY
SUPPORT FOR THE SHIFT OF COMPETENCIES TO
THE EUROPEAN LEVEL

Analyses have shown so far, firstly, that the differences in support for a competence shift between policy areas are a matter of the problem scope and, to a lesser degree, the problem load. Secondly, they have shown that differences between countries can be at least partly explained by a globalization of the economy hypothesis, i.e., the more countries are dependent on trade, the stronger the support. Results also show that there are national institutional factors related to the structure of organized interests that put a constraint on support for shifting competencies and that the degree of resistance varies with the strength of vested interests, particularly in the corporatist arena.

In order to come close to a fuller explanation of differences in support for shifting competencies to the European level, a regression model will be tested, introducing all the factors under consideration so far. From Table 9.1 we know that problem load and scope account for 34 percent of the variance in support. Introducing the dependency of a country on foreign trade adds about 10 percent. Introducing union density and privileges of the union systems instead of foreign trade also adds roughly 10 percent and finally all variables add another 5 percent (Table 9.5).

TABLE 9.5. Full Model of the Explanation of Differences in Support for Shifting Policy Competencies to the European Level

	Model 1 beta	Model 2 beta	Model 3 beta	Model 4 beta
Problem Load	0.13***	0.14**	0.14***	0.14***
Problem Scope	0.53***	0.51***	0.51***	0.51***
Foreign Trade Dependency		0.32***	-	0.29***
Union Density			-0.31***	-0.19***
Legal Regulation of Union Systems			-0.09	-0.17***
Explained Variance (adj. R^2)	0.34***	0.43***	0.46***	0.53***

Aggregate regression, 408 cases (policy fields times groups [14 MEP; 10 MNP]).
*   sign. at .05.
**   sign. at .01.
*** sign. at .001.

Altogether, this model thus accounts for 53 percent of the variance in support for shifting authority. From the scatterplot of estimated scores and empirical scores it is obvious that the found explanatory model is quite firm and reliable. Points scatter nicely around the regression line and there are only some outliers (see Figure 9.5).

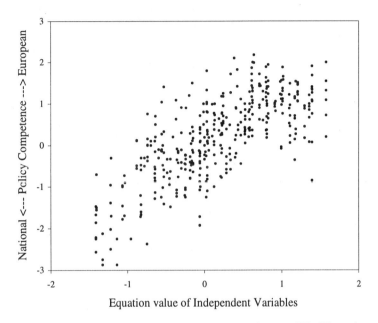

Correlation between estimated and empirical values 0.74 (sign. p = .000; 408 cases).

FIG. 9.5. Competence Level: Estimated and Empirical Preferences

INSTITUTIONAL FACTORS: POWER OF NATIONAL PARLIAMENTS AND SHIFTING OF AUTHORITY

In the previous sections we investigated some factors promoting and constraining competence shift that are valid for members of the EP as well as for members of national parliaments. We now fully concentrate on the national level and ask about the sources of support for and resistance against a shift of authority by members of national parliaments.

This perspective might allow us to gain insight into the sources of conflict and tension between national and supranational levels in the course of European integration. Since we are interested in national differences, it is to be expected that factors of resistance and support might be found mainly in the institutional contexts of the national political systems. Do different national institutional settings result in more or less support of the transfer of power to the European level, and why? To address this question, we turn to the role and strength of national parliaments in policy-making.

It has been pointed out recently that "legislatures have been transformed from law-making to ... law-effecting institutions" (Norton 1996b: 3). The literature reports a substantial shift of legislative power toward executive dominance in the making of public policies (Norton 1996b: 5). While this might be a general trend, in fact, a great variety of interplay and counterplay of parliaments and governments can be found across Europe.

The strength of parliaments in the legislative process thus could be imagined as a continuous variable reaching from exclusive government power to exclusive parliamentary power. From organization theory as well as from the rational actors approach it is known that, if possible, organizations and actors tend to increase their power, scope, and size rather than to give something away. This tendency is stronger when the organizations and actors are already strong. This would suggest that strong parliaments put some constraint on shifting authority. This hypothesis is also plausible from the perspective of democratic theory. Given that the European level still suffers from some institutional deficits with respect to democratic control of government action, it is easy to understand that legislators who have strong democratic control capacities at the national level would not like to exchange this situation for one where democratic control is more doubtful. Thus, one can formulate the following hypothesis:

The more powerful a national parliament is, the more its members resist a shift of policy competencies to the European level.

Though the idea behind this distribution-of-power hypothesis seems to be quite clear, finding adequate measures is more difficult. The relationship of executive and legislature, especially the question of the strength of parliament versus government, is one of the big questions of politics but seems seldom to be targeted in comparative research (Olson 1994 :93). However, the excellent research of Döring and associates about national parliaments in Europe provides very valuable indicators in this respect. In an exploratory factor analysis, Döring found three dimensions of agenda control to be indicative of the strength of parliament vis-à-vis government (Döring 1995a: 664). The first factor indicates the degree to which the parliament or the government has control over the agenda (plenary timetable, timetable committees, hearings, etc.). The second factor could be interpreted as the strength of committees in the legislative process. The third factor describes the degree to which the plenum has the power to reverse the voting order, which gives it more freedom to determine the policy results. Döring calls the first "Government priorities", the second "Committee drafting", and the third "Whips' power". Scores for all three factors have been added in this analysis in order to construct an overall measure of plenary power.

The evidence shown in Figure 9.6 clearly indicates strong support of our hypothesis. Although the data have to be read carefully due to the small number of cases, the correlation is quite high (Pearson's r = -.52).

As we can see, the more powerful a parliament is vis-à-vis the government, the less MNPs support a transfer of authority to the European level. Without the two outliers, Sweden and Italy, the correlation would be almost perfect (-.94), and there might be some very good reasons why Italy and Sweden differ from the general pattern. The Swedish case could be explained by a general attitude of scepticism toward the ongoing integration process of the European Union. For Italy, a good explanation might be more difficult to find. An ad hoc hypothesis is that Italian MPs are to a great extent unsatisfied with the outcomes of the national political systems. In contradiction of our general hypothesis, this might lead to a strong parliament being strongly in favour of shifting competencies to the EU, i.e., of giving power away in order to produce more satisfactory outcomes.

But does this strong correlation for the mean competence score also hold for different policy areas? To explore this question, a classification scheme of policies developed by Roller (1991) has been utilized to differentiate policy areas. The classification by Roller is based on a concept invented by Almond and Powell (1978) and consists of seven categories named action goals, six of which could be used here. These action goals are: international security, national security, wealth,

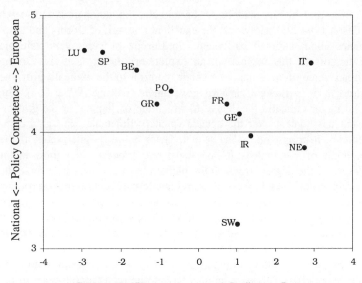

Government Power <------------> Parliament Power

Note: Entries are predicted values.

FIG. 9.6. Competence Level and Distribution of Power

equality, and environment (Roller 1991: 16). Wealth has been divided
into two action goals: infrastructure and macro-management.

Table 9.6 shows the action goals and how the seventeen policy variables have been assigned to them. The action goals in Table 9.6 are
sorted according to their problem scope derived from Figure 9.1.

The results for policy areas presented in Table 9.7 confirm the general tendency quite well. Although the correlations have to be read very
carefully due to the small number of cases, the relationship confirms
our hypothesis at the level of individual issues as well. Whereas the
inclusion of all eleven countries produces correlations high enough to
speak of a quite strong (but not significant) relationship (reaching from
-.39 for equality to -.54 for the infrastructure component of wealth), the
interrelation becomes much more impressive with the deletion of the
two deviant cases identified above (see Table 9.7). In order to explore
the relationship across policy fields somewhat more, regression analyses have been performed as shown in Figure 9.7. We find the effect
indicated by the correlation analysis confirmed and we can conclude

TABLE 9.6. Classification of Policy Fields

Action Goal (according to Roller 1991)	Policy Area (Variable in Dataset)
Environment	Protection of the environment
International Security	Security and defense Foreign policy Developing countries
Wealth: Macro-management	Agriculture/fisheries Economic policy Monetary policy
National Security	Fighting crime Immigrants and refugees
Wealth: Infrastructure	Regional development Broadcasting/press Research
Equality	Unemployment policies Health Social policy Education Taxation policy

that strength of parliament is a clear constraint to the shift of authority to the European level *in all policy fields.* But another question arises: Could the extent to which a policy field is already Europeanized, i.e., policy competence already rests with the EU, be seen as a limitation on shift of authority?

The assumption behind this question is well-known as the ceiling-effect: the higher the degree of Europeanization in a particular policy field already is, the lower the support for a further shift of policy competence to the EU. Figure 9.7 seems to confirm this assumption. Looking at the predicted values plotted in the figure, it is quite obvious that the gradient of the regression lines for policy goals with a relatively low level of Europeanization is much steeper than the gradients for policy goals with a relatively high level of Europeanization. The lowest gradient is for the most Europeanized policy domain, environment (.05). The coefficient is considerably higher for national security (.11) and the macro-management component of wealth (.10), and highest for

TABLE 9.7. Distribution of Power and Shift of Policy Competencies to the European Level (Correlations)

Action Goal	Pearson's R
Overall Competence Score	-.96***
Environment	-.78**
International Security	-.69*
Wealth: Macro-management	-.61
National Security	-.82**
Wealth: Infrastructure	-.79**
Equality	-.83**

*   sign. at .05
**   sign. at .01
***   sign. at .001.

Note: The correlations have been computed without the two outliers Italy and Sweden (N=9)

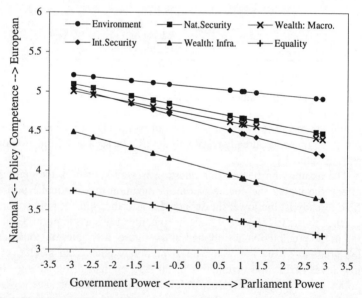

Note: Entries are predicted values.

FIG. 9.7. Policy-specific Level of Competence and Distribution of Power (Linear Regressions)

international security (.14) as well as the infra-structure component of wealth (.14). An exception to the general pattern can be found for equality, which is less Europeanized than any other policy domain, but only shows a relatively moderate gradient coefficient of .10. Does this already provide us with enough evidence to assume that the power of parliaments does matter or have we neglected an important factor? It might well be that our findings coincide with cultural differences between countries affecting attitudes toward integration and competence shift. In order to check, a multivariate regression analysis has been performed.

Since we found a strong relationship between the mean support for shifting competencies between MEP-country groups and the corresponding MNPs, the mean MEP position might serve as an *independent* yardstick for a possibly culturally determined position toward integration. Introducing this variable into a regression model computed for the countries described in Table 9.7, we indeed find a strong relationship (beta = .58). However, if we introduce parliamentary power as a variable, the country effect vanishes completely, and the effect of parliamentary power remains nearly as high as in the bivariate model (beta = -.95). Hence, our doubts can confidently be put aside. It is the institutions that matter.

CONCLUSIONS

This chapter took a multidimensional approach to the explanation of support for shifting authority to the European level. Cross-country variations in attitudes toward competence shift clearly show that a search for explanation has to go beyond the individual level, given the relative homogeneity and convergence of social structures across the member states of the EU. Therefore the search strategy had to be found at the macro-level of differences between countries: differences in their situation; differences in the effects of EU integration on their national settings; and differences in their institutions. There are two big strands of discussion concerning the convergence or divergence of countries: one is the debate about globalization; the second the debate about institutions as constraints and facilitators of action. From these discussions we derived a set of hypotheses. With respect to globalization, we

196   *Problems and Institutional Change*

investigated whether the globalization of problems and the globalization of the economy matter. With respect to institutional hypotheses,
we tested on the one hand whether national settings of interest groups
and interest intermediation and the capacity of national parliaments
democratically to control their governments place constraints on the
shift of authority. Results give clear evidence that globalization is a
condition favouring support for policy shift, be it related to problems or
the to economy. On the other hand, institutional factors like the
strength of the intermediary system or the national parliaments clearly
put limits on support for competence shift. The more powerful national
settings, the less political actors are ready to give away their capacity to
influence decisions.

10

Policy Evaluations

MICHAEL MARSH

EASTON (1967) and others have argued that regime support is dependent to some degree on political outputs, and that approval of specific policies feeds back into support for the political system as a whole. This process also plays a part in the idea of spillover, which has been an important element in theories about the progress of European integration since the 1960s. For neo-functionalist theorists of that time, spillover provided the dynamic for integration. It did so in several ways. First of all, it was argued, successful policy-making would provide support for more such action. This was a claim made originally by "functionalists" such as Mitrany (1966) whose work, first published long before the Treaty of Rome was signed, was developed by the neofunctionalists (e.g. Haas 1964). A second spillover mechanism was the need for more authority to complete previously agreed tasks. An expansion of EU authority might be required to fulfil something already agreed. This would be most significant when authority was required in a second area in order to complete the tasks in the first one. Either way, spillover could contribute to the gradual extension of EU authority.

The apparent inevitability of the dynamic implicit in the spillover concept was widely criticized, particularly when the forward march of European integration stalled in the 1960s and 1970s. Lindberg and Scheingold (1970: 135-40) admitted that "forward linkage" to other policy areas and increased authority was only one of the possible outcomes. Stressing the importance of policy success, they suggested that "output failure" could result in the weakening of authority and the reassertion of national competencies. Even successful policy-making might result only in a new equilibrium, with no implications for other policy areas. If Lindberg and Scheingold's reservations signalled the clear acceptance of spillover as a possibility rather than an inevitability among neo-functionalists, other commentators suggested very strict limits to the dynamic. Most notably, Stanley Hoffman (1966) asserted that there could be no spillover from low politics (economic cooperation) to the "high" politics of foreign and defence policy, and was sceptical about the operation of the process even within particular areas, arguing from the realist assumption that national self-interest provided the only dynamic behind integration.

Some saw signs of spillover in the renewed emphasis on the European project evident in the Single European Act and the Maastricht Treaty, but others spotted only more evidence of intergovernmental negotiations (see Muttimer 1989, Moravcsik 1991). Evidence for both conclusions came from policy analysis, as did the original considerations on spillover in the EU in the work of Haas (1964) in the 1960s.

Yet attitudes as well as actions are part of the spillover thesis. While the spillover process has generally been considered as operating at the elite level, in the wake of the referendums on the Maastricht Treaty, more attention has been paid to mass publics. A growing literature on the sources of mass support for the EU, which seems to provide evidence for the existence of a link between mass perceptions of the impact of EU policy on their national economies and their support for the EU itself. Among mass publics, the best results have been obtained using measures of mass perceptions of the EU's impact (Eichenberg 1998; Marsh 1999). Expecting a link between changes in objective conditions and changes in support for the EU may be unrealistic as it ignores the importance of the struggle between political elites to claim credit and apportion blame for such conditions (although see Gabel 1998).

There has to date been little attempt to trace the basis of support for the European project among elites. Do their views on the future of integration stem from their perceptions of its past success? How far is their support for the EU, and support for increasing the responsibilities of the EU, related to satisfaction with EU outputs to date? Does satisfaction feed into greater support for the EU (as neo-functionalist theory would suggest), to support for more integration, or neither, or both? How much difference can be seen between economic and other issue areas? Unlike the mass public, parliamentarians in both national parliaments and the EP can be expected to have views about different areas of policy. It is thus possible, in principle, to contrast the impor-

tance of the different policy areas. First of all though, we need to find
out what parliamentarians think of the record of EU policy-making.

ELITE POLICY EVALUATIONS

Members of national parliaments and of the European parliament were
asked for their assessment of the activities of the EU in seventeen different policy areas: "Do you think the EU has done a good or a bad job
in the following areas in the last five years?" Respondents were asked
to mark their response on a seven-point policy scale with very good (1)
and very bad (7) at the extremes.

Table 10.1 shows the mean scores for each of the 17 areas, first for
MEPs and secondly for MNPs.[1] The most striking thing about these
results is the level of dissatisfaction revealed. No policy has an average
policy evaluation indicating satisfaction; that is, a rating below 3.5—
the mid point of the scale. It is hard to know whether this is good or
bad for Europe, since we do not know what elites would say about the
outputs of their own national governments. However, taken at face
value, it does indicate that parliamentarians as a whole think the EU
"could do better" on all issues. The second point is that while MEPs
and MNPs are pretty much in agreement with respect to their relative
satisfaction with different areas, MEPs seem to discriminate a little
more between policies. The latter's assessments range from regional
development at one extreme, which gets an average rating of 3.66, to
unemployment at the other, which scores 5.52. In contrast, among
MNPs the range is from 3.90 (monetary policy) to 5.40 (unemployment). Among MEPs five items score below 4.0 and five score at or
above 5.0, while the corresponding figures for MNPs are only one and
one respectively. Comparing the two columns of figures, differences in
absolute levels are most apparent for the issues like defence, foreign
policy and environmental protection for which the scores are closest to
the ends of the scale. However, scores for unemployment also are
relatively close to the end of the scale, yet it is evaluated similarly.
These differences are not due to the differing national or party composition of the two samples. Weighting the analysis either by nation or
party group leaves the basic pattern unchanged.

TABLE 10.1. Evaluations of EU Policy, by Institution, Authority, Load, and Scope

	MEP	MNP	Authority	Load	Scope	Load plus scope	Load minus authority
Regional development	3.66	3.90	3	2	1	3	-1
Protection of the environment	3.83	4.36	3	3	3	6	0
Developing countries	3.91	4.47	2	2	3	5	0
Research	3.91	4.10	2	2	2	4	0
Monetary policy	3.93	3.86	2	1	3	4	-1
Agriculture/fisheries	4.19	4.54	4	3	3	6	-1
Education policy	4.35	4.38	2	1	1	2	-1
Economic policy	4.37	4.42	3	2	2	4	-1
Health policy	4.41	4.56	2	1	1	2	-1
Broadcasting/press	4.49	4.57	na	1	2	3	na
Social policy	4.74	4.86	2	2	1	3	0
Taxation policy	4.99	4.71	2	1	1	2	-1
Immigrants and refugees	5.00	4.96	na	3	3	6	na
Fighting crime	5.18	4.82	1	2	2	4	1
Security and defence	5.44	4.70	2	2	3	5	0
Foreign policy EU has	5.45	4.64	2	2	3	5	0
Unemployment policies	5.52	5.40	na	3	1	4	na
Correlation with MEPs policy evaluations			-0.48*	0.12	-0.05	0.03	0.39*
Correlation with MNPs policy evaluations			-0.29	0.38	-0.15	0.11	0.44*

* $p < .10$

na = not available

Note: Authority scores from Schmitter 1996; Scope and Load from Wessels and Kielhorn, Chapter 9.

Regardless of institution, what accounts for the differing assessments of parliamentarians? One possibility is that assessments are linked to current levels of EU authority: that parliamentarians are less (or more) critical of the EU in areas where it has more authority. Table 10.1 also shows assessments of EU authority in each area upon the ratification of the Single European Act, taken from Schmitter (1996a). There is some sign of a negative relationship between authority and dissatisfaction: that is, areas where the EU has more power are those where its performance is considered better. Among MEPs the correlation is -.48 and among MNPs it is -.29. Neither of these is strong given the small number of cases involved (14), and only the MEP coefficient is significant at the .10 level, but the results are suggestive of a relationship that brings more criticism on the EU for what it does not do than for what it does.

Wessels and Kielhorn (Chapter 9) have shown that approval for the EU having political authority depends on the type of issue area, with some areas having either more scope, or more need for the EU to play a role (see also Sinnott 1995). Other columns in Table 10.1 show the respective "load" and "scope" for different areas, and their weight in combination. However, in neither group is any correlation significant at the .10 level. What does seem more powerful is the contrast between authority and load: what the EU does and how important an issue is. The correlation between load/authority difference and dissatisfaction is .35 for MEPs and .52 for MNP across the 14 policy areas. Both of these correlations are significant, and again point to dissatisfaction lying more in what the EU has not done than what it has done. If we score broadcasting, unemployment and immigration areas as 1, and to date the EU has had little authority in these areas, correlations rise to .50 and .77 for MEPs and MNPs and to .55 and .50 in the case of authority/evaluation. European governments at the EU summit in 1998 started to give a higher priority to EU policy on unemployment. Judging by these results, this is perhaps long overdue in the eyes of parliamentary elites.

Even if the emphasis on tackling unemployment through EU action is relatively new, the scope of EU authority has widened in a number of areas since 1992. Our surveys were generally carried out in 1996 by which time the Maastricht provisions were coming into effect. Taking the figures suggested for the post Maastricht period produces similar, though marginally weaker, results. But given the changing authority pattern over the period, and the frame of reference as the last five years provided by the question wording, the basic finding, that the EU is blamed more for what it does not do than for what is does do, remains valid.

While the differences between the ratings of individual policy areas are interesting and suggest some priorities for EU action in the future, it is also important to look at the broader picture. The respondents' assessments of the 17 issue areas can be added to provide a single measure of policy evaluation. The greater the approval expressed for individual issue areas, the greater the overall approval score. This summation can be done in many ways but we have chosen to do it in the most simple way: by adding up the score for each item. In this way we constructed two indices, one for the narrowly economic issue areas and one for the rest. The first contains assessments of agricultural policy, monetary policy, economic policy and taxation policy; the second contains the assessments of the other policy areas. These do not form strong scales, indicating that individuals do discriminate between issue areas. A widely used indicator of unidimensionality, Cronbach's alpha, is .64 for the economy scale for MEPs and .62 for MNPs; for the rest it is .82 and .86 for the MEPs and MNPs, respectively. Ideally alpha should be in excess of .90 at least. Nonetheless, we think it is reasonable to sum the items here on the assumption that being satisfied in more areas indicates a higher level of overall policy satisfaction. Table 10.2 shows summary statistics for the two scales. Each is standardized as a seven-point scale, with lower scores indicating more satisfaction.

As might be expected from the previous analysis in Table 10.1, there is little difference in average levels of satisfaction but the kurtosis

TABLE 10.2. Satisfaction with Economic and Non-Economic Policy Areas, by Institution

Variable	Mean	Std Dev	Kurtosis	N
MEPs				
Economic policy	4.39	1.02	-0.08	282
Other policy	4.61	0.72	0.40	267
All	4.55	0.71	0.50	261
MNPs				
Economic policy	4.37	0.96	0.40	1254
Other policy	4.58	0.81	1.50	1177
All	4.52	0.78	1.68	1150

statistic indicates that the distribution of MNP evaluations is more peaked than that of MEPs. Economic policy assessments are also more diverse than are other policy assessments. This is true both for MEPs and MNPs.

While the differences observed between MEPs and MNPs are not simply a function of party or national differences, there is of course a difference in the assessments of different political and national groups. Table 10.3 shows differences between countries in terms of overall assessments are relatively small. We used the overall policy satisfaction scale here as the small Ns in many subgroups make comparison across the two groups impossible in most instances. Only the parliamentarians from Greece and to a much lesser extent Ireland are significantly more satisfied with policy than the average parliamentarian, while Swedish, French, and Belgian parliamentarians are significantly more critical. While elites from some of the newer and less affluent countries seem more often to be less dissatisfied, and those from the older, often richer original six entrants more critical there are too many exceptions to either generalization to suggest a clear pattern.

Table 10.4 shows party families too are broadly similar, at least with respect to the "centre" parties. Christian democrats are significantly

TABLE 10.3. Policy Assessment by Country

Country	Mean	Cases
Greece	3.36*	67
Ireland	4.15*	63
Finland	4.26	10
Portugal	4.37	61
Spain	4.38	144
Luxembourg	4.41	29
United Kingdom	4.44	24
Netherlands	4.54	73
Germany	4.58	303
Austria	4.64	9
Italy	4.66	108
Belgium	4.68*	131
Sweden	4.70*	233
France	4.78*	151
Denmark	5.69	5
All	4.52	1411

* Indicates significant difference from overall mean, p < .05.

less dissatisfied with policy, while social democrats, liberals and conservatives are all very close to the mean levels and to one another. The remaining groups, particularly the radical left, Greens, the extreme right and unattached, are significantly more critical, a pattern evident in most analysis of Euro support by party (see Hix and Lord 1997 for example). There is considerable diversity within each family, although in the non-centrist parties this is largely in terms of degrees of disapproval, rather than a diversity of approval/disapproval. Even so, in all groups the average deputy is at the dissatisfied rather than the satisfied end of the policy satisfaction scale.

THE IMPLICATIONS OF POLICY EVALUATIONS

The causes of variable policy assessments are difficult to pin down. Party and national differences could be a function of differences in the ways that policies have impacted on different communities, or of ideological or cultural differences in the evaluation of those policies, but in either case patterns are not very distinct. What is of more interest here, however, are the consequences of the policy evaluations, and the implications they have for the future. How far does satisfaction with policy outputs spill over into support for extending integration as theorists as diverse as Haas and Easton would suggest? Alternatively, is

TABLE 10.4. Policy Satisfaction by Party Group

	Mean	N
PPE/Christian Democrats	4.24*	407
ELDR/Liberals	4.49	183
PSE/Social Democrats	4.52	490
UPG/Conservatives	4.58	150
ARE/Regionalists	4.64	14
V/Greens	5.22*	54
EDN/Nationalists	5.36*	11
GUE/Radical Left	5.41*	50
Parties not belonging to EP-Party Groups	5.26*	29
Not classified	4.87	7
All	4.52	1395

*   Indicates significant difference from overall mean, $p < .05$

such support at best effectively contained within an issue area, as critics such as Hoffman would lead us to believe?

Providing even a tentative answer to these questions forces us to make a number of assumptions about the way in which assessments of policy evaluations and judgements about EU competencies might impact on one another. We have a number of measures of different attitudes, all taken at the same time, and in order to talk about the implications of one for another we have to specify the way in which these interrelate. The core idea is that favourable policy evaluations give rise to confidence in the institutions that make policy and support for more integration. The spillover from favourable evaluation to support for greater responsibility may be direct, or flow indirectly through the increased confidence in EU decisions. Figure 10.1 illustrates the possible influences of policy evaluation on support for more authority.

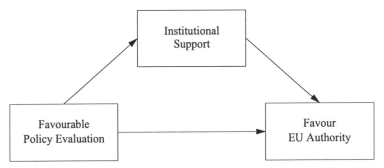

FIG. 10.1. General Spillover Model

Two more features can usefully be added to this model. The first is the distinction between economic and other policy areas. This applies both to evaluation and to judgements of competence. The interrelationships here are those already illustrated. Secondly, we should allow the possibility that more general assessments of the impact of the EU could affect policy evaluation, and might have more influence on support for further efforts than those based on particular policy evaluations. That is, something more general and diffuse than evaluations of specific policies might determine attitudes towards integration.

Full operationalization of these concepts is explained in the appendix of this chapter. In brief they are as follows, all taken from the MEP/MNP surveys:

- General EU impact—combined assessment of extent to which the EU over-regulates, damages the national economy and treats the nation unfairly in the EU budget
- Economic/Other policy evaluation; as explained above
- Institutional support: confidence in EU decisions
- Support EU authority in economic areas: extent to which people think that the EU rather than the national governments should legislate in Economic/Other policy areas
- Support for EU authority in non-economic areas: approval of increasing authority of EU
- Support more integration: favour increase in EU role in policy-making.

The complex interrelationships between these variables mean the model cannot be estimated as a single regression equation. Rather, we must estimate a set of equations. The underlying model and its estimated parameters are shown in Figures 10.2 and 10.3, using data on MEPs and MNPs respectively.[2] Each arrow indicates the assumed direction of the relationship. Where there is no arrow, there is assumed to be no link. Numbers attached to the arrows are standardized (partial) regression coefficients, indicating the direct impact of one variable on another, controlling for others as appropriate. Standardized variables are expressed in terms of their own standard deviations. A coefficient of, for instance, .33 indicates that a change of one standard deviation in the independent variable would bring about a change of one third of a standard deviation in the dependent variable. (Standard deviations for all variables in the model are shown in the appendix of this chapter or in Table 10.2.) The coefficients within each box show R^2, and indicate the proportion of variance explained in that variable by those antecedent to it.

Both sets of results tell a similar tale with respect to the impact of policy evaluation on support for an increase in EU authority. It is modest, and what impact such evaluation does have is indirect, via greater confidence in EU decisions and support for a greater degree of EU authority in that broad policy area. Nonetheless, about 25 percent of variance is explained in support for more EU authority among MEPs, and about 15 percent is so attributable in the case of MNPs. Neither among MEPs nor MNPs is there any significant direct link between policy evaluation and support for more EU authority in general. Even so, there is evidence for the argument that elites who evaluate policy

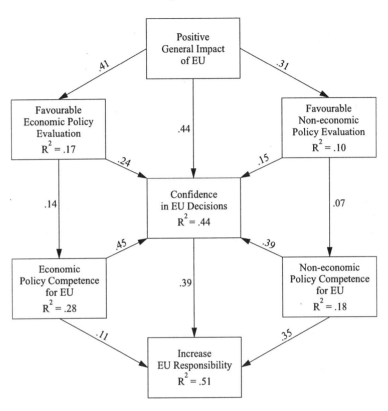

FIG. 10.2. Spillover Model for MEPs

more favourably are more inclined to support a stronger EU role in an area, and support an increase in EU authority more generally.

Assessments of economic policy have much more impact on support for EU decision-making than do non-economic policy assessments. In the case of MNPs, there are no significant links at all between the evaluation of non-economic policies and confidence in the EU or support for more EU authority in general. In the case of MEPs, there is a small but significant link with confidence in EU decisions. By contrast, all links from the economic policy assessment variables are significant, and quite strong in the case of the link to confidence in decisions.

There are also some notable differences between the two sets of results. This is most evident in the relationship between the general impact measures and the policy evaluation measures. In the case of MNPs, there is simply no significant relationship between the two, whereas for MEPs, general impact explains 17 percent of variance for the economic policy evaluations and 10 percent for the evaluation of other policy. A second difference is that for MEPs the explained variance is 51 percent and for MNPs only 31 percent. At most points in the model, the relationship is stronger for MEPs than for MNPs.

The contrast between the apparent spillover from the economic evaluations and the lack of it in the non-economic area might be considered to be due to the disparate nature of the non-economic policies included in the index. It is possible that some of these, including the two "high" politics items, defence and foreign policy, might actually

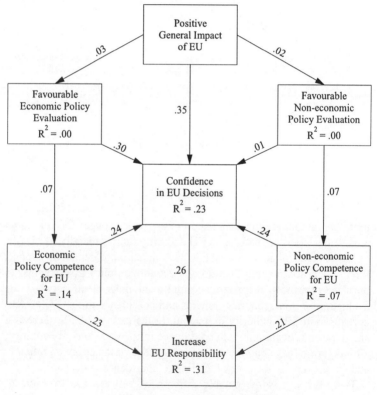

FIG. 10.3. Spillover Model for MNPs

exhibit spillover. However, experiments with alternative formulations, for instance separating the foreign and security policies from the rest and running the model with three types of policy, or simply with two types, economic and defence/foreign policy, told much the same story of the predominance of the economic items. This analysis thus confirms the lack of spillover in the "high" politics area, bearing out the assertion made by Hoffman (1966) that was discussed earlier. Furthermore, a stepwise regression, including all seventeen policy variables along with confidence in EU decisions as predictors of support for more EU authority underlined the importance of agriculture and monetary policy as most significant, both components of the economic policy scale. Neither foreign policy, nor defence and security policy, featured here.

CONCLUSIONS

This brief chapter set out to examine the evidence for spillover among parliamentary elites: to assess the extent to which support for more integration could be said to stem from approval of what has been done so far. We started by examining assessments of 17 policy areas. Evaluations varied quite naturally between the different areas. While MEPs were no more or less critical than MNPs, they did seem to have a wider variety of viewpoints across the many issues. There was some evidence to suggest that criticism of policy-making to date stemmed rather more from omission than from commission: areas in which the EU had greater responsibility evidenced less criticism. Criticism was greatest where the issue most demanded political action and yet the EU had least authority to act.

The implications of policy evaluations for parliamentarians' willingness to support increased EU competencies was then examined. We did not find the strong link between favourable policy evaluation and support for more integration that underpins the functionalist and neo-functionalist approach to the understanding of European integration, but there was evidence of a modest, but largely indirect effect. There was also evidence that such spillover was more apparent in the case of economic policy. In general there was almost no evidence of spillover in the non-economic area.

For the most part MEPs and MNPs do not differ much either in their assessments of EU policy or in the manner in which this affects their views on more integration. MEPs' views on the latter are, however, more explicable in terms of the variables used here: more variance is explained. While this may mean that MNPs' attitudes stem from a different set of causes, it is more reasonable to suggest that the difference is due to the greater interest in and knowledge about the details of EU policy among MEPs. They have thought about some of these questions a little more, and so there is less random error or "noise" in their answers. The greater variety of response shown in Table 10.1 is consistent with this interpretation.

NOTES

1   All unweighted.
2   This model was estimated by maximum likelihood methods using the AMOS program. An initial estimation with independent error terms for each of the endogenous variables gave much the same results as those in Figures 10.2 and 10.3 but the fit of the model was poor. Allowing covariation between the error terms for each of the issue evaluation and issue perception variables greatly improved the fit without altering the estimated parameters very much. For the model as a whole chi square is 93.3 with df 14; CFI = .98, AGFI = .94 and RMSEA = .06. For MEPs covariance is .48 between evaluation error terms and .75 between the competence error terms; for MNPs the coefficients are .59 and .67. This may be interpreted substantively as the probable effect of factors like nationality and party on the parliamentarians' attitudes.

APPENDIX

General Impact of EU is an index constricted by averaging responses to three statements, each measured on a seven-point agree strongly/disagree strongly scale. These are:
- "The EU subjects member states to too much regulation"
- "The EU has greatly harmed the <national> economy"
- "The financial contribution of < nation> to the EU is too high compared to what other member states contribute"

The polarity of the index was reversed to make low scores negative.

The economic and non-economic policy competence indexes are produced by averaging responses to the questions: "To what extent should each of the following policy areas be decided at the national level and to what extent at the European level," where on a seven-point scale 1 denoted policy-making exclusively at the national level and 7 policy-making exclusively at the European level. Policy areas were identical to those employed in the policy evaluation indexes.

Confidence in EU decisions is measured by responses to the question: "How much confidence do you have that decisions made by the EU will be in the interest of your country?" Response options were: a great deal of confidence, a fair amount of confidence, not very much confidence, no confidence at all. The first response was given 4, the next 3, the next 2 and no confidence was scored 1. Finally, attitudes towards further extensions of EU authority were measured by the question: "One of the major issues presently facing the EU is the increasing of the range of responsibilities of the EU. Do you favour or are you against increasing the range of responsibilities of the EU?" Respondents were asked to indicate their answer on a seven-point scale where one extreme was very much in favour and the other very much against. This is scored 1-7 where higher number indicates support for increasing responsibilities.

Details of scores on these variables are given below.

TABLE A.1. Variables Included in Model

Variable	Mean	Std Dev
Economic policy competence: 1 National ... 7 European	4.34	1.16
Non-Economic policy competence: 1 National ... 7 European	3.80	0.91
Impact of EU on nation: 1 Bad ... 7 Good	4.71	1.07
Economic policy evaluations: 1 Bad ... 7 Good	2.63	0.97
Non economic policy evaluations: 1 Bad ... 7 Good	2.75	0.67
Increase EU policy/responsibility: 1 Against ... 7 In favour	3.59	1.78
Confidence in EU decisions: 1 No ... 4 Yes	1.80	0.67

Note: All missing values replaced with appropriate MEP/MNP mean for that variable.

11

Institutional Change and the Future Political Order

BERNHARD WESSELS

INTRODUCTION

ONE of the major challenges for the future is to solve the problem of democratic decision-making and political representation in the European Union. The current institutional order is far from sufficient to satisfy the demands. The satisfaction of members of parliament with the existing political order in the European Union is rather low. Neither are they particularly satisfied with the policy performance of the EU or with the working of democracy in general. Representatives at the European and the national level share these views (Table 11.1). Even if there were not a public debate about the quality and form of democracy in the European Union, this situation would demand institutional change. One of the major problems, if not the most important problem, is how to arrange representation at the two levels and how to link them. On the one hand, this is a purely technical problem of co-ordination. On the other hand, it is a problem of political order in general. Clearly, the technical co-ordination problems and the problems of political institutional order are interrelated. At the moment, and for day-to-day politics, technical co-ordination problems are of more practical relevance. For the future, the problem of political order is of greater relevance. Without further institutional development, one might imagine a situation similar to that of a cultural gap (Ogburn 1950), except that in this case the gap is a widening one between state-building and democracy.

TABLE 11.1. Parliamentarians' Satisfaction with the Working of Democracy in the European Union and in Their Countries

	MEP		MNP	
	EU %	own country %	EU %	own country %
very satisfied	5	14	3	15
fairly satisfied	46	58	47	65
not very satisfied	37	22	40	17
not at all satisfied	13	7	10	3
N = 100 %	310	1392		

It is not at all clear which institutional means might help to narrow, or even to avoid, the gap. The debate about the future political order of the European Union is very complex and inspired by many different considerations. Members of parliament at the national level might have a different view than members of the European Parliament, the political left other views than centre or conservative parties. This chapter evaluates the institutional changes parliamentarians in Europe envisage.

DEMAND FOR INSTITUTIONAL CHANGE

One of the major problems of the multi-level policy-making and representation of the European Union is co-ordination and control. Who one believes should be co-ordinated in action and who should be controlled clearly depends on the political order one has in mind. Should parliaments or governments play a larger role? Should national parliaments have better means to control their governments' action at the European level? Should control be organized at the European or national level?

Democracy has to solve the problems both of efficient policy-making and of democratic representation (Shepsle 1988). The first can be regarded as a co-ordination problem; the second is a two-sided problem. It relates to control and accountability on the one hand and to the link between representatives and represented on the other. Judging from the views of parliamentarians with respect to all three aspects, i.e., better co-ordination, better control, and better linkages, institutional improvements can be made.

Judging from the demands for institutional improvements, co-ordination between levels seems to be the most central concern of parliamentarians at both levels. At both levels almost two-thirds favour joint committees to debate community proposals and joint committee meetings. There is basically no difference in judgement in this respect between MNPs and MEPs. The proposal to have a cabinet minister in national governments responsible for European affairs is strongly supported by European-level parliamentarians (82 percent), but less strongly by members of national parliaments (63 percent). In contrast, stronger links between European Commissioners and members of national parliaments are more strongly favoured by national parliamentarians. On the one hand, these results clearly indicate that representatives at both levels perceive a major co-ordination problem. On the other hand, they also reveal differences with respect to the latter two proposals, which might stem from different views on the role of the institutions from which they come. A cabinet minister for European affairs clearly would strengthen the European level. A stronger link between commissioners and national parliamentarians would strengthen the national influence on European politics (Figure 11.1).

Improvement of democratic control and accountability also seems to be of central concern for parliamentarians in Europe. One institutional means would be to make the debates about legislative proposals in the Council of Ministers a matter of public record. This clearly would increase transparency as well as the possibility to hold ministers accountable. Almost 90 percent of the members of the European Parliament favour this proposal; for members of national parliaments the figure is 75 percent, somewhat lower but still very high. Another possibility would be to have "instructed ministers," i.e., ministers attending the Council should follow the instructions of their national parliaments. Two-thirds of MNPs and about 57 percent of MEPs favour this proposal. A third aspect of control is the recruitment of the European Commission. More than 60 percent of the members of the European Parliament want the Commission to be elected by the European Parliament, while only 42 percent of the MNPs favour parliamentary election of the Commission. These figures indicate that parliamentarians in Europe see even more need for change of control mechanisms than for co-ordination. But again, differences in strength of demands between

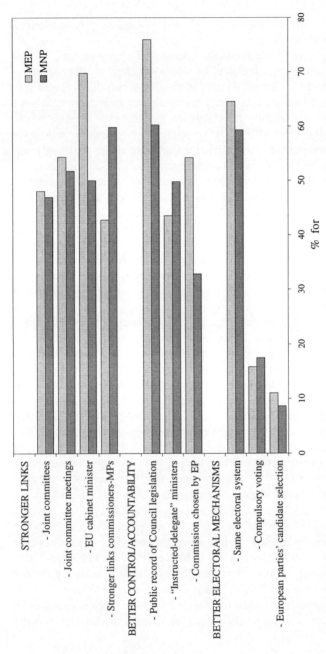

Fig. 11.1. Evaluation of Proposals for Institutional Change

Judgements based on a seven-point scale ranging from 1 (very much for) to 7 (very much against). Percentages represent portion of answers with scale values of 1, 2, and 3.

levels are visible. They follow the same patterns as for co-ordination: those strengthening European level politics are more favoured by members of the European Parliament; those strengthening control capacities at the national level are more favoured by national parliamentarians (Figure 11.1).

The last aspect, strengthening the linkages between elected and electorates, is clearly crucial for political representation. In an institutional sense, this relates to elections as the most central means of translating the wishes of the represented into distributions of power (Dahl 1971, 1975; Held 1996: 204). European elections still do not really compare to national elections. The 1999 European elections will be the first in which a proportional system is used in all countries, but European elections still are not equal elections, given that the number of voters per seat differs strongly between countries. This disproportionality exists for a good reason, to provide fair representation of smaller countries in the European Parliament. It is not at all clear whether members of parliament in Europe have this problem in mind when asking for the same electoral system in all member-states, but it is evident that parliamentarians at both the European and the national level regard a common single electoral system as necessary for European elections. More than two-thirds favour this. On the other hand, compulsory voting is regarded as a means of improving the electoral link by only a small number of MPs. Surprisingly, the proportion of parliamentarians supporting a European way of candidate selection for European elections is even lower than that for compulsory voting. Selecting candidates by European rather than national parties is regarded as the most effective means of overcoming the weakness of the European party system in the (scientific) debate (Franklin, van der Eijk, and Marsh 1996). The figures indicate, however, that parliamentarians do not see much need to change the system of candidate recruitment. The implication is that they do not see much need to strengthen the European parties either (Figure 11.1). Since support for this measure is low on both levels, one might conclude that MEPs as well as MNPs are relatively satisfied with the national routes to the European Parliament.

Some of these evaluations of proposals for institutional change obviously are related to the question of distribution of power or influence. In this respect, members of the European Parliament and the national parliaments clearly have a common view. First, their judgements about

the actual distribution of influence are very similar. Both groups regard
the Council of Ministers as the most influential institution in European
politics, followed by the European Commission, and the national governments, in that order. All three of these actors are regarded as having
much or very much influence. The European Parliament occupies a
middle position closer to "little" than "very much" influence, while the
national parliaments are least influential in the perceptions of European
parliamentarians. It is not surprising that this distribution of power does
not fit the interests of parliamentarians. Both groups of parliamentarians want more influence for the European as well as the national parliaments, with members of national parliaments even more supportive
than members of the EP. They also want the other three institutions to
have somewhat reduced influence (Figure 11.2). The resulting power
structure would not be a reversal of the existing one. Rather, the result
would be a more equalized distribution of power in which the European
Parliament would have equal influence with the Council of Ministers.

The power structure members of the European and national parlia-
ments envisage clearly gives parliaments at both levels a larger role.
This is the most obvious expression of the claim that democracy in the
European Union must be based on a stronger role of parliaments and

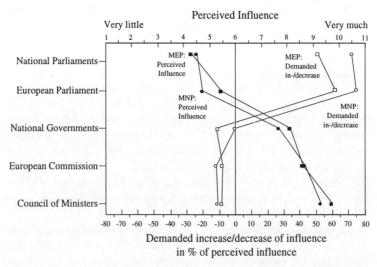

FIG. 11.2. Perceived Influence of Institutions of European Policy-making and
Demanded Increase or Decrease of Influence

therefore more strongly on directly democratically legitimized representation. It points to what Scharpf (1996a) has highlighted recently, that the democratic deficit is not confined to the European level, but includes the national level as well. Strengthening parliaments at both levels seems to be the strategy that parliamentarians prefer.

The institutional measures to improve co-ordination, control, and linkages elaborated above only weakly relate to the demand for a change in the power structure, but although the relations are rather weak, they reveal typical patterns. Institutional changes toward improvement of democratic control and accountability are related to the demand for more power for parliaments, in particular for the European Parliament, and a decrease in power of the national governments and the Council of Ministers. Improvement of linkages for representation is positively related to demand for more power for the European Parliament as well as the European Commission (Table 11.2).

These findings suggest that there might be more behind the demands for institutional improvements than just the wish to improve co-ordination between levels. They suggest that these demands might be based on different views about the future political order.

VIEWS ON THE FUTURE POLITICAL ORDER OF THE EUROPEAN UNION

With respect to the possible future of the political order in the European Union, models ranging from more technocratic and regulatory to full-fledged democratic systems are under discussion. The debate is both complex (Zürn 1995) and basically inspired by existing political models. The major alternatives can described in opposing terms: intergovernmentalism vs. parliamentarism or confederation vs. federation (W. Wessels 1996). These contrasts are not necessarily identical, since federalism can have a parliamentary as well as a presidential form. In the discussions about the future political order, however, they often coincide. The reason is that parliamentarism at the European level cannot be conceived without some kind of federal political order, given that the European Union is composed of different nations and the subsidiarity principle of the Union.

TABLE 11.2. Institutional Changes and Demanded Power Change

Demanded Change in Power Structure (Demanded − Perceived Influence)	Summary Measures for Improvements of		
	Coordination	Control	Links
National Parliaments	.15***	.12***	.08**
European Parliament	.14***	.30***	.28***
National Governments	.12***	-.14***	-.18***
European Council	.01	-.05	.20***
Council of Ministers	.08*	-.24***	.03

Entries are correlation coefficients.
*** sign. p < .000
** sign. p < .001
* sign. p < .010

The basic characteristic of the two most prominent alternative models of political order can be summarized quite parsimoniously. The intergovernmental model is based on the sovereignty of nation states. It is a kind of "pooling of sovereignties" (W. Wessels 1996: 23). The pooling of authority finds its representation in the Council. Parliament does not play a role in this model, at least not at the European level. At the national level, it is the basis of the legitimation of national governments acting at the European level.

The parliamentary model, sometimes equated with the federal model, would require a total rearrangement of the existing institutional setting. The role of the European Parliament at the European level would become similar to that of national parliaments in the member states. There is wide variation with respect to the concrete competencies of parliaments, their role in policy-making, etc. (Norton 1996a). However, national parliaments are legislative bodies and they elect governments.

There are many more implications of these two general models with respect to divisions of power and the shape of the concrete institutional setting, but basically they can be distinguished by the locus of democratic legitimation. In the intergovernmental model, the power of the European level comes from a pooling of authority of sovereign states, with national governments having the final say regarding the scope of the power of the European level. In the parliamentary model, at least if fully developed, power at the European level is high and its locus is the parliament.

Although the question of preferred political order cannot be directly addressed with our surveys, it can be indirectly addressed by making use of two indicators relating to the power of the European Union on the one hand and to the legislative authority of the European Parliament on the other hand. Combining these two questions, models of political order can be differentiated which come very close to the distinction between intergovernmentalism and parliamentarism. Conceptionalizing the two dimensions in simple dichotomies and combining them leads to a four-fold table, presenting the principle alternatives (Table 11.3).

If this classification is applied as a more gradual concept, comparing views of parliamentarians of different countries according to the proportions who either favour or not a system with high power and a European Parliament with high legislative competencies, three of the four cells defined in Table 11.3 show cases. Parliamentarians of Denmark, Sweden, Finland, France, and Ireland fall into the category weak state. Only about 15 to 35 percent favour a strong European Parliament and between 0 and 45 percent favour a European Union with increased responsibilities. But in France and Ireland, only a few percentage-points are missing to make the majority of their parliamentarians supporters of a strong intergovernmental order. Parliamentarians of Luxembourg and Portugal particularly favour strong intergovernmentalism, but those of Greece, the Netherlands, and Austria also fall in this category although being somewhat short of a majority for a strong parliamentary system. Representatives of Great Britain, Germany and even more those of Belgium, Spain, and Italy favour "strong parliamentarism" (Figure 11.3).

The question of where these differences in supranationalist orientations come from cannot be addressed here. However, given the distribution of countries, it is obvious that neither length of membership nor federalism at home determines the preferences for a particular political order (see Beyers 1998 for an exploration of some hypotheses). The differences indicate that there is no cross-nationally common view of

TABLE 11.3. Models of Political Order

		Responsibilities of the European Union	
		low	high
Power of the EP to pass laws which directly apply in the member states	low	Weak State	Strong Intergovernmentalism
	high	Weak Parliamentarism	Strong Parliamentarism

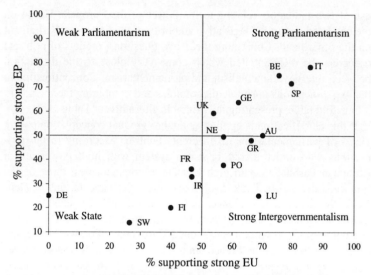

Based on a seven-point scale where 1 indicates very much in favour of a strong EU or EP and 7 indicates being against. Percentage of answers favouring.

FIG. 11.3. Preferences for Models of Political Order

parliamentarians on the future political order. Without a common perspective, however, it is unlikely that clear decisions on the future political order can easily be achieved.

The situation is even more complicated when differences between levels are taken into account. In some countries, potential tensions between the European level perspective and the national perspective are very strong. In particular in France, Luxembourg, and the Netherlands, majorities of members of national parliaments favour a different political order than their counterparts in the European Parliament. The direction of difference is most obvious: members of national parliaments in these countries tend to favour either a weak state or strong intergovernmentalism; MEPs in these countries favour strong parliamentarism (Table 11.4). It is also evident that the group classifications may be unstable where only plurality positions exist. Again, these findings indicate that it will not be easy to achieve a consensus about the future development of the political order at the EU-level, either between levels or within groups.

TABLE 11.4. Plurality/Majority Preference for Political Order of MEP and MNP

	Weak State	Strong Intergov-ernmentalism	Weak Parliamentarism	Strong Parliamentarism
AU				MEP (p)
BE				MEP; MNP
DE	MEP			
FI	MEP			
FR	MNP			MEP
GE				MEP; MNP(p)
GR		MNP (p)		MEP
IR	MEP; MNP			
IT				MEP; MNP
LU		MNP (p)		MEP
NE	MNP (p)			MEP
PO	MEP; MNP			
SP				MEP; MNP
SW	MEP; MNP			
GB				MEP

MEP = Members of the European Parliament (without [p] majority position, otherwise plurality position)
MNP = Members of National Parliaments (without [p] majority position, otherwise plurality position)

The struggle, if there will be one, is also a struggle about the distribution of power between institutions and between levels. Starting with a look at parliaments and their role, these four models clearly envisage quite different power distributions. Those favouring a weak state at the European level show high demand for an increase of influence of national parliaments, but much less desire for a power injection for the European Parliament. On the other side, MPs who favour the model of strong parliamentarism at EU-level clearly want to see a huge increase in power for the European Parliament but only a little one for national parliaments (Figure 11.4). However, whatever model they favour, parliamentarians share the view that parliaments in Europe need more power. The only difference is how much. This is different with respect to non-parliamentary institutions having a say in European politics. Those favouring a weak state at the European level want to see an increase in the power of national governments and a status quo situation for the Council of Ministers—the institutions on which the national level has major influence. Conversely, they want to see a decrease in the power of the European Commission. A weaker role for national

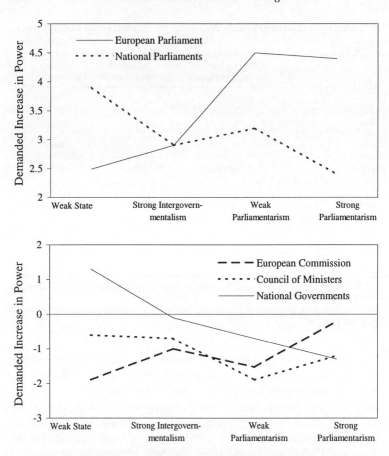

FIG. 11.4. Models of Political Order and Demanded Change
in Power Distribution Between Institutions

governments is most strongly favoured by those who prefer a strong European parliamentary system. Parliamentarians in favour of this model also want to see less influence for the Council of Ministers. That the construction of the European system is also a struggle about the distribution of power does not make it easier to come to grips with this most urgent task. To make things even more complicated, ideology matters as well.

THE ROLE OF IDEOLOGY

Cross cutting national and level differences, ideology also influences institutional preferences. According to Hix and Lord (1998: 209), the left-right dimensions and anti- or pro-integration attitudes define the cleavage system in the European Parliament. Hooghe and Marks (1999) explicitly argue that contestation in the European Union is defined by a two-dimensional political space: social democracy versus market liberalism constitutes one dimension; nationalism versus supranationalism the other. They argue that regulated capitalism is supported by the political left, neoliberalism by the political right.

The definitions of the neoliberal model on the one hand and the regulatory model on the other almost mirror the distinction between weak state and strong parliamentarism at the European level. The neoliberal project means insulating markets from political interference, implying resistance to a supranational Euro-polity. The model of regulated capitalism seeks to create a liberal democracy capable of regulating markets and redistributing resources. Central to this project is the deepening of democracy (Hooghe and Marks 1999: 82-8).

With respect to articulated need for institutional change in the fields of better co-ordination, better control and accountability, and better electoral linkage, empirical results support the hypothesis that ideas about political order and its improvements relate to ideology. In particular, better control is favoured more by the political left than by the right, fitting with the claim that a model of regulated capitalism is concerned also with deepening of democracy (Table 11.5). The question of power distribution also reflects differences in ideology. The political left clearly favours an increase in the power of the European Parliament more than the right, and disfavours an increase of powers of the European Commission and the Council of Ministers, which again indicates the concern with democratic means.

These findings suggest that supranationalism has its political home more with the left than the right. This is also reflected in the level of support for a strong European Union and a strong European Parliament. Whereas about seventy percent of the most leftist support both strong EU and strong EP, on the right only one-third are for a strong EP and almost a half for a strong EU (Figure 11.5).

TABLE 11.5. Left-Right Ideological Position, Institutional Change and
Preferred Political Order

	Correlation with Left-Right Self-placement
Better coordination (summary score)	.06
Better control (summary score)	.25***
Better electoral link (summary score)	.13***
Demand for increase in power of:	
- national parliaments	.04
- the European Parliament	.20***
- national governments	-.17***
- European Commission	.01
- Council of Ministers	-.18***

*** sig .000

Ideology is also reflected in preferences regarding a future political order. Two-thirds of the leftist MEPs and a small majority (52 percent) of leftist MNPs favour a strong parliamentary state. The corresponding figure for the political right is 25 percent for both levels. The majority of the political right favours a weak European state (Table 11.6). Ideology determines preferences for a future political order in a similar way at the European and the national level. This might be a sign that ideology can form a shell in which consensus can be reached across levels.

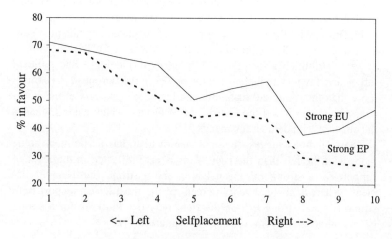

FIG. 11.5. EU-Power, EP Power, and Ideology

TABLE 11.6. State Model[a] and Political Ideology[b]

	MEP			MNP		
	Left %	Centre %	Right %	Left %	Centre %	Right %
Weak state	18	20	68	27	40	54
Strong non-parliamentary state	9	9	4	13	19	17
Weak parliamentary state	7	9	4	8	7	4
Strong parliamentary state	66	61	25	52	34	25
n = 100 %	122	142	28	390	776	175

a Combination of attitudes toward a European Parliament which had the power to pass laws directly and attitudes toward increasing range of responsibilities of the EU. Both 7-point scales, first three highest categories in favor against rest, combined as follows: not in favour of strong EP or strong EU: weak state; in favour of strong EU but not EP: strong non-parliamentary state; in favour of a strong EP but not EU: weak parliamentary state; in favour of strong EP and strong EU: strong parliamentary state.
b Left-Right self-placement on a 10-point scale, where 1 is left and 10 is right. 1, 2, 3 coded as left; 4, 5, 6, 7 coded as center; 8, 9, 10 coded as left.

But the finding also shows that tensions within levels might persist because they are founded in ideological differences.

CONCLUSION

This rather descriptive view of preferences for institutional change and political order shows what is obvious in the day-to-day debates about the future of the European Union. There seems to be no easy, and more importantly, no consensual solutions to overcome the existing problems. The whole bundle of ideas about changing Europe institutionally seems to be quite constrained in the minds of parliamentarians. Evaluations of concrete institutional reforms and more general preferences for a political order show the same pattern. On the one hand, this might be a good sign, since if ideas about concrete measures match ideas of a more general kind, the chance is higher that the outcome will be something that is internally consistent.

On the other hand, differences between parliamentarians of different countries and at different levels can result in very different opinions about the changes needed. There is no obvious majority position that has a chance to get through without serious opposition. Furthermore, there is a clear ideologically-based split in the envisaged prospects of the future Union. Ideology seems to be a mighty shell in this respect. It seems that differences between countries and between levels are cancelled out to a certain degree by ideological positions. But differences between the political left and political right are so striking that ideology on the one hand unites and on the other hand divides. Even if one of the ideological groups could claim that it represents the majority, it would be doubtful that it could implement its own vision of political order. The implementation of a political order at the European level needs consensus as a base. Majority decisions would not be accepted. Given the differences and tensions in attitudes between countries, levels, and ideological groups, it seems that consensus is far from feasible. If this is true, the same applies for the construction of a European political order.

PART IV

The European Parliament,
the National Parliaments,
and European Integration

12

Parliaments and Democracy in Europe in the Era of the Euro

RICHARD S. KATZ AND BERNHARD WESSELS

WHAT is now the European Union has been in a state of flux virtually since its inception as the European Coal and Steel Community in 1952. Progress toward "an ever closer union" has taken place in many steps that have involved both broadening and deepening of the Union: expanding the number of member states from 6 to 9 to 11 to 12 to 15; expanding the range of questions within the purview of Union institutions; expanding the level of Union activity and control over those policy areas in which it is involved. Arguably, however, the establishment of monetary union and the advent of the Euro as the single currency in 11 of the member states, represents the most fundamental change in the character of the Union since its founding.

Assuming that there is a real threshold between inter-governmentalism and the formation of a new, and at least semi-sovereign, entity, one could easily argue that with the introduction of the Euro, the EU has crossed that threshold. With the establishment of a single European Central Bank, the member states have, for the first time, ceded full authority over one of the traditional core responsibilities and powers of sovereign states to the supranational level. The magnitude of this step has been widely recognized, of course, not least in the decisions of those member states that elected not to join to Euro area.

Notwithstanding the tremendous political implications of monetary union, most of the discussion about and arguments for the Euro have focused on economics. Such concerns as efficiency in accounting, reduction in the costs of insuring against currency fluctuations, transparency of pricing, the relative market power of the EU versus the United States and the possibility of establishing a European rival to the dollar as the dominant currency of international trade have dominated the public discussion. The focus on such questions continues the pattern of debate that was typical of the first half century of the European Project, and which formed the basis of the so-called permissive consensus under which European integration is said to have progressed, at least until the difficulties surrounding the ratification of the Maastricht Treaty called it into question. Put simply, economic advantage trumped concern with democratic norms; so long as advocates of further integration could claim that their agenda either was dictated by the realities of economic "globalization" and the exigencies of "the market," or indeed simply that their policies would improve the economic well-being of citizens, there was very little discussion of the political costs involved.

It has not been our purpose in this book, and it is not our purpose in this concluding chapter, either to support or to question the economic arguments that have in any case been thoroughly debated elsewhere. We observe, however, that the idea of basing further progress toward European integration on a permissive consensus has been substantially challenged since the signing the Maastricht Treaty. As we suggested in the first chapter of this book, one reason why the Maastricht Treaty rather than the Single European Act proved to be the flashpoint is precisely because of its objective of establishing a single European currency.

Money is of central political concern for two types of reasons. One is substantive. If the state of the economy is one of the key determinants of government popularity and electoral success (Lewis-Beck 1990), then loss of power by national governments over monetary policy is of tremendous significance. On one hand, there will be increased (and perhaps also increasingly justified) temptation to "blame it on Europe" when the economy turns downward, as capitalist economies inevitably do from time to time. A parallel tendency to blame painful economic policies on globalization has been apparent for many years, but in the "blame it on Europe" scenario, the target is much more easily identified. The virtually inevitable result will be to increase the visibility of the lack of democratic accountability at the European level. Even if the capacity of political decision-makers really to manipulate the economy is often exaggerated, the obvious inability of voters to use the political decision-makers as scapegoats by turning them out of office is likely to have a significant effect in eliminating an important safety valve, and in focusing popular discontent on institutions rather than on individuals.

The other type of reason why money is of such central concern is symbolic. Aside from a national language, money is the most obvious symbol of nationhood. While changing money at the border may be both a nuisance and an expense, it emphasizes the differences between "us" and "them." Every time the citizen makes a purchase, there is a tangible reminder of national sovereignty and distinctiveness.

We make these points not because we are unconcerned here with the economic wisdom of monetary union, but because monetary union has added even greater weight and immediacy to the problem of the democratic deficit in the European Union, and in European political life more generally. Whether real or an illusion, whether based on dereliction by the framers of existing European institutions or on their inability to meet an impossible goal, the problem of maintaining or establishing democratic accountability at both the supranational and the national levels has taken on renewed urgency in the era of the Euro.

Of course, the problem of institutional reform that has been accentuated by monetary union is not the only pressing issue on the European agenda, but it is implicated in many of them. There is pressure for further harmonization within policy areas already heavily penetrated by Europe. An example is the proposal for greater coordination of tax regimes and standardization of tax rates. On a purely economic level, this proposal obviously is in the economic and political interest of countries with higher tax rates since, to the extent that higher rates were agreed, it would allow them to minimize the competitive disadvantages they suffer when advantageous tax rates can be used by other countries to attract business, while to the extent that their tax rates are lowered, they can externalize the political fall-out resulting from budget cuts and service reductions. But as this suggests, it also involves further ceding of authority to the supranational level, with the same kinds of accountability and legitimacy problems that are raised by the Euro. Similarly, while further shifts of authority to the European level may be necessary if environmental concerns are to be addressed, and while preservation of the environment may be to the general advantage of all Europeans, neither protection nor restoration of the environment will be without costs. Under the current institutional structure of the EU, this means, contrary to normal democratic practice, giving the authority to impose those costs to officials who, effectively and/or in the public's mind, are accountable to no one. Again, policies that may be justified for nonpolitical reasons have the effect of highlighting the democratic inadequacies of current institutional arrangements.

The problems of democratic legitimation also will be aggravated by proposals to increase the range of EU competencies. For a common European defence or foreign policy to advance beyond the current ineffective system of ad hoc consultation would require the member states to make a further substantial cession of one of the core powers of sovereign states. Likewise, to cede control over external borders or internal security to the supranational level also would strip the national states of a key characteristic of sovereignty.

Supranational coordination is perfectly compatible with national sovereignty, so long as each state retains the right to veto or opt out of common decisions. As has been recognized in the expansion of the EU to include Austria, Finland, and Sweden, however, coordination and national vetoes and opt-outs become increasingly unworkable as the number of member states increases. This is already seen to require more decisions by majority (whether qualified or not) voting. Even some of the basic organizational practices of the EU, like the require-ment that every member state have one judge on the European Court of Justice and at least one member of the Commission would become unworkable were the EU to be joined by a significant number of Mid-dle and East European states. Both the increased use of majority voting and the possibility that some member states will not be represented on all EU bodies would further undermine the path of legitimation that runs from the voters through their national governments and ultimately to the EU, since they raise the possibility that a state will become committed by decisions in whose making it had no voice, and the probability that states will become committed by decisions in whose making they were out voted. If European integration is to advance along any of these dimensions, it will be necessary to address the institutional question and its relation to democratic legitimation. This book has tried to elaborate and explain the problems and tensions, the prerequisites and possible solutions, to the ever urgent question of the role of parliaments as reflected in the attitudes and opinions of members of parliaments in the era of the Euro.

A SUMMARY OF FINDINGS

As we have demonstrated in this book, studying the attitudes and opinions of members of the European Parliament and of the national parliaments of the member states is an apt way to address questions about the future both of the structure of the EU and about its policies. Because of the centrality of representative bodies to all western conceptions of democracy in large states (e.g., Mill 1861: ch. 3), it is clear that any resolution of the problems of European accountability and legitimation will have to involve a major role for parliaments. Which level of parliament (national or European), and how the role for parliament will be institutionalized, are still open questions. What is not open to question is that any successful strategy for democratic legitimation must include a significant role for some level of parliament.

The question of the democratic deficit and perceptions of it, is not commonly addressed at the elite level rather than at the mass level. Traditionally, discussion of the democratic deficit has instead figured in debates concerning mass-support models (Niedermayer and Sinnot 1995b). However, since the European political system is still in the making, and still an elite project despite the larger role now played by public opinion; and since whatever the democratic pretensions either of the EU or of its member states, decisions about Europe—like decisions about virtually every other question—generally are taken by elites and then justified to the electorate, elite preferences and expectations are particularly important to any assessment of alternative futures and their possibilities. While public opinion must play a central role in any democracy, public opinion in most cases is reactive rather than proactive, and much of what it reacts to is the proposals and decisions of elites.

Our research has suggested a number of conclusions about the possible futures of the European project. Many of these have been elucidated in the various chapters, but it is useful to recapitulate the principal findings here, bringing together the related findings of different chapters. What then are the conclusions that we can draw from this study, and what are their implications for the future of European integration?

One conclusion is that an identifiable, professional, European parliamentary elite is emerging. The idea that was often expressed in the early days of the directly elected European Parliament—that it would become a dumping ground or retirement sinecure for politicians whose national political careers had faltered, a comfortable junket for political amateurs or a cushy reward for party supporters, or merely an early stepping stone for a career in domestic politics—have been refuted. MEPs look very much like MNPs both in the mix of their demographic characteristics and in their professional backgrounds. While there are more MEPs who aspire to national political careers than there are MNPs whose career hopes would lead to EU institutions, there is a substantial corps of MEPs who see their professional political futures at the European level. Similarly, while national as well as European level interest groups are in frequent contact with MEPs, there is an apparent separation between MEPs whose attention is focused primarily on national groups and those whose primary focus is on European level organizations. Just as in the national parliaments, where there are some MPs who see themselves primarily as members of local political systems who happen, for the time being, to be representing their localities at the national level, and other MPs who perceive themselves primarily to be participating in a national political system made up of various constituencies (whether defined by geography or interest or demographics) one or more of which they are representing, so in the European Parliament there is a mix of national members who happen to be working in Europe and European members who happen to represent their particular national or sub-national constituencies.

We also found that MEPs have developed a stake both in the institutions of the European Union in general, and in the European Parliament in particular. The "where you stand depends on where you sit" hypothesis is clearly supported with regard to attitudes toward Europe. In comparison to MNPs from the same countries, the members of the European parliament are more likely to believe that the democratic legitimacy of the EU should be based on European elections, that the competencies of the EU should be increased, and especially to favour a greater role for the European Parliament in the process of EU decision-making. Particularly in this last respect, however, while there is a significant difference between the views of MEPs and MNPs, with the former more strongly favouring an increased role for the EP, there is also a great similarity. MPs at both levels appear dissatisfied with the current role of parliament at both levels. MNPs also favour an increased role for the EP, they simply do not favour it as strongly as

MEPs, while MEPs favour an increased role for the national parliaments as well as for their own institution. Thus, while we find some evidence of an emerging European elite, we also find evidence of an emerging "EP branch" of a broader European parliamentary class.

Overall, there is considerable evidence that the EP is developing, and indeed has developed, the pool of talent and a body of members with the mix of attitudes and role orientations that would be required for it successfully to play a central role in the European Union. This appears to have three sources. The first is simply the general location of the members of the European Parliament, and indeed of the pool of candidates from which they are selected, in a European elite, much of which is pro-Europe and pro-parliament. If, as most observers would agree has been the case, European integration has been primarily an elite project, it is not surprising to find that members of the elite are generally supportive of it. And if, as is also clearly the case, parliament plays a central role in the dominant "legitimizing myth" of European democracy (Wildenmann 1986), it is not surprising to find that individuals who have made their careers in democratic politics are generally supportive of a strong parliamentary role.

The second reason why the EP has developed a membership adequate for a central role in the governing of Europe lies in patterns of recruitment. Whether through self-selection or party selection, candidates are coming forward, being nominated to winnable constituencies or placed in winnable positions on party lists, and then ultimately entering the chamber of the EP, who both have the necessary skills to serve effectively and who have attitudes that are favourable to the European project. Finally, the third basis of these developments is socialization within the EP. In contrast to earlier studies, our ability to compare the views expressed by newcomers to the EP when they were still unelected candidates with the opinions expressed by the same individuals after they had served in the EP for a relatively brief period enabled us to detect the impact of socializing processes that take place quite quickly. While these forces were found to be modest, they nonetheless were there. We also found patterns that are consistent with a (possibly longer-term) more complex process of socialization affecting not so much individual attitudes about Europe as the way in which patterns of attitudes are structured.

Against this background of similarity among MEPs and between MEPs and MNPs, we also found significant, and more importantly, understandable, differences. First, as already suggested, there are significant differences across levels: that is between MEPs and MNPs. MPs tend to be more favourably disposed toward the political level and the particular parliament in which they are serving than they are toward the political system and parliament at the other level. MEPs tend to be more pro-Europe with regard to the level at which various problems should be addressed. MEPs also tend to be more pro-EP with regard to the level at which increased parliamentarization of European affairs should be focused.

Second, we found differences across policy areas. The willingness of MPs, and presumably of members of the European political elites more generally, to see policy competence transferred to the European level appears to be strongly influenced both by the nature of specific problem areas and by the ways they have been dealt with at the national level.

Some policies are dealt with at the European level more easily than others because they affect all member states in roughly the same way; other policies, because they are important to some countries but not to others, are less natural candidates for Europeanization. We found that the greater the convergence of the problem load, i.e., the greater convergence of problems across countries, the greater was the willingness of elected representatives to see authority shifted to the supranational level.

Even more significant than the convergence of problem load was problem scope. Some problems can be addressed more effectively at the European level because, by their very nature, they are border-crossing in character, while others problems can be addressed effectively on a national or subnational basis. The classic example of a border-crossing (high scope) problem is, of course, air-borne pollution, but with the advance of the single-market ideals of free movement of capital and people other problems that in the past could have been regarded as having low cross-border scope such as immigration and monetary policy have joined the environment, defence, and foreign policy as high scope policy areas. We found that the higher the cross-border problem scope, the greater was the willingness of elected representatives to see authority shifted to the supranational level.

Shifts of authority to the supranational level naturally unsettle existing patterns of policy and policy-making at the national level. We found that the more satisfactory and the more entrenched those patterns are, the less was the enthusiasm expressed for transfer of authority to the European level. In particular, in contrast to the hypothesis that European integration would spell the end of corporatist decision-making, and in contrast as well to the hypothesis that national level corporatism would be translated to the European level as a way of maintaining corporatist arrangements, we found that the strength of corporatist groups has a constraining impact on Euro-enthusiasm; the stronger national corporatist arrangements are, the less willing representatives are to see authority shifted to the European level in those policy domains for which corporatism is most relevant.

As this suggests, the third major set of differences is between nations. Increased globalization, national specialization, and trade all have reduced the "economic sovereignty" of all states in the sense that they are less able to carry on an autonomous economic life. The level of economic independence from which these trends started, and the degree to which they have left individual nations enmeshed in, and dependent on, an inter-national economy varies, however. In the limiting case of prior complete self-sufficiency, ceding of economic policy-making to the European level would involve a substantial loss of sovereignty and of autonomous control. In the other limiting case—total dependence on international trade and globalized markets—however, increased authority at the European level might well represent an opportunity at least to participate in the making of effective economic policy in place of near total lack of control. On the basis of this reasoning, we anticipated that MPs from countries whose economies are more internationally dependent would be more favourably disposed toward increased competence for the EU, and this hypothesis was confirmed by our analysis.

In the same vein as the (confirmed) hypothesis that greater strength of the social partners in domestic corporatist arrangements would be associated with lesser enthusiasm for shifting competencies to the European level, we also expect that members of national parliaments that are relatively strong will be less likely to favour weakening those parliaments by transferring authority to the European level, where parliament obviously is relatively weak. Again our hypothesis was supported, with the qualification that an institutionally strong but effectively unsatisfactory parliament (i.e., the Italian case) does not disincline MPs to support transferring authority to the European level.

Finally, we found that experience with the EU and national strength within it also bear on the degree to which MPs express "pro-European" views. MPs from countries that have been members of the EEC/EC/EU for longest tend to be the most pro-European. Similarly, MPs from the countries that have the greatest weight within the EU (the biggest countries, with more MEPs, more members of the Commission, and more heavily weighted votes in the Council), also tend to express more pro-European views.

ALTERNATIVE FUTURES

No one knows what direction the course of further European integration will be, or, indeed, even if there will be further progress toward a more integrated Europe. It is, however, possible on the basis of the enormous scholarly, journalistic, and political literatures on the subject, to suggest in general terms a number of potential or alternative futures. Each has attractive features, but each also has liabilities both in the shape of serious impediments to being achieved and in the shape of negative consequences if it were to be approximated. Allusion has already been made to many of these attractions and also many of these problems in the preceding chapters. Here again we bring some of these points together.

The first possible future to consider is the model of Europe as an emerging supra-state, i.e., the project of the Euro-federalists. The assumption underlying this model is that as the European Union comes to exercise ever more of the functions traditionally associated with the sovereignty of national states, it also will adopt institutions and practices like those currently found at the national level. The problem of democratic legitimation at the European level would then simply be the problem of national democratic legitimation, but now reproduced on a continental scale.

There are two related problems that would have to be overcome before such a scenario could be realized, however. On one hand, this scenario requires the development of a real European party system, not just a series of loose federations of broadly similar, or similarly denominated, national parties. On the other hand, it also requires the development of a single European demos: an acceptance of membership in a single political community such that the losers of elections or parliamentary decisions would see the resulting decision as having been legitimately made by a majority of "us" rather than having been arbitrarily and illegitimately imposed on "us" by a majority of "them." Neither of these conditions appears to be close to realization.

In fact, one can distinguish two variants of the Euro-federalist model: a parliamentary type and a presidentialist type. The need for strong parties is most obvious in the parliamentary type, since this would require that the European government be able to command a coherent and continuous majority in the EP. If a European government is to be legitimate because it emerges from European parliamentary elections several conditions must be met. First, the choices offered voters in one country must be equivalent to those offered voters in the others; if French voters have one set of options and German voters have another, there can be no European majority choice. Second, the distinctions among the choices offered must be based on relevant, i.e., European level, questions; so long as European elections are treated by voters and parties as second-order national elections, they cannot impart legitimacy at the European level. Third, there must be cross-nationally recognized and recognizable European party leaders. Together, these imply the existence of cohesive European parties, able to propose coherent policy programs to the voters and then to take responsibility for their implementation. While the presidentialist model would require less party cohesion in the European Parliament, it would require even stronger party organization outside the parliament since it would require each party eventually to present a single presidential candidate rather than merely a team of leaders. Moreover, if the European electorate is to choose a head of government in a meaningful direct election, the number of candidates, and thus the number of parties presenting candidates, would have to be severely limited, again implying the existence of strong pan-European parties.

Our analysis, however, suggests that there are very serious obstacles to be overcome before a real European party system could emerge. There are still quite substantial differences among national parties of the same European denomination, both with regard to the "European question" of how much and what kind of Europe there should be, and with regard even to the "simpler" questions of what policies the EU should pursue on questions that are already agreed to be within its purview. In many cases, these cross-national differences are as big or bigger than the cross-party differences. Until the primary distinction is left versus right (or positions on some equivalent dimension) rather than British versus Italian or Swedish versus Portuguese, there can be no European party government. Moreover, the emergence of an effective European party system at the parliamentary level would require MEPs to see their primary point of reference to be their EP party groups rather than their national parties, and their primary peer group to be MEPs of the same party group but different countries rather than MEPs from their own country who are members of different party groups. What we found, however, is that those MEPs whose role perceptions most emphasize the ideals of party government are more, rather than less, orientated toward their national parties.

The question of developing a European demos is beyond the immediate focus of our research (although see the companion volume of Schmitt and Thomassen 1999), but we can say that such a shift in mass thinking is only likely to occur in response to messages sent by the political elites. Thus, the fact that those politicians who are most committed to party government understand that to refer to party at the *national level* is likely to impede the formation of a single European demos as well.

The second possible future is the model of Europe as a confederation, in which sovereignty continues to be located primarily at the national level, and democratic legitimacy, as well as decision-making authority, is "delegated" by the national governments to the European Union. As an abstract ideal, this model corresponds to John C. Calhoun's (1943) theory of "concurrent majorities." While written in an earlier century and for a different (and already more strongly federated) system, the theory corresponds quite well to the ideal of a European confederation of sovereign states.

The essential problem that Calhoun's theory addresses is how one can have popularly (we would now say democratically) legitimated government in the absence of a single people for whom simple majority rule (i.e., national party government) would be appropriate. The answer Calhoun offers is to require majority acceptance of decisions not by an overall majority, but by a majority of *each* of the constituent peoples. In this way, no one of the constituent peoples can ever feel that it has had a policy forced upon it by some combination of the other peoples. This, of course, is precisely analogous to the justification for the national veto at the European level, and Calhoun's answer to the question of why any group would ever consent to a decision that is not to its own advantage—and indeed why every group would not always try to blackmail the others into accepting decisions that would be particularly to its own advantage—is the same as that offered at the European level for restrained use of the national veto option. So long as every people/nation perceives itself to be better off with the confederation than it would be were the confederation to be dissolved, they will be willing to compromise and to accept short term costs to preserve their long term gains.

As a strategy for European legitimation, concurrent majorities has three essential prerequisites, two of which have been substantially undermined by the course that European integration actually has taken, and the third of which arguably never was present. First, concurrent majorities would require unanimity among the member states. This could be expressed as a unanimous (albeit perhaps compromised and bundled) vote in the Council, or by unanimous coincidence of national majorities in the European Parliament, or by unanimous acceptance by majorities in the national parliaments. Except for modification of the treaties themselves, however, there has been steady movement (generally described as progress) away from requiring unanimity in favour of decision by qualified or even simple majority.

Second, concurrent majorities requires that there be sufficient commonality of interest that everyone will see the long term gains to outweigh the short term costs. The more the EU has expanded geographically, the more problematic this has become, and the more difficult the compromises required. An early and dramatic example of this problem came with the British budgetary question in 1979 (Dinan 1994: 109), but more recently even Germany has begun to question whether it is "getting its money's worth" from the EU. If the EU expands geographically again to include an even more diverse set of members, and if its competencies are expanded into more policy areas in which there is not a fundamental harmony of interest, this problem will be further exacerbated.

Third, concurrent majorities requires that those consenting to decisions on behalf of their nations be democratically authorized to do so. In part the difficulty is that so long as European affairs are marginal to national politics, it is problematic to assert that the mandate conveyed to national governments by national elections extends to their participation as members of the Council of Ministers in decisions made in

Brussels. Given the de facto status of European elections as second-order national elections, this problem applies to the European Parliament with nearly as much force as it applies to the members of the Council. This effectively has been true since the formation of the ECSC, and *faute de mieux* is why the idea of a permissive consensus has been important. Moreover, beyond the question of whether national elections can convey European legitimacy, there is the question of whether, in the absence of decision-making by unanimity (and probably with this decision rule as well), the Europeanization of decision and the externalization of blame by national politicians is undermining the capacity of, and perhaps also the self-interest of, national political systems to legitimate the European enterprise in any form.

The third future would be for a pluralist, technocratic, Europe. This would be a system arguably like the present, in which decisions are made by technocrats informed by, but not fundamentally accountable to, a variety of "popular" inputs—from MEPs, from the national governments, from European and national interest organizations, etc. Some, of course, would claim that this is really the way in which all liberal democratic governments in mass societies operate. And if there has indeed been a permissive consensus, it has been produced by the success of policies made in this way.

As we observed in earlier chapters, however, whatever the efficiency or efficacy of pluralist technocracy, at best it engenders tolerance, not legitimacy. Moreover, it engenders a highly conditional tolerance, that may not be transferable from one policy arena to another, even if the overall balance is positive. To date, most attention to a breakdown of the permissive consensus has focused on the mass level, but we find analogous trends at the elite level. It is evident that members of parliaments are not satisfied to leave decisions to the Eurocrats and their networks, but rather insist that there must be more weight accorded to parliament. Further, the lack of an obvious democratic mandate makes European institutions an easy target for politicians wishing to curry popular favour by denouncing bureaucratic indifference to, and isolation from, the needs of ordinary people, even when the decisions made are objectively near optimal.

The other problem with pluralist technocracy as a future for Europe is that it may not be efficient; that is, it may not generate good policies. As is known from long experience at the national level, representation of interests through pluralist networks does not treat all interests and citizens equally; instead, it privileges the well funded over the poorly funded, and it privileges interests that are organized for other reasons over those that must form organizations primarily for the purpose of influencing policy. Thus, it tend to privilege business over labour, and both business and labour over consumers. Intermediation by interest groups tends to "disaggregate the citizen," emphasizing only certain varieties of needs. And, as our research shows, the process of intermediation by interest groups continues to be strongly oriented toward the national level, and so does not necessarily favour increased integration, even when it would be generally beneficial.

CONCLUSION

As is true for any political system, how and whether the institutions and practices of the European Union could be made more democratic depends first of all on one's definition of democracy (Katz 1997). Once the definitional question is addressed, one can go on further to ask whether the real world circumstances will allow improvements to be made, and at what cost. Depending on one's definitions and assessments of conditions, it is conceivable that one might conclude that the EU as currently structured is as democratic as it can possibly be, or at least that it is democratic enough. We are not of that opinion, but this is not the place try to resolve the proper meaning or standard of assessment of democracy. Rather, we begin this concluding section with the observation that whatever definition is in their heads, and whatever their judgements regarding the range of possibilities, most observers of, and most participants in, the process of building and operating the EU believe it to be democratically deficient. As a practical matter, the democratic deficit is a problem because most of the relevant actors think it is. And if one takes the position, which most of those actors do, and which we as a consequence have done in developing this analysis, that the correct standard against which to judge EU democracy is that of parliamentary party government, then the democratic deficit is not just perceptual—it is real as well.

The democratic deficit also is serious. Governance is both cheaper and more effective when based on willing compliance, and compliance is more reliably voluntary when the government is regarded as legitimate. In this case, citizens obey because they believe they should, not merely because they believe it to be in their immediate private interest. It would tremendously advance the cause of European union if the democratic deficit were to be substantially reduced, but this will not be easy.

Perhaps the biggest problem is that of numbers. Individual citizens do not feel effective in the EU largely because there is no way in which the average citizen can be effective in such a large polity. This, of course, is true at the national level as well—once one moves beyond the scope of a moderate sized town, there does not appear to be a significant difference with regard to democratic legitimacy among big, very big, and gigantic (Dahl and Tufte 1973). At the national level citizens can feel effective as parts of various groups. But neither the range of groups nor the sense of direct citizen involvement in, and personal identification with, those groups that is typical at the national level as yet exists at the European level. Whereas at the national level citizens can feel effective as participants in party politics, there are no real European parties, and European questions generally are marginalized by national parties. Much more than at the national level, the problem of size at the European level is complicated by the absence of a true European demos.

The impact of the number problem also is mitigated at the national level simply because the national states are older, and benefit from habitual acceptance that the EU does not have. The last time there was a serious challenge to the legitimacy of the nation-state was in the "national revolutions" of the 19th century. While the Franco-Prussian War in the 19th century, and the two world wars of the 20th century all brought about territorial adjustments, it is nearly two centuries since there was any question but that Europe was comprised of nation-states, and that the primary political identity of the individual was as a citizen of one of them. The only exceptions, German and Italian unification and then the collapse of the Austro-Hungarian empire, are simply belated victories of a principle that had already been widely accepted even within those territories themselves. The European Union and a formal articulation of the ideal of a European citizenship is not yet a decade old, dating only from the Treaty of Maastricht in 1992. Without the patina of age to distract attention from the degree to which reality falls short of the democratic ideal, the problems at the European level seem particularly acute.

The institutional development of the EU will be complicated. On one hand, there is the problem of conflicting interests. First, there are conflicts of interest among the member states, based, among other things, on different patterns of industrial and agricultural production, different patterns of intra-European and intercontinental trade, different traditions of social provision. Second, there are conflicts of interest among institutional actors at the national level and at the European level; members of parliaments generally want more parliamentary oversight and control of the executive, while members of cabinets and bureaucrats want more autonomy. Third, there are conflicts of interest between the levels. Cross-cutting all of these, there are conflicts of ideology, with the left generally favouring a more federal solution than the right. In this regard the potential conflict of interest between European and national levels that was one focus of much of this book is complicated by the addition of the regional and local levels as well. On the other hand, the institutional development of the EU will be complicated by continuing rapid changes. Among these are changes in the world, European, and national business cycles; changes in the membership of the Union; changes in the range and depth of European competencies; changes in public tolerance, expectations, and demands. Each of these changes will present new problems as well as having the potential to reopen conflicts once thought resolved. The resolution of these problems will be difficult, but it is precisely the things that make their resolution difficult that make the search for solutions imperative if Europe is to continue to provide peace and prosperity for its citizens in the 21st century.

Appendix

The European Representation Study

THE whole project on which this book rests is the European Representation Study. This study consists of four distinct survey operations: the European Election Study 1994 (EES 94), the European Candidates Study 1994 (ECS 94), the Study of Members of the European Parliament 1996 (MEP 96), and the European Members of Parliament Study (MNP 96). This appendix reports technical details of the candidates' and MPs' surveys, which have been used in this book. Results of and details about the voters survey, i.e. the European Election Study 1994 (EES 94) can be obtained from the companion volume "Political Representation and Legitimacy in the European Union," edited by Hermann Schmitt and Jacques Thomassen, Oxford University Press 1999.

The three elite components of the study to which we now turn were jointly prepared by a research group consisting of Richard Katz (Baltimore, MD), Pippa Norris (Cambridge, MA), Jacques Thomassen (Enschede), and Bernhard Wessels (Berlin). Herman Schmitt participated in most meetings of the group to ensure comparability with the voters study.

THE 1994 EUROPEAN CANDIDATES STUDY (ECS94)

The European Candidates Study 1994 was carried out by mail questionnaire, in the weeks ahead of the 1994 European Parliament election, in ten of the then twelve member-countries of the EU. It was co-ordinated by Jacques Thomassen and carried out by himself, Peter Geurts and Henk van der Kolk in the Netherlands; by Tom Bryder in Denmark; Cecile Chavel in France; Irene Delgado and Lourdes Lopez Nieto in Spain; Peter Linch and Pippa Norris in Great Britain; Michael

Marsh in Ireland; Georgio Sola and Louisa Gardella in Italy; Maria José Stock in Portugal; Bernhard Wessels and Achim Kielhorn in Germany; Lieven de Winter in Belgium and Luxembourg; and 1995 in Sweden by Martin Brothen, Peter Esaiasson and Sören Holmberg. Overhead funds were provided by the University of Twente. Table A.1 shows for each country the number of interviews and the return rate.

The data are available from the *Zentralarchiv für Empirische Sozialforschung*, Cologne, Germany (Study Number 3077).

TABLE A.2. ECS 94: Number of Interviews and Return Rates

	Number of interviews	Return rate
Belgium	117	35
Britain	134	38
Denmark	105	57
France	104	13
Germany	395	34
Ireland	12	23
Italy	137	10
Luxembourg	33	55
Netherlands	125	51
Portugal	24	8
Spain	74	4
Sweden[a]	514	86
Overall	1726	35

a   Swedish elections to the European Parliament 1995

THE 1996 MEP STUDY (MEP 96) AND THE MNP STUDIES (MNP 96)

The study among the members of the European Parliament (MEP 96) was co-ordinated by Bernhard Wessels and funded by the *Deutsche Forschungsgemeinschaft*. The survey was carried out by INFRATEST BURKE in Spring 1996. The study among the members of the national parliaments (MNP 96) was co-ordinated by Bernhard Wessels and Jacques Thomassen. National study directors were Irene Delgado and Lourdes Lopez Nieto in Spain; Louisa Gardella in Italy; Sören Holmberg, Martin Brothen, and Peter Esaiasson in Sweden; Manina

Kakepati in Greece; Christina Leston Bandeira in Portugal; Michael Marsh and Mary Clare O'Sullivan in Ireland; Bernhard Wessels and Achim Kielhorn in Germany; Lieven de Winter and Patrick Dumont in Belgium and Luxembourg; and Colette Ysmal in France. Overhead funds for this part of the study were provided by the universities of Mannheim and Twente and the *Wissenschaftszentrum Berlin*. Table A.2 informs about fieldwork period, number of interviews, return rates, and representativity of both the MEP Study and the MNP Studies.

Given the great variation in return rates, the question of representativity of the studies is of major importance. Representativity has been tested for party and gender and, where data were available, for age (and for the MEP study also for nation). The Duncan index of dissimilarity, measuring deviations between the original and the sample distributions, shows that altogether sample deviations from the real distributions are acceptably low in most studies. For both the MEP Study and the MNP studies, the deviation of party composition in the samples from their universes is about eight percentage points; it is about one for gender compositions and about three for age composition. For individual national studies the Duncan index is below ten in most cases except for party and age for some countries. A methodological caveat may remain for those countries with extreme low return rates. However, since most analyses reported in this book describe relations between variables rather than distributions of individual variables, this potential problem should be minimised.

The data of both studies are available from the *Zentralarchiv für Empirische Sozialforschung*, Cologne, Germany (Study Numbers 3078 [MEP 96] and 3079 [MNP 96]).

TABLE A.2. Summary Table of Returns for MEP- and MNP-Studies (MEP 96, MNP 96)

Study	Fieldwork	Number of Respondents	Return Rate	Duncan Index of Dissimilarity[a] regarding			
				Country	Party	Gender	Age Groups
MEP-Study	20.05.- 21.6.1996	314	50.2	9.11	7.99	0.32	3.50
MNP-Studies:	(29.4.1996-10.7.1997)	1367	37.6	n.a.	7.01	1.45	2.97
- Belgium[b]	3.6.1996-28.4.1997	87	58.0	n.a.	7.20	0.60	4.00
- France	2.7.1996-10.7.1997	146	25.3	n.a.	7.70	0.40	6.90
- Germany	21.5.-6.8.1996	317	47.2	n.a.	6.80	1.50	5.60
- Greece	15.4.-31.7.1996	60	20.0	n.a.	16.30	0.70	11.30
- Ireland	9.7.-25.10.1996	71	42.8	n.a.	3.20	0.00	-
- Italy	June-Oct. 1996	94	14.9	n.a.	18.30	2.40	-
- Luxembourg	12.6.1996-28.2.1997	28	46.7	n.a.	14.10	3.10	-
- Netherlands	29.4.-19.7.1996	65	43.3	n.a.	10.70	3.60	-
- Portugal	13.6.-4.8.1996	54	23.5	n.a.	8.50	0.50	-
- Spain	Autumn 1996	130	37.1	n.a.	4.90	2.80	-
- Sweden	5.3.-10.12.1996	315	90.3	n.a.	1.80	1.30	0.80

a   Duncan Index of Dissimilarity measures the percentage point differences between distributions, in this case between distribution in the universe and the sample. It ranges from 0 (no difference) to 100 (100 percent difference).

b   House of Representatives.

n.a.   not applicable.

-   not available.

References

ABERBACH, JOEL D., PUTNAM, ROBERT D., and ROCKMAN, BERT A., *Bureaucrats and Politicians in Western Democracies* (Cambridge: Harvard University Press, 1981).

ÁGH, ATTILA, *The Emergence of East Central European Parliaments* (Budapest: Hungarian Centre of Democracy Studies, 1994).

ALEMANN, ULRICH VON, and WESSELS, BERNHARD (eds.), *Verbände in vergleichender Perspektive—Beiträge zu einem vernachlässigten Feld* (Berlin: Sigma, 1997).

ALMOND, GABRIEL A., and POWELL, G. BINGHAM JR., *Comparative Politics* (Boston: Little Brown, 1978).

——, —— and MUNDT, ROBERT J., *Comparative Politics: A Theoretical Framework* (New York: Harper Collins, 1993).

ALVAREZ, R. MICHAEL, GARRETT, GEOFFREY, and LANGE, PETER, 'Government Partisanship, Labor Organization, and Macroeconomic Performance', *American Political Science Review,* 85 (1991), 539-56.

ANDERSEN, SVEIN, and BURNS, TOM, 'The European Union and the Erosion of Parliamentary Democracy: A Study of Post-parliamentary Governance', in Svein S. Andersen and Kjell A. Eliassen (eds.), *The European Union: How Democratic Is It?* (London: Sage, 1996), 227-52.

—— and ELIASSEN, KJELL A. (eds.), *The European Union: How Democratic Is It?* (London: Sage, 1996a).

—— and ——, 'EU-Lobbying: Between Representativity and Effectiveness', in Svein S. Andersen and Kjell A. Eliassen (eds.), *The European Union: How Democratic Is It?* (London: Sage, 1996b), 41-55.

ARMINGEON, KLAUS, *Staat und Arbeitsbeziehungen – Ein internationaler Vergleich, Abschlußbericht für die DFG über das geförderte Projekt 'Regulierung der Arbeitsbeziehungen'* (Heidelberg: mimeo, 1992).

ATTINÀ, FULVIO, 'The Voting Behaviour of European Parliament Members and the Problem of Europarties', *European Journal of Political Research,* 18 (1990), 557-79.

AVERY, WILLIAM P., 'Eurogroups, Clientela, and the European Community', *International Organizations*, 29 (1975), 949-72.

BAKER, MIKE, 'Voluntary Group Lobbying in the EC', *European Access*, (1992), 8-9.

BARDI, LUCIANO, 'Transnational Party Federations, European Parliamentary Party Groups and the Building of Europarties', in Richard S. Katz and Peter Mair (eds.) *How Parties Organize. Change and Adaptation in Party Organizations in Western Democracies* (London: Sage, 1994), 357-72.

BARNOUIN, BARBARA, *The European Labor Movement and European Integration* (London/Wolfeboro: Frances Pinter, 1986).

BENTLEY, ARTHUR F., *The Process of Government* (Cambridge: Belknap Press of Harvard University Press, 1967) (first published: Chicago: Chicago University Press, 1908).

BENZ, ARTHUR, 'Ansatzpunkte für ein europafähiges Demokratiekonzept', in Beate Kohler-Koch (ed.), *Regierung in entgrenzten Räumen*, PVS-Sonderheft 29/1998 (Opladen: Westdeutscher Verlag, 1998), 345-68.

BERGER, SUZANNE, and DORE, RONALD (eds.), *National Diversity and Global Capitalism* (Ithaca/London: Cornell University Press, 1996).

BEYERS, JAN, 'Where Does Supranationalism Come From?', *European Integration online Papers* (EIoP), 2 (1998), (http://eiop.or.at/eiop/texte/1998-009a.htm).

BLONDEL, JEAN, 'Are Ministers "Representatives" or "Managers", "Amateurs" or "Specialists"? Similarities and Differences Across Western Europe', in Hans-Dieter Klingemann, Richard Stöss, and Bernhard Wessels (eds.), *Politische Klasse und politische Institutionen* (Opladen: Westdeutscher Verlag, 1991), 187-207.

BONHAM, G. MATTHEW, 'Participation in Regional Parliamentary Assemblies: Effects on Attitudes of Scandinavian Parliamentarians', *Journal of Common Market Studies,* 8 (1970), 325-36.

BOWLER, SHAUN, and FARRELL, DAVID, 'Parliamentary Norms of Behaviour: The Case of the European Parliament', European Policy Research Unit Working Paper no. 4/93, Manchester, 1993.

BRZINSKI, JOANNE BAY, 'Political Group Cohesion in The European Parliament', in Carolyn Rhodes and Sonia Mazey (eds.), *The State of The European Union, Vol 3, Building a European Polity?* (Boulder: Lynne Rieder Publishers, 1995), 135-58.

BUCK, PHILIP W., *Amateurs and Professionals in British Politics 1918-59* (Chicago: The University of Chicago Press, 1963).

BUDGE, IAN, NEWTON, KENNETH, et al., *The Politics of the New Europe* (London/New York: Longman, 1997).

BUZAN, BARRY, 'The Interdependence of Security and Economic Issues in the "New World Order"', in Richard Stubs and Geoffrey R. D. Underhill (eds.), *Political Economy and the Changing Global Order* (London: Macmillan Press, 1994), 92-112.

CALHOUN, JOHN C., *Disquisition on Government* (New York: Peter Smith, 1943).

CALMFORS, LARS, and DRIFFILL, JOHN, 'Bargaining Structure, Corporatism and Macroeconomic Performance', *Economic Policy, 3* (1988), 13-61.

CAMERON, DAVID R., 'Social Democracy, Corporatism, Labor Quiescence, and the Representation of Economic Interest in Advanced Capitalist Society', in John H. Goldthorpe (ed.), *Order and Conflict in Contemporary Capitalism: Studies in the Political Economy of Western European Nations* (Oxford: Oxford University Press, 1984), 143-78.

CASTLES, FRANCIS G., and WILDENMANN, RUDOLF (eds.), *Visions and Realities of Party Government* (Berlin: de Gruyter, 1986).

CHUBB, BASIL, 'Going About Persecuting Civil Servants: The Job of the Irish TD', *Political Studies,* 11 (1963), 272-86.

CHURCH, CLIVE H., and PHINNEMORE, DAVID, *European Union and European Community: A Handbook and Commentary on the Post-Maastricht Treaties* (New York: Harvester/Wheatsheaf, 1994).

CONVERSE, PHILIP E., and PIERCE, ROY, *Political Representation in France* (Cambridge: Harvard University Press, 1986).

COPELAND, GARY W., and PATTERSON, SAMUEL C., *Parliaments in the Modern World* (Ann Arbor: University of Michigan Press, 1994).

CORBETT, RICHARD, JACOBS, FRANCIS, and SHACKLETON, MICHAEL, *The European Parliament* (London: Cartermill International, 1995), 3rd edition.

COTTA, MAURIZIO, 'Direct Elections of the European Parliament: A Supranational Political Elite in the Making', in Karlheinz Reif (ed.), *European Elections 1979/81 and 1984* (Berlin: Quorum Publishers, 1984).

CZADA, ROLAND, 'The Impact of Interest Politics on Flexible Adjustment Policies', in Hans Keman, Heikki Paloheimo, and Paul

F. Whiteley (eds.), *Coping with the Economic Crisis* (London et al.: Sage 1987), 20-53.

DAHL, ROBERT A., *Polyarchie, Participation and Opposition* (New Haven: Yale University Press, 1971).

——, 'Governments and Political Oppositions', in Fred I. Greenstein and Nelson W. Polsby, *Macropolitical Theory, Handbook of Political Science*, Vol. 3 (Reading: Addison-Wesley, 1975), 115-74.

—— and TUFTE, EDWARD, *Size and Democracy* (Stanford: Stanford University Press, 1973).

DAHLERUP, DRUDE, 'From a Small to a Large Minority: Women in Scandinavian Politics', *Scandinavian Political Studies,* 11 (1988), 275-98.

DAMGAARD, ERIK, *Parliamentary Change in the Nordic Countries* (Oslo: Scandinavian University Press, 1992).

DAVIDSON, ROGER H., and OLESZEK, WALTER J., *Congress and Its Members* (Washington, DC: CQ Press, 1994).

DEHOUSSE, RENAUD, 'European Institutional Architecture after Amsterdam: Parliamentary System or Regulatory Structure?', European University Institute, Working Paper Robert Schuman Centre, RCS No 98/11, 1998.

DELORS, JACQUES, *Le Noveau concert européen* (Paris: Jacob, 1992).

DINAN, DEMOND, *Ever Closer Union?* (New York: Lynne Reiner, 1994).

DÖRING, HERBERT, 'Is Government Control of the Agenda Likely to Keep "Legislative Inflation" at Bay?', in Herbert Döring (ed.), *Parliaments and Majority Rule in Western Europe* (Frankfurt/New York: Campus and St. Martins Press, 1995a), 654-87.

—— (ed.), *Parliaments and Majority Rule in Western Europe* (Frankfurt/New York: Campus/St. Martin's Press, 1995b).

DUFF, ANDREW, 'Building a Parliamentary Europe', *Government and Opposition*, 29 (1994), 147-65.

EASTON, DAVID, *A Systems Analysis of Political Life* (New York: Wiley, 1967).

ECONOMIC AND SOCIAL COMMITTEE OF THE EUROPEAN COMMUNITIES, *European Interest Groups and their Relationship with the Economic and SocialCcommittee* (Westmead: Saxon House, 1980).

EHRENHALT, ALAN, *The United States of Ambition* (New York: Times Books, 1992).

EICHENBERG, RICHARD C., 'Measurement Matters: Cumulation in the Study of Public Opinion and European Integration', paper presented at the Annual APSA Convention, Boston, September 1998.

VAN DER EIJK, CEES, and FRANKLIN, MARK N., with ACKAERT, JOHAN, et al., *Choosing Europe? The European Electorate and National Politics in the Face of Union* (Ann Arbor: University of Michigan Press, 1996).

EISING, RAINER, and KOHLER-KOCH, BEATE, 'Inflation und Zerfaserung: Trends der Interessenvermittlung in der Europäischen Gemeinschaft', in Wolfgang Streeck (Hrsg.), *Staat und Verbände, Sonderheft 25 der Politischen Vierteljahresschrift* (Opladen: Westdeutscher Verlag, 1994), 176-206.

EPSTEIN, LEON, *Political Parties in Western Democracies* (New Brunswick: Transaction Books, 1980).

ESAIASSON, PETER, and HOLMBERG, SÖREN, *Representation From Above. Members of Parliament and Representative Democracy in Sweden* (Aldershot: Dartmouth, 1996).

FALKNER, GERDA, 'Corporatist Governance and Europeanisation: No Future in the Multi-level Game?', *European Integration online Papers* (EIoP), 1 (11), 1997 (http://eiop.or.at/eiop/texte/1997-011a.htm).

FELDMAN, GERALD D., and HOMBERG, HEIDRUN, *Industrie und Inflation: Studien und Dokumente zur Politik der deutschen Unternehmer 1916-1923* (Hamburg: Hoffmann und Campe, 1977).

FOWLER, LINDA L., and MCCLURE, ROBERT D., *Political Ambition: Who Decides to Run for Congress* (New Haven: Yale University Press, 1989).

FRAENKEL, ERNST, *Deutschland und die westlichen Demokratien* (Stuttgart et al.: Kohlhammer, 1968).

FRANKE, JAMES L., and DOBSON, DOUGLAS, 'Interest Groups: The Problem of Representation', *The Western Political Quarterly*, 38 (1985), 224-37.

FRANKLIN, MARK, VAN DER EIJK, CEES, and MARSH, MICHAEL, 'The Electoral Connection and the Democratic Deficit', in Cees van der Eijk and Mark Franklin, *Choosing Europe?* (Ann Arbor: The University of Michigan Press, 1996), 366-90.

GABEL, MATTHEW, *Interests and Integration: Market Liberalization, Public Opinion and European Union* (Ann Arbor: University of Michigan Press, 1998).

GALLAGHER, MICHAEL, and MARSH, MICHAEL, *Candidate Selection in Comparative Perspective* (London: Sage, 1988).

——, LAVER, MICHAEL, and MAIR, PETER, *Representative Government in Modern Europe* (New York: McGraw Hill, 1995).

GATSIOS, KONSTANTINE, and SEABRIGHT, PAUL, 'Regulation in the European Community', *Oxford Review of Economic Policy* 5 (1989), 37-60.

GEER, JOHN, *Nominating Presidents. An Evaluation of Voters and Primaries* (New York: Greenwood Press, 1989).

——, 'Campaigns, Competition, and Political Advertising: A Look at Some Evidence', paper presented at the Annual Meeting of American Political Science Association, Washington D.C, September 1993.

GLAGOW, MANFRED, and SCHIMANK, UWE, 'Gesellschaftssteuerung durch korporatistische Verhandlungssysteme. Zur begrifflichen Klärung', in Jürgen W. Falter, Christian Fenner, and Michael Th. Greven (eds.), *Politische Willensbildung und Interessenvermittlung* (Opladen: Westdeutscher Verlag, 1984), 539-46.

GOLDEN, MIRIAM, 'The Dynamics of Trade Unionism and National Economic Performance', *American Political Science Review*, 87 (1993), 439-54.

GRANT, WYN, *Pressure Groups, Politics and Democracy in Britain* (London: Philip Allan, 1989).

GREENWOOD, JUSTIN, GROTE, JÜRGEN R., and RONIT, KARSTEN (eds.), *Organized Interests and the European Community* (London: Sage, 1992).

GRENDSTAD, GUNNAR, *Europe by Cultures. An Exploration in Grid/Group Analysis* (University of Bergen: Department of Comparative Politics, 1990).

—— and SELLE, PER (eds.), *Kultur som levemåte. Hierarki, egalitarianisme, individualisme, fatalisme* (Oslo: Det nordiske samlaget, 1996).

GUÉHENNO, JEAN-MARIE, *The end of the nation-state* (Minneapolis: Univ. of Minnesota Press, 1995).

HAAS, ERNST G., *The Uniting of Europe: Political, Social and Economic Forces* (Stanford, CA: Stanford University Press, 1958).

——, *Beyond the Nation-State: Functionalism and International Organization* (Stanford, CA.: Stanford University Press, 1964).

References 259

HANDLEY, DAVID, 'Public Opinion and European Integration: The Crisis of the 1970s', *European Journal of Political Research*, 9 (1981), 335-64.

HAYWARD, JACK, *The Crisis of Representation in Europe* (London: Frank Cass, 1995).

HELANDER, VOITTO, 'Finland', in Pippa Norris (ed.), *Passages to Power: Legislative Recruitment in Advanced Democracies* (Cambridge: Cambridge University Press, 1997), 56-75.

HELD, DAVID, *Models of Democracy* (Stanford: Stanford University Press, 1996).

HICKS, ALEXANDER, 'Social Democratic Corporatism and Economic Growth', *Journal of Politics*, 50 (1988), 677-704.

HILDEBRANDT, KAI, and DALTON, RUSSELL J., 'Die neue Politik— Politischer Wandel oder Schönwetterpolitik?', in Max Kaase (ed.), *Wahlsoziologie heute—Analysen aus Anlaß der Bundestagswahl 1976*, Politische Vierteljahresschrift 18 (2/3) (Sonderheft) (1977), 230-56.

HIRST, PAUL, and THOMPSON, GRAHAME, 'Globalization and the Future of the Nation State', *Economy and Society*, 24 (1995), 408-42.

HIX, SIMON, 'The Transnational Party Federations', in John Gaffney (ed.), *Political Parties and the European Union* (London and New York: Routledge 1996), 308-31.

—— and LORD, CHRISTOPHER, *Political Parties in the European Union* (New York: St. Martin's Press, 1998).

HOFFMAN, STANLEY, 'Obstinate or Obsolete; the Fate of the Nation State and the Case of Western Europe', *Daedalus*, Summer (1966), 862-915.

HOLLAND, MARTIN, 'Candidates for the Career Politician in Britain and Its Consequences', *British Journal of Political Science*, 11 (1986), 249-63.

HOLMBERG, SÖREN, 'Election Studies the Swedish Way', *European Journal of Political Research*, 25 (1994), 309-22.

—— and ESAIASSON, PETER, *De folkvalda* (Stockholm: Bonniers, 1988).

HOOGHE, LIESBET, and MARKS, GARY, 'The Making of a Polity: The Struggle over European Integration', in Herbert Kitschelt, Peter Lange, Gary Marks, and John Stephens (eds.), *Continuity and*

Change in Contemporary Capitalism (Cambridge: Cambridge University Press, 1999), 70-97.

INGLEHART, RONALD, 'An End to European Integration?' *American Political Science Review,* 61 (1967), 91-105.

——, 'Long-Term Trends in Mass Support for European Unification', *Government and Opposition,* 12 (1977a), 150-77.

——, *The Silent Revolution* (Princeton: University of Princeton Press, 1977b).

——, *Culture Shock* (Princeton: University of Princeton Press, 1991).

JACOBS, FRANCIS, and CORBETT, RICHARD, *The European Parliament* (Essex: Longman, 1990).

JANSSEN, JOSEPH, 'Postmaterialism, Cognitive Mobilization and Public Support for European Integration', *British Journal of Political Science,* 21 (1991), 442-68.

JENSEN, TORBEN K., 'Risk Perception Among Nordic Parliamentarians: Economy, Ecology and Social Order', in Peter Esaiasson and Knut Heidar (eds.), *Beyond Westminster and Congress. The Nordic Experience* (Columbus: Ohio State University Press, forthcoming).

KARVONEN, LAURI, and SELLE, PER, *Women in Nordic Politics* (Aldershot: Dartmouth Press, 1995).

KATZ, RICHARD S., 'Intraparty Preference Voting', in Bernard Grofman and Arend Lijphart (eds.), *Electoral Laws and Their Political Consequences* (New York: Agathon Press, 1986a), 85-103.

——, 'Party Government: A Rationalistic Conception', in Francis G. Castles and Rudolf Wildenmann (eds.), *Visions and Realities of Party Government* (Berlin: de Gruyter, 1986b), 31-71.

—— (ed.), *Party Governments: European and American Experiences* (Berlin: de Gruyter, 1987).

——, *Democracy and Elections* (Oxford: Oxford University Press, 1997).

—— and MAIR, PETER, 'Changing Models of Party Organization and Party Democracy: The Emergence of the Cartel Party', *Party Politics,* 1 (1995), 5-28.

KAZEE, THOMAS, *Who Runs for Congress?* (Washington, DC: CQ Press, 1994).

KERR, HENRY H., 'Changing Attitudes Through International Participation: European Parliamentarians and Integration', *International Organization,* 27 (1973), 45-83.

KING, ANTHONY, 'Modes of Executive-Legislative Relations: Great Britain, France and West Germany', *Legislative Studies Quarterly*, 1 (1976), 11-36.

——, 'The Rise of the Career Politician in Britain and Its Consequences', *British Journal of Political Science,* 11 (1981), 249-63.

KIRCHNER, EMIL JOSEF, *Trade Unions as a Pressure Group in the European Community* (Westmead: Saxon House, 1978).

—— and SCHWAIGER, KONRAD, *The Role of Interest Groups in the European Community* (Aldershot: Gower, 1981).

KOHLER-KOCH, BEATE, 'The Strength of Weakness', Working Paper AB III/10, MZES, Mannheim, 1995.

——, 'Die Gestaltungsmacht organisierter Interessen', in Markus Jachtenfuchs and Beate Kohler-Koch (eds.), *Europäische Integration* (Opladen: Leske + Budrich, 1996), 193-222.

——, 'Organized Interests in the EC and the European Parliament', paper prepared for the Colloque "Pluralisme, Lobbyisme et Construction Europeenne", March 20-22, Bruxelles, 1997.

KRUGMAN, PAUL R., 'Making Sense of the Competitiveness Debate', *Oxford Review of Economic Policy,* 12 (1996), 17-25.

LADRECH, ROBERT, 'Political Parties in the European Parliament', in John Gaffney (ed.), *Political Parties and the European Union* (London and New York: Routledge, 1996), 291-307.

LANGE, PETER, and GARRETT, GEOFFREY, 'The Politics of Growth: Strategic Interaction and Economic Performance in the Advanced Industrial Democracies, 1974-1980', *Journal of Politics,* 47 (1985), 792-827.

—— and MEADWELL, HUDSON, 'Typologies of Democratic Systems: From Political Inputs to Political Economy', in Howard J. Wiarda (ed.), *New Directions in Comparative Politics* (Boulder/San Francisco/Oxford: Westview Press, 1991), 82-117.

LANZALACO, LUCA, 'Coping with Heterogeneity: Peak Associations of Business within and across Western European Nations', in Justin Greenwood, Jürgen R. Grote, and Karsten Ronit (eds.), *Organized Interests and the European Community* (London: Sage, 1992), 173-205.

LAPRAT, GÉRARD, 'Parliamentary Scrutiny of Community Legislation: An Evolving Idea', in Finn Laursen and Spyros A. Pappas (eds.) *The*

Changing Role of Parliaments in the European Union (Maastricht: European Institute of Public Administration, 1995).

LAURSEN, FINN, and PAPPAS, SPYROS A. (eds.), *The Changing Role of Parliaments in the European Union* (Maastricht: European Institute of Public Administration, 1995).

LAVER, MICHAEL, and SHEPSLE, KENNETH A., 'How Political Parties Emerged from the Primeval Slime: Party Cohesion, Party Discipline, and the Formation of Governments', in Shawn Bowler et al. (eds.), *Party Cohesion, Party Discipline and the Organization of Parliaments* (Columbus: Ohio State University Press, forthcoming).

LEDUC, LAWRENCE, 'Elections and Democratic Governance', in Lawrence LeDuc, Richard G. Niemi, and Pippa Norris (eds.), *Comparing Democracies: Elections and Voting in Global Perspective* (Thousand Oaks: Sage, 1996), 343-63.

LEHMBRUCH, GERHARD, 'Neo-Corporatism and the Function of Representative Institutions', paper prepared for presentation at the conference "Representation and the State", Stanford University, Oct. 11-15, 1982a.

—— and SCHMITTER, PHILIPPE C. (eds.), *Patterns of Corporatist Policy-Making* (London/Beverly Hills: Sage, 1982b).

LEIJENAAR, MONIQUE, and NIEMOLLER, KEES, 'The Netherlands', in Pippa Norris (ed.), *Passages to Power: Legislative Recruitment in Advanced Democracies* (Cambridge: Cambridge University Press, 1997), 114-36.

LEWIS-BECK, MICHAEL, *Economics & Elections* (Ann Arbor: University of Michigan Press, 1990).

LIJPHART, AREND, *Democracies; Patterns of Majoritarian and Consensus Government in Twenty-One Countries* (New Haven: Yale University Press, 1984).

——, 'Democratic Political Systems: Types, Cases, Causes and Consequences', *Journal of Theoretical Politics,* 1 (1989), 33-48.

—— and CREPAZ, MARKUS M. L., 'Corporatism and Consensus Democracy in Eighteen Countries: Conceptual and Empirical Linkages', *British Journal for Political Science,* 21 (1991), 235-56.

LINDBERG, LEON, and SCHEINGOLD, STUART, *Europe's Would-be Polity: Patterns of Change in the European Community* (Englewood Cliffs: Prentice-Hall, 1970).

LIPSET, SEYMOR MARTIN, 'Values, Education, and Entrepreneurship', in Seymor Martin Lipset and Aldo Solari (eds.), *Elites in Latin America* (New York: Oxford University Press, 1967), 3-60.

—— and ROKKAN, STEIN, 'Cleavage Structures, Party Systems, and Voter Alignments. An Introduction', in Seymour Martin Lipset and Stein Rokkan (eds.), *Party Systems and Voter Alignments* (New York: Free Press, 1967a), 1-64.

—— and ——, *Party Systems and Voter Alignments* (New York: Free Press, 1967b).

LODGE, JULIET, and HERMAN, VALENTINE, *Direct Elections to the European Parliament* (London: Macmillan, 1982).

LOEWENBERG, GERHARD, and PATTERSON, SAMUEL, *Comparing Legislatures* (Boston: Little Brown, 1979).

LOVENDUSKI, JONI, *Women and European Politics* (Sussex: Wheatsheaf Books, 1986).

—— and NORRIS, PIPPA (eds.), *Gender and Party Politics* (London: Sage, 1993).

MAJONE, GIANDOMENICO, 'The Rise of the Regulatory State in Europe', *West European Politics,* 17 (1994), 77-101.

MANUEL, FRANK, and MANUEL, FRITZIE, *Utopian Thought in the Western World* (Cambridge, Mass.: Belknap Press, 1979).

MARKS, GARY, 'Neocorporatism and Incomes Policy in Western Europe and North America', *Comparative Politics,* 18 (1986), 253-77.

MARQUAND, DAVID, *Parliament for Europe* (London: Jonathan Cape, 1979).

MARSH, MICHAEL, 'Policy Support for the European Union', in Jacques J. Thomassen and Hermann Schmitt (eds.) *Political Legitimacy and Representation in the EU* (Oxford: Oxford University Press, 1999).

—— and NORRIS, PIPPA (eds.), *Political Representation in the European Parliament,* Special Issue of the European Journal of Political Research, 32 (1997).

MATTHEWS, DONALD, *U.S. Senators and their World* (New York: Vintage Books, 1960).

MCALLISTER, IAN, 'Australia', in Pippa Norris (ed.), *Passages to Power: Legislative Recruitment in Advanced Democracies* (Cambridge: Cambridge University Press, 1997), 15-32.

MEZEY, MICHAEL L., 'Parliament in the New Europe', in Jack Hayward and Edwards C. Page, *Governing the New Europe* (Cambridge: Polity, 1995), 196-223.

MILL, JOHN STUART, *Considerations on Representative Government* (London: Parker, Son, and Bourne, 1861).

MITRANY, DAVID, *A Working Peace System* (Chicago: Quadrangle Books, 1966).

MORAVCSIK, ANDREW, 'Negotiating the Single European Act: National Interests and Conventional Statecraft in the European Community', *International Organization,* 45 (1991), 19-55.

MUTTIMER, DAVID, '1992 and the Political Integration of Europe: Neo-Functionalism Reconsidered', *Journal of European Integration,* 13 (1989), 75-101.

NEWMAN, MICHAEL, *Democracy, Sovereignty and the European Union* (New York: St. Martin's Press, 1996).

NIEDERMAYER, OSKAR, 'Trends and Contrasts', in Oskar Niedermayer and Richard Sinnott (eds.), *Public Opinion and Internationalized Governance* (Oxford: Oxford University Press, 1995a), 53-72.

—— and SINNOT, RICHARD (eds.), *Public Opinion and Institutionalized Government* (Oxford: Oxford University Press, 1995b).

NORRIS, PIPPA, 'Women Politicians: Transforming Westminster?' *Parliamentary Affairs,* 49 (1996), 91-104.

—— (ed.), *Passages to Power: Legislative Recruitment in Advanced Democracies* (Cambridge: Cambridge University Press, 1997a).

——, 'Towards a More Cosmopolitan Political Science?', *European Journal of Political Research,* 31 (1997b), 17-34.

——, and LOVENDUSKI, JONI, *Political Recruitment: Gender, Race and Class in the British Parliament* (Cambridge: Cambridge University Press, 1995).

NORTON, PHILIP (ed.), *National Parliaments and the European Union* (London: Frank Cass, 1996a).

——, 'Parliaments: A Framework for Analysis', in Philip Norton (ed.), *Parliaments in Western Europe* (London: Frank Cass, 1996b), 1-9.

NUGENT, NEILL, *The Government and Politics of the European Community* (Durham: Duke University Press, 1989).

——, *The Government and Politics of the European Union* (Durham: Duke University Press, 1994).

OFFE, CLAUS, 'The Attribution of Public Status to Interest Groups: Observations on the West German Case', in Suzanne Berger (ed.),

Organizing Interests in Western Europe (Cambridge et al.: Cambridge University Press, 1981), 123-58.

OGBURN, WILLIAM F., *On Culture and Social Change* (Chicago: Chicago University Press, 1950).

OLSON, MANCUR, *The Logic of Collective Action* (Cambridge: Harvard University Press, 1971).

——, *Democratic Legislative Institutions. A Comparative View* (Armonk, NY/London: M.E. Sharpe, 1994).

PAPPI, FRANZ URBAN, and SCHNORPFEIL, WILLI, 'Das Ausschußwesen der Europäischen Kommission', in Thomas König, Elmar Rieger, and Hermann Schmitt (eds.), *Das europäische Mehrebenensystem* (Frankfurt: Campus, 1996), 135-59.

PEDERSEN, MOGENS N., 'Europarties and European Parties: New Arenas, New Challenges and New Strategies', in Svein S. Andersen and Kjell A. Eliassen (eds.), *The European Union: How Democratic Is It?* (London: Sage, 1996), 15-39.

PHILLIPS, ANNE, *Democracy and Difference* (Cambridge: Polity Press, 1993).

POLSBY, NELSON, 'The Institutionalization of the U.S. House of Representatives', *American Political Science Review,* 62 (1968), 144-68.

POWELL, G. BINGHAM, *Contemporary Democracies* (Cambridge: Harvard University Press, 1983).

PREWITT, KENNETH, 'Political Efficacy', in: *International Encyclopedia of the Social Sciences Vol. 12*, (New York: MacMillan/Free Press, 1968), 225-8.

PUTNAM, ROBERT D., *The Comparative Study of Political Elites*, (Englewood Cliffs, NJ.: Prentice Hall, 1976).

RANNEY, AUSTIN, *The Doctrine of Responsible Party Government* (Urbana: University of Illinois Press, 1962).

REIF, KARLHEINZ (ed.), *European Elections 1979/81 and 1984* (Berlin: Quorum Publishers, 1984).

——, and SCHMITT, HERMANN, 'Nine Second-Order National Elections: A Conceptual Framework for the Analysis of European Election Results', *European Journal of Political Research,* 8 (1980), 3-44.

RIDDELL, PETER, *Honest Opportunism* (London: Hamish Hamilton, 1993).

RIKER, WILLIAM H., *Liberalism against Populism: A Confrontation between the Theory of Democracy and the Theory of Social Choice* (Prospect Heights: Waveland Press, 1982).

RISSE, THOMAS, 'To Euro or Not to Euro? The EMU and Identity Politics in the European Union', European University Institute, Working Paper Robert Schuman Centre, RCS No 98/9, 1998.

ROKKAN, STEIN, 'Norway. Numerical Democracy and Corporate Pluralism', in Robert A. Dahl (ed.), *Political Oppositions in Western Democracies* (New Haven: Yale University Press, 1966), 70-115.

ROLLER, EDELTRAUD, *Ein analytisches Schema zur Klassifikation von Politikinhalten,* Discussion paper FS III 91-201, Wissenschaftszentrum Berlin für Sozialforschung (WZB), 1991.

ROMETSCH, DIETRICH, and WESSELS, WOLFGANG (eds.), *The European Union and Member States* (Manchester/New York: Manchester University Press, 1996).

ROSE, RICHARD, *The Problem of Party Government* (London: Macmillan, 1974).

RUGGIE, JOHN G., 'Trade, Protectionism and the Future of Welfare Capitalism', *Journal of International Affairs,* 48 (1994), 1-12.

SANI, GIACOMO, and SARTORI, GIOVANNI, 'Polarization, Fragmentation and Competition in Western Democracies', in Hans Daalder and Peter Mair (eds.), *Western European Party Systems, Continuity and Change* (London: Sage, 1983), 307-40.

SCARROW, SUSAN E., 'Political Career Paths and the European Parliament', *Legislative Studies Quarterly,* 22 (1997), 253-63.

SCHARPF, FRITZ W., 'The Joint-Decision Trap', *Public Administration,* 66 (1988), 239-87.

——, *Optionen des Föderalismus in Deutschland und Europa* (Frankfurt a. M.: Campus, 1994).

——, 'Economic Integration, Democracy and the Welfare State', MPIfG Working Paper 96/2, Cologne, 1996a.

——, 'Negative and Positive Integration in the Political Economy of European Welfare States', in Gary Marks, Fritz W. Scharpf, Philippe C. Schmitter, and Wolfgang Streeck (eds.), *Governance in the European Union* (London: Sage, 1996b), 15-39.

——, 'Interdependence and Democratic Legitimation', MPIfG Working Paper 98/2, Cologne, 1998.

SCHATTSCHNEIDER, ELMER E., *Party Government* (New York: Rinehart, 1942).

SCHENDELEN, RINUS VAN, 'Images of Democratic Representation in the European Community', in Hans-Dieter Klingemann, Richard Stöss, and Bernhard Wessels (eds.), *Politische Klasse und politische Institutionen* (Opladen: Westdeutscher Verlag, 1991), 357-71.

SCHIMMELPFENNIG, FRANK, 'Legitimate Rule in the European Union', Tübinger Arbeitspapiere zur internationalen Politik und Friedensforschung, Tübingen, 1996.

SCHLESINGER, JOSEPH, *Ambition and Politics* (Chicago: Rand McNally, 1966).

SCHMALZ-BRUNS, RAINER, 'Bürgerschaftliche Politik—ein Modell der Demokratisierung der Europäischen Union', in Klaus Dieter Wolf (ed.), *Projekt Europa im Übergang* (Baden-Baden: Nomos, 1997), 63-89.

SCHMID, JOSEF, *Wohlfahrtsverbände in modernen Wohlfahrtsstaaten* (Opladen: Leske + Budrich, 1996).

SCHMITT, HERMANN, and THOMASSEN, JACQUES (eds.), *Political Representation and Legitimacy in the European Union* (Oxford: Oxford University Press, 1999a).

—— and ——, 'European Parliament Groups: An Emerging Party System?', in Hermann Schmitt and Jacques Thomassen (eds.), *Political Representation and Legitimacy in the European Union* (Oxford: Oxford University Press, 1999b).

SCHMITTER, PHILIPPE C., 'Imagining the Future of the Euro-Polity with the Help of New Concepts', in Gary Marks, Fritz W. Scharpf, Philippe C. Schmitter, and Wolfgang Streeck (eds.), *Governance in the European Union* (London:Sage, 1996a), 121-50.

——, 'Imagining the Present Euro-Polity with the Help of Past Theories', in Gary Marks, Fritz W. Scharpf, Philippe C. Schmitter, and Wolfgang Streeck (eds.), *Governance in the European Union* (London: Sage, 1996b), 1-14.

—— and GROTE, JÜRGEN R., 'The Corporatist Sisyphus: Past, Present and Future', EUI-Working Papers, SPS No. 97/4, 1997.

—— and LEHMBRUCH, GERHARD (eds.), *Trends toward Corporatist Intermediation* (Beverly Hills/London: Sage, 1979).

—— and STREECK, WOLFGANG, 'The Organization of Business Interests', WZB discussion paper IIM/LMP 81-13, 1981.

—— and ——, 'Organized Interests and the Europe of 1992', in Norman J. Ornstein and Mark Perlman (eds.), *Political Power and Social Change* (Washington, DC: AEI Press, 1991), 46-67.

268   *References*

SCHUMPETER, JOSEPH, *Capitalism, Socialism and Democracy* (London: George Allen and Unwin, 1976 [1942]), 5th edition.

SCULLY, ROGER M., 'Becoming Europeans? Socialization Processes in the European Parliament', paper presented at the 1997 American Political Science Association Meetings, Washington, D.C., 1997.

SHEPSLE, KENNETH A., 'Representation and Governance', *Political Science Quarterly*, 103 (1988), 461-84.

SIDJANSKI, DUSAN, 'Pressure Groups and the European Economic Community', in Michael Hodges (ed.), *European Integration* (London: Penguin Books, 1972), 401-20.

SINNOTT, RICHARD, 'Policy, Subsidiarity, and Legitimacy', in Oskar Niedermayer and Richard Sinnott (eds.), *Public Opinion and Internationalized Governance* (Oxford: Oxford University Press 1995), 246-76.

SMITH, JULIE, 'How European Are European Elections,' in John Gaffney (ed.), *Political Parties and the European Union* (London and New York: Routledge, 1996), 275-90.

STINCHCOMBE, ARTHUR L., 'Social Structure and Politics', in Fred I. Greenstein and Nelson W. Polsby (eds.), *Macropolitical Theory, Handbook of Political Science Vol. 3* (Reading, Mass.: Addison-Wesley, 1975), 557-622.

STREECK, WOLFGANG, 'Neo-Voluntarism: A New European Social Policy Regime?', in Gary Marks, Fritz W. Scharpf, Phillippe C. Schmitter, and Wolfgang Streeck (eds.), *Governance in the European Union* (London: Sage, 1996), 64-94.

STROM, KAARE, 'Democracy as Political Competition', in Gary Marks and Larry Diamond. (eds.), *Reexamining Democracy. Essays in Honor of Seymour Martin Lipset* (London: Sage, 1992), 27-46.

SUMNER, WILLIAM GRAHAM, *Folkways* (Boston: Ginn & Co., 1907).

THOMAS, SUE, *How Women Legislate* (Oxford: Oxford University Press, 1994).

THOMASSEN, JACQUES, 'Political Communication between Political Elites and Mass Publics; The Role of Belief Systems', in Warren Miller et al., *Political Representation in Western Societies* (Oxford: Oxford University Press, forthcoming).

—— and SCHMITT, HERMANN, 'Policy Representation', *European Journal for Political Research,* 32 (1997), 165-84.

THOMPSON, MICHAEL, ELLIS, RICHARD, and WILDAVSKY, AARON, *Cultural Theory* (Boulder: Westview Press, 1990).

TRUMAN, DAVID B., *The Governmental Process* (New York: Knopf, 1951).

TSEBELIS, GEORGE, 'Conditional Agenda-Setting and Decision-Making inside the European Parliament', *The Journal of Legislative Studies*, 1 (1995), 65-93.

TSOUKALIS, LOUKAS, 'The European Agenda: Issues of Globalization, Equity and Legitimacy', The Robert Schuman Centre, Jean Monnet Chair Papers, No 98/49, 1998.

VALLANCE, ELIZABETH, 'Do Women Make a Difference? The Impact of Women MEPs on Community Equality Policy', in Mary Buckley and Malcolm Anderson (eds.), *Women, Equality and Europe* (London: Macmillan, 1988).

—— and DAVIES, ELIZABETH, *Women of Europe: Women MEPs and Equality Policy* (Cambridge: Cambridge University Press, 1986).

VISSER, JELLE, 'In Search of Inclusive Unionism', *Bulletin of Comparative Labor Relations*, Bulletin 18-1990 (1990).

—— and EBBINGHAUS, BERNHARD, 'Making the Most of Diversity?', in Justin Greenwood, Jürgen R. Grote, and Karsten Ronit (eds.), *Organized Interests and the European Community* (London: Sage), 206-37.

WAHLKE, JOHN C., EULAU, HEINZ, BUCHANAN, WILLIAM, and FERGUSON, LEROY C., *The Legislative System: Explorations in Legislative Behavior* (New York: John Wiley, 1962).

WALLERSTEIN, MICHAEL, 'Centralized Bargaining and Wage Restraint', *American Journal of Political Science*, 34 (1990), 982-1004.

WEBER, MAX, 'Parlament und Regierung im neugeordneten Deutsch–land', in Max Weber, *Gesammelte politische Schriften*, herausgege–ben v. Winkelmann, Johannes (Tübingen: UTB [Mohr Siebeck], 1988) 5. Aufl. (first published: München: Drei-Masken-Verlag, 1921).

——, 'Politik als Beruf', in Max Weber, *Gesammelte politische Schriften* (Tübingen: Mohr, 1958).

WEILER, JOSEPH H. H., 'European Neo-Constitutionalism: In Search of Foundations for the European Constitutional Order', *Political Studies*, 44 (1996), 517-33.

WESSELS, BERNHARD, 'Gruppenbindungen und rationale Faktoren als Determinanten der Wahlentscheidung in Ost- und Westdeutschland', in Hans-Dieter Klingemann and Max Kaase (eds.), *Wahlen und*

Wähler. Analysen aus Anlaß der Bundestagswahl 1990 (Opladen: Westdeutscher Verlag, 1994), 123-60.

——, 'Development of Support: Diffusion or Demographic Replacement?', in Oskar Niedermayer and Richard Sinnott (eds.), *Public Opinion and Internationalized Governance* (Oxford: Oxford University Press, 1995), 105-36.

——, 'Systems of Economic Interest Groups and Socio-Economic Performance', paper prepared for delivery at the 1996 Annual Meeting of the American Political Science Association, Division 25 "Comparative Politics of Advanced Industrial States", Panel 25-12 "Liberalization and National Organizational Responsiveness", The San Francisco Hilton and Towers, August 29-September 1, 1996.

——, 'Germany', in Pippa Norris (ed.), *Passages to Power: Legislative Recruitment in Advanced Democracies* (Cambridge: Cambridge University Press, 1997a), 76-97.

——, 'Organizing Capacity of Societies and Modernity', in Jan W. van Deth (ed.), *Private Groups and Public Life, Social Participation, Voluntary Associations, and Political Involvement in Representative Democracies* (London: Routledge, 1997b), 198-219.

——, 'Social Alliances and Coalitions: The Organizational Underpinnings of Democracy in West Germany', in Dietrich Rueschemeyer, Marilyn Rueschemeyer, and Bjorn Wittrock (eds.), *Participation and Democracy East and West: Comparisons and Interpretations* (New York: M.E. Sharpe, 1998) (also published as WZB Discussion Paper FS III 96-204).

——, 'Whom to Represent? Role Orientations of Legislators in Europe', in Hermann Schmitt and Jacques Thomassen (eds.), *Political Representation and Legitimacy in the European Union* (Oxford: Oxford University Press, 1999), 215-45.

——, KIELHORN, ACHIM, and THOMASSEN, JACQUES, 'Political Representation in Europe: European Members of Parliament Study', Codebook of the Integrated Dataset of Members of European Parliament and Members of National Parliaments, Berlin, 1997.

WESSELS, WOLFGANG, 'Institutions of the EU system: models of explanation', in Dietrich Rometsch and Wolfgang Wessels (eds.), *The European Union and Member States* (Manchester/New York: Manchester University Press, 1996), 20-36.

WILDENMANN, RUDOLF, 'The Problematic of Party Government', in Francis G. Castles and Rudolf Wildenmann (eds.), *Visions and Realities of Party Government* (Berlin: de Gruyter, 1986), 1-30.

WILSON, GRAHAM K., *Interest groups* (Oxford: Basil Blackwell, 1990).

ZÜRN, MICHAEL, 'Über den Staat und die Demokratie in der Europäischen Union', in Michael Zürn and Ulrich K. Preuß, Probleme einer Verfassung für Europa, ZERP discussion paper 3/95, (Bremen: Universität Bremen, Zentrum für Europäische Rechtspolitik, 1995), 1-40.

Index

278   *Index*